National Redeemer
Owain Glyndŵr in Welsh Tradition

National Redeemer

Owain Glyndŵr in
Welsh Tradition

Elissa R. Henken

CORNELL UNIVERSITY PRESS
ITHACA, NEW YORK

First published 1996 by Cornell University Press

Library of Congress Cataloging-in-Publication Data

Henken, Elissa R.
  National redeemer : Owain Glyndŵr in Welsh tradition / Elissa
Henken.
      p.   cm.
  Includes bibliographical references and index.
  ISBN 0-8014-3268-5 (alk. paper). -- ISBN 0-8014-8349-2 (pbk. : alk.
paper)
  1. Glendower, Owen, 1359?–1416? 2. Wales--History--1284–1536--
Historiography.   3. Nationalism--Wales--Historiography.
  4. Revolutionaries--Wales--Biography.   5. Princes--Wales--Biography.
  6. Heroes--Wales--Biography.   7. Folklore--Wales.   8. Legends--
Wales.   I. Title.
  DA716.G5H46   1996
  942.9′041′092--dc20
  [B]   96–10286
                                                                         CIP

International Standard Book Number 0-8014-3268-5 (cloth)
International Standard Book Number 0-8014-8349-2 (paper)

Printed in Great Britain

For
Mariamne and Jonathan

Contents

Acknowledgments

During my years of work on this study, many people have given crucial assistance and support. Mary Ellen Brown and Brynley F. Roberts taught, guided and encouraged me, and from the earliest stages helped shape this study by forcing me to answer difficult questions. Each demonstrated unending patience in helping me through the agonies of redefining the project and rethinking the materials. Dr Roberts has continued to teach me, clarifying myriad matters of language, bibliography, history and culture with a generosity of time and spirit which can never be measured or repaid. Carl Lindahl provided the difficult questions and invaluable suggestions of the later stages, helping me both hone and broaden my thinking. Mary Burdett-Jones and Philip Henry Jones, in addition to providing food and comfort to a weary folklorist, shared their expert and often arcane knowledge, solving puzzles and offering, always, yet one more example. Siân Gruffudd, Marged Haycock, Alun Jones, Modlen Lynch and Tony Parkinson facilitated my fieldwork by taking me places, introducing me to people, and occasionally assisting with interviews. Siân Gruffudd also gave invaluable assistance by transcribing field tapes, as did the late Erina Morris. Trefor M. Owen, Curator (1970–87), and Robin Gwyndaf, Assistant Keeper, provided access to the archives of the Welsh Folk Museum (now the Museum of Welsh Life). Cledwyn Fychan generously shared his own field research. Dozens of strangers gave their time, knowledge and patience in answering my questions. Henry A. Fischel, William Hansen, and Roger L. Janelli read the early drafts and Charles C. Doyle read the last drafts; all gave important guidance and suggestions. Robert Van Horn Dover, Simon Gatrell, J.E. Caerwyn Williams and Alysa J. Ward contributed their own expert assistance. Julia J. Brody and George S. Brody supported my fieldwork, giving me time to carry out my initial research. The American Association of

University Women gave funding so that I could write for a period undistracted by financial concerns. Friends, some already named as well as Dana L. Everts-Boehm, Susan Domowitz, Allena Opper, Ceridwen Lloyd-Morgan, Rhiannon Roberts, Mariamne H. Whatley and Jonathan T. Henken, provided along with their essential encouragement the protective warmth of their friendship and necessary distractions from the work. For all of this generosity in time, energy and support, I am truly grateful.

ELISSA R. HENKEN

Abbreviations

AP[2]	Ifor Williams, ed., and Rachel Bromwich, trans., *Armes Prydein*.
Arch Camb	*Archaeologia Cambrensis*.
AT	Antti Aarne and Stith Thompson, *The Types of the Folktale*.
AWC	Amgueddfa Werin Cymru (Museum of Welsh Life, previously Welsh Folk Museum).
BBC	J. Gwenogvryn Evans, ed., *The Black Book of Carmarthen*.
BBCS	*Bulletin of the Board of Celtic Studies*.
BL	British, Library, London.
BT	J. Gwenogvryn Evans, ed., *The Book of Taliesin*.
BT–Haycock	Marged Haycock, 'Llyfr Taliesin: astudiaethau ar rai agweddau'.
CMCS	*Cambridge Medieval Celtic Studies*.
DWB	*The Dictionary of Welsh Biography Down to 1940*.
EVW	Margaret Enid Griffiths, *Early Vaticination in Welsh*.
GHC	Islwyn Jones, ed., *Gwaith Hywel Cilan*.
GLM	Eurys I. Rowlands, ed., *Gwaith Lewys Môn*.
GTA	T. Gwynn Jones, ed., *Gwaith Tudur Aled*.
IGE[2]	Henry Lewis, Thomas Roberts, and Ifor Williams, eds., *Cywyddau Iolo Goch ac Eraill*.
JAF	*Journal of American Folklore*.
JFI	*Journal of the Folklore Institute*.
LlDC	A.O.H. Jarman, ed., *Llyfr Du Caerfyrddin*.
Motif	Stith Thompson, *Motif-Index of Folk-Literature*.
NLW	National Library of Wales, Aberystwyth.
RBP	J. Gwenogvryn Evans, ed., *The Poetry in the Red Book of Hergest*.
THSC	*Transactions of the Honourable Society of Cymmrodorion*.
TYP	Rachel Bromwich, ed., *Trioedd Ynys Prydein*.

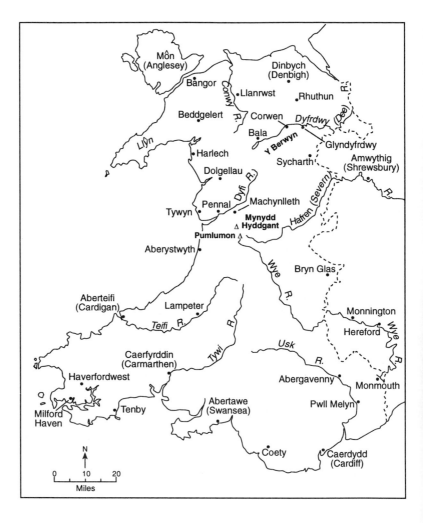

Places associated with Owain Glyndŵr's legendry. (*Cartographic Services Laboratory, University of Georgia*)

1

Introduction

The patterns of folklore structure – and are structured by – our worldviews. Ever responsive to changing needs and contexts, whether personal or socio-political, they express our perceptions and affect our expectations. Existing in neither fixed nor superorganic form, patterns shift and re-form, influenced by interaction with literary and popular genres as well as by circumstances. Folklore and history, too often misapprehended as unrelated opposites, never cease their constant interplay – each shaping the other: traditional expectations shape readings of the past and decisions for the future; events refine and reshape traditional expectations. Developed from a group's experience, folklore provides paradigms for subsequent experiences. Collective perceptions of the past – the hopes and frustrations, victories and defeats related in legend and ritual, history and literature – create and define a people's self-identity.

This study concerns Owain Glyndŵr,[1] an actual Welsh nobleman of the fifteenth century, who took on the traditional role expected of him and who has continued, throughout centuries of socio-political change and narrative shifts, to serve the Welsh as they required. It is about one polysemous hero in one particular culture, but it is also about how, in the confluence of folklore, history and literature, people create and maintain their group identity, using heroes and reworking folklore as necessary to give them the strength and cultural tools to survive and accomplish their aims.

When Owain Glyndŵr led the last major rebellion of the Welsh against the English, 1400–15, he assumed a role which had been established centuries earlier and which he would continue to fill for at least another five or six centuries. An historical figure, he became a focal point for legendry and nationalist sentiment, and his life, shaped by traditional and cultural necessities, was viewed as following the same pattern as had been established for preceding Welsh heroes. This study examines both the traditional elements which comprise the figure of Glyndŵr, and the ways in which he functions in Welsh culture.

Glyndŵr's most important role is as a national redeemer-hero, the hero whose coming (whether for the first time or after a long absence) is awaited so that he might restore the nation to its former glories. The redeemer-hero, who appears in many places in Europe, is of particular significance in Wales, where he is part of the mythology of Welsh consciousness, inextricably linked with the theme of the loss of Britain and with the hope of regaining 'the crown of London'. Glyndŵr stands seventh in a line of eight major redeemers whose pattern, well-established in Wales long before his time, carried its own expectations. Tradition held not only that the hero would come, but also what he would do when he arrived in order to destroy the enemy and restore the golden age. The pattern is so strong, rooted firmly in popular understanding, that it enables or causes people to shape legends about historical figures according to the heroic pattern and to view historical events – both past and contemporaneous – in terms of this pattern as well.

In this study, I examine the development of the redeemer-hero and the establishment of his pattern in the centuries preceding Owain Glyndŵr, as they can be discerned in early histories and prophecy which appear in both verse and prose forms (Chapter 2). Then in studying the literary and historical documentation subsequent to Glyndŵr, I examine the manner in which people's expectations of him and their view of his life placed Glyndŵr in the established pattern (Chapter 3).

However, Owain Glyndŵr is not only a redeemer-hero; the traditions about him belong to several different types of hero and demonstrate different aspects of his character. This wealth of different lines of tradition, in showing that Glyndŵr is not one-dimensional, indicates Glyndŵr's importance in Welsh culture. He is a figure who must satisfy many cultural needs and about whom legends accrue. As discussed in Chapter 4, he is, amongst other roles, also a trickster, an outlaw and a war leader.

The legendry which places Glyndŵr in these various traditional roles is still strong in the areas in which he lived and fought and where he continues to serve as a local hero. His role on a national level, however, is quite different. While in certain areas traditional knowledge of him has become more limited, he has at the same time become for many a symbol of Welsh nationalism. His struggle and his traditional characteristics, especially as a redeemer-hero, have made him a natural representative of nationalist aspirations, for as one writer notes, he is 'the most compelling of the emblematic heroes of the Welsh resistance'.[2] The nationalists were able to build on traditional perceptions of him to create a strong symbol. In the last chapter of this study, I examine his appearance as a local hero and his use as a symbol and a rallying cry in modern Welsh politics.

Historical Background

Various aspects of Glyndŵr's life and wars are discussed in greater detail in the following chapters, but a brief history may be useful at this point.

Owain ap Gruffydd Fychan, or Owain Glyndŵr as he was later called, was born in the middle of the fourteenth century, probably in 1349, 1354 or 1359, with 1354 as the year generally favoured by historians. His father, Gruffydd Fychan ap Madog, descendant of the kings of Powys, was baron of Glyndyfrdwy and Cynllaith Owain in north-east Wales, and his mother Helen, daughter of Thomas ap Llywelyn ab Owen, represented the royal line of Deheubarth in southern Wales. Glyndŵr studied for seven years at the Inns of Court in London, which was a place not only for the study of law but also for the training of young gentlemen. Glyndŵr then took up military service, though the details about this period are not clear. He may have served as an esquire to Richard II or even served under Henry Bolingbroke, who later became his greatest enemy. In any case, he definitely did fight in Richard's Scottish wars in 1385 and 1387. Sometime during this period, possibly in 1383, he married Margaret, daughter of David Hanmer of Maelor, an important justice of the king's bench. Together they had six sons and three daughters, of whom only the daughters and one son survived their father. Glyndŵr lived as a wealthy nobleman, enjoying both revenue and bounty from his estates. His home at Sycharth was the well-appointed estate of a Welsh gentleman, serving as a culture centre visited by itinerant bards.

The disruption to Glyndŵr's comfortable and successful life came when Henry Bolingbroke deposed Richard II and became King Henry IV. Dissatisfaction with conditions under English rule had been growing in Wales for a very long time. Matters had steadily worsened since 1282, when Welsh independence had been lost and Edward I had begun building castles in Wales. English rule became more and more restrictive. The Englishmen put in charge of local affairs were generally concerned not with the welfare of the local Welsh inhabitants, but rather with the benefits to the English, both themselves and the Crown. English laws, which often conflicted with the needs and expectations of Welsh culture, were found to be even more oppressive when enforced by these men who were completely lacking in sympathy. Other laws, specifically limiting the rights of the Welsh, only added to the hardship. Much of the hardship was economic. For example, under the new system, the Welsh were expected to pay heavy taxes with money, which until then had not been a major part of the economy. Added to all these problems, the Black Death struck in 1348–50, recurring periodically thereafter. The noblemen did not suffer as much economically as did the other classes, but they, along with Welsh churchmen, were generally kept out of important positions. When Henry became king in 1399, he levied a new set of especially heavy taxes. With resentment towards the English ever deepening, when Owain Glyndŵr rose, the Welsh, both peasants and nobles, were ready to rise with him.

Glyndŵr's rebellion was precipitated by conflict with Reginald Grey, lord of Rhuthun. The two men had neighbouring lands, and dispute arose over a certain piece which Grey seized. When Glyndŵr sought redress through Parliament, he was rebuffed. Parliament's response to warnings against such an attitude in the face of growing Welsh dissatisfaction was, 'What care we for bare foot rascals?'³ Although questioned by later historians, early histories report that Grey, who was already close to the king, purposely turned Henry against Glyndŵr. One of the most persistent stories claims that, charged with delivering to Glyndŵr a summons to join Henry in battle in Scotland, Grey withheld the summons (or delayed until it was too late to respond) and then told Henry that Glyndŵr had refused to come. In the summer of 1400, Glyndŵr realized that he would get no satisfaction within the English system. On 16 September, a group of supporters declared him prince of Wales, and on 20 September, the eve of St Matthew's Day, when the town was crowded for the fair, Glyndŵr attacked Rhuthun. He then attacked several other places before his men were scattered by English forces. Glyndŵr was declared an outlaw and his lands made forfeit. However, this was only the beginning of the uprising: Parliament soon began to take matters seriously when it noticed that Welsh students and labourers working in England were returning to Wales in order to take part, and responded with yet more restrictive measures and punitive laws. Glyndŵr, apparently, bided his time in the mountains.

In the summer of 1401, Glyndŵr had a major victory at the battle of Mynydd Hyddgant, on the banks of the Hyddgen, near Pumlumon. Glyndŵr's small army was surrounded by a large one (the early histories record 120 men surrounded by 1,500 men, including Flemings from the south-west), but Glyndŵr's forces won. This success brought more supporters to Glyndŵr's side. In the autumn, Henry took over the Cistercian monastery of Strata Florida, which he and his men proceeded to defile, while Glyndŵr wrote to Robert III of Scotland and the Irish lords asking for help. In 1402, during which a great comet appeared and was interpreted as portending Glyndŵr's victory, Glyndŵr, again fighting in the North, captured Grey and held him for ransom. Next he had a great victory at Bryn Glas near Pilleth in Maelienydd (Radnorshire),⁴ where he captured Sir Edmund Mortimer. Grey was eventually ransomed by Henry for 10,000 marks, but Mortimer, who through his grandfather had better claim than Henry to the throne, and whose nephew had been declared heir presumptive by King Richard, was a potential threat to Henry. Mortimer was not ransomed. He and Glyndŵr became allies, bonded by Mortimer's marrying Glyndŵr's daughter Catherine. Through Mortimer, Glyndŵr made friends with Sir Henry Percy (Hotspur), Mortimer's brother-in-law. Grey, too, eventually made peace with Glyndŵr and married his daughter. King Henry did try to lead a great force into Wales, but was turned back by fierce storms. However, the king's son Prince Henry (Hal) and his forces managed to destroy Glyndŵr's homes at Sycharth and Glyndyfrdwy in early 1403. Later that year, while King Henry was engaged in his Scottish wars, Percy began to make his move to link forces with Mortimer and Glyndŵr. The king received warning and intercepted him at Shrewsbury, where Percy was killed. The alliance was continued by Percy's father, the earl of Northumberland, and in the Tripartite Indenture of 1405, plans were made to divide the realm amongst the three men. King Henry followed his victory at Shrewsbury with a trip into Wales to strengthen his castles, but did not remain.

The castles at Aberystwyth and Harlech fell to Glyndŵr's forces in 1404 and became valued bases for his campaign. Summoning four men from every commote (a Welsh administrative district), Glyndŵr called a parliament to meet in Machynlleth. Probably, he was officially crowned prince of Wales there, but of even greater importance, he began to establish Wales as an independent state. He was helped and guided in this by clerics already experienced in administration, most particularly by Gruffudd Young, archdeacon of Merioneth and Glyndŵr's chancellor, John Trevor, bishop of St Asaph, Lewis Byford, bishop of Bangor, and also Glyndŵr's brother-in-law John Hanmer. In July of 1404, Hanmer and Young concluded a treaty with the king of France.

The following year, Glyndŵr's troops, which had been threatening the English border, suffered two grievous defeats, the first near Grosmont and the more serious one at Pwll Melyn near Usk, where Glyndŵr's son Griffith was captured and his brother Tudur was killed. Another parliament was called, this time at Harlech. French forces (approximately 2,500 men) landed at Milford Haven and joined Glyndŵr's 10,000 men. Together they took Haverfordwest, Tenby, Carmarthen and Cardigan, and pushed straight through South Wales into England. They were approaching Worcester when Glyndŵr apparently decided his forces were overextended and withdrew. It is believed by many historians that this is the decisive point at which, had he engaged Henry in battle, he would have won, but that lack of sufficient support led him to forsake the opportunity. In September of that year, Henry once again led a large army into Wales and once again was driven back by the weather.

In 1406 Glyndŵr called the parliament in Pennal, which gave its name to some of Glyndŵr's noblest policies, such as establishing universities in North and South Wales and establishing an independent Welsh church, free of England and Canterbury. Towards this end, it was decided to support the disputed papacy in Avignon. It was in this year, however, that the tide of war began to turn. Henry defeated the Scottish king and thus was able to turn more attention and effort towards Wales. The English advantage in sea power and castles (which could be provisioned from the sea) and numerical superiority in men and arms began to overwhelm Glyndŵr's forces, who had been living mainly off the land and through pillaging and who, though quite numerous for such a small nation, were outnumbered by England. In 1407 Glyndŵr fended off one attack on the castle at Aberystwyth, but in the following year it fell. Harlech fell in 1409, and Glyndŵr's family was taken into captivity. The uprising only gradually faded, however, with the mountains of central Wales still serving as Glyndŵr's stronghold. In 1410, Glyndŵr still held his home area in Powys, and from there he attacked the Shropshire border in a battle which lost him some of his most faithful supporters – Rhys Ddu, Philip Scudamore and Rhys ap Tudur. In 1412 he captured his old enemy Dafydd Gam, and in 1415 Gruffudd Young was still representing him in France. English forces were maintained in Wales to protect against Glyndŵr, and in 1415 Henry V offered a pardon to Glyndŵr and his supporters if they would only submit. Glyndŵr would not. Nothing more is known of him after that time.[5] Nevertheless, as will be seen in the subsequent chapters, Glyndŵr left a legacy of hope for a free and independent Welsh state. His war is not lost, only unfinished.

Sources

In studying Owain Glyndŵr, the development of the heroic pattern into which he was placed, the traditions which developed from his life and wars, and his assumption of the role of nationalist symbol, I relied upon a wide variety of sources, ranging from twelfth-century manuscripts containing sixth-century texts to twentieth-century fieldwork. These sources include poetry, prophecies, histories, antiquarian reports, folklore collections, nationalist journals and political writings. Although many of these are discussed at relevant points in the following chapters, some general discussion before proceeding will be helpful.

Most of the material about the redeemer-heroes who preceded Owain Glyndŵr appears in verse, particularly in vaticinations. Vaticinatory poetry, of which the earliest extant Welsh examples appear to come from the early tenth century, draws on a variety of bardic skills, including prophecy, knowledge of tradition and political acumen. Poets played an important role in Welsh society, possibly continuing their earlier function as counsellors to priest-kings. Their primary activity appears to have been as panegyrists but, credited with divinatory powers, they were also seers. Moreover, they were guardians of knowledge. They were trained not only in such matters as metre and alliteration but also in traditional lore such as genealogy, history, mythology and legendry. So even though the overt purpose of the poems may be praise, the praise is conveyed through reference to events, both immediate and past, to notable figures and to legendry. Furthermore, the poets' praise of a king reaffirmed his right to rule and at the same time reiterated society's values, reminding both king and people what standards of honour and generosity were to be expected. The bards were active members of the court, sometimes themselves warriors, but always attentive to political and social needs.

Because poetry was an oral form, very little of the early verse has survived. The first poets of whom anything is known are the *Cynfeirdd* (early poets) Taliesin and Aneirin of the sixth century, but they were composing as part of an already well-established, highly-developed poetic tradition. Their poetry and that of later poets, whose work was often attributed to the earlier ones, appears to have been first written down in the ninth century, though the earliest extant manuscripts are from the thirteenth century. *Llyfr Du Caerfyrddin* (Black Book of Carmarthen), compiled *c*.1250, *Llyfr Taliesin* (Book of Taliesin), *c*.1300–25, and *Llyfr Coch Hergest* (Red Book of Hergest), *c*.1400, were the most useful for this particular study.

Generally, the *canu darogan* or vaticinations were consciously political propaganda. Often they were predated so that the 'predictions' which they contained about events already passed were accurate, thus lending greater authority to statements about the future, of which the most important were promises of the coming of a great leader and of eventual Welsh victory over the Saxons. A.O.H. Jarman explains that 'the prophecies were propagandist poems designed to sustain the morale of the people, and in particular of the soldiery, in the face of continuing enemy successes, and they were composed in language which was simple and comprehensible compared with the difficult diction deliberately cultivated by the court poets of the later princes'.[6] They may have been easily comprehended at the time, but corrupt texts, changes in vocabulary and ignorance about the details underlying the allusions make them much more difficult to understand now. Nonetheless, they do indicate traditions in common use, such as that of the returning hero; they do reveal on what traditional expectations the poets were building as they tried to guide the community. Though it can be argued that the early poetry belonged to the aristocracy, ignoring as it did the everyday concerns of the lower classes, the poetry must nevertheless have relied on commonly held lore and beliefs because it also served as part of the structure which bound the people and the ruler together. In reiterating the values of the culture and laying out the present's foundations in the past, the poets posited a shared worldview necessary for maintaining society's fabric.

Though times and rulers changed, the role of the poet stayed essentially the same for centuries, and with it the type of information conveyed through the poetry. The *Gogynfeirdd* (fairly early poets) or *Beirdd y Tywysogion* (poets of the princes), writing in the twelfth and thirteenth centuries when the Welsh were straining against the Normans to keep their independence, concentrated on the same matters as did earlier poets – on praising their patrons in both eulogy and elegy, on genealogy, on history and on narrative. Later, *Beirdd yr Uchelwyr* (poets of the gentry), who flourished *c*.1350–*c*.1650, continued the tradition.

The allusive quality of the poetry of the *Gogynfeirdd* and *Beirdd yr Uchelwyr* may have been intensified, making it more difficult for modern scholars to understand, but that very allusive quality provides evidence that the poets were indeed referring to shared knowledge. The references may be esoteric now, but at that time the histories and stories were part of the common lore.[7]

In this study, the poetry was most useful as a source of attitudes about the redeemer-hero and for expectations of specific redeemers within specific political and social contexts. The poetry also provides a few glimpses of Glyndŵr as a warrior and a lord, but the major source of information on Glyndŵr's life and wars is a series of chronicles. The oldest Welsh account, 'Annals of Owen Glyn Dŵr', was compiled around 1422 and is preserved in Aberystwyth, NLW Peniarth MS 135, which was written in the sixteenth century by Gruffudd Hiraethog. It is also copied in Aberystwyth, NLW Panton MSS 22 and 23. The next major account, Aberystwyth, NLW Mostyn MS 158, was composed *c.*1548 by Elis Gruffydd, a soldier attached to the garrison at Calais. Then in 1584, David Powel, a cleric and historian, published *The Historie of Cambria, now called Wales*, which includes passages concerning Glyndŵr. Although writing after the Acts of Union of 1536 and 1542, of which he highly approved as being 'beneficiall to the common people of Wales',[8] Powel was only mildly critical of Glyndŵr, who he says did not really have claim to the title prince of Wales. In contrast, he was highly critical of Henry IV, who 'conceiuing great hatred against them [the Welsh], shewed himself a manifest oppressor of all that nation, making rigorous lawes against them . . . lawes both vnreasonable and vnconcionable (such as no prince among the heathen euer offered to his subjects)'.[9] Part of Powel's reason for publishing was a desire to redress an imbalance. He complained of the

> slanderous report of such writers, as in their bookes do inforce euerie thing that is done by the Welshmen to their discredit, leauing out all the causes and circumstances of the same; which doo most commonlie not onelie eleuate or dissemble all the iniuries and wrongs offered and done to the Welshmen, but also conceale or deface all the actes worthie of commendation atchieued by them. Search the common Chronicles touching the Welshmen, and commonlie thou shalt find that the King sendeth some noble man

or other with an armie to Wales, to withstand the rebellious attempts, the proud stomachs, the presumptuous pride, stirre, trouble and rebellion of the fierce, vnquiet, craking, fickle and unconstant Welshmen, and no open fact laid downe to charge them withall, why warre should be leuied against them, nor yet they swaruing abrod out of their owne countrie to trouble other men. Now this historie dooth shew the cause and circumstances of most of those warres, whereby the qualitie of the action may be iudged.[10]

He then went on to declare that the Welsh have the right to defend themselves and their land from greedy foreigners. Nevertheless, despite this early warning against unqualified acceptance of English views, subsequent historians, writing under English rule, often showed an English bias. In the 1660s, Robert Vaughan of Hengwrt, an antiquarian and collector of manuscripts, wrote a history of Owain Glyndŵr (preserved in Aberystwyth, NLW Panton MS 53, pp.49–60), which was the first full account of Glyndŵr's life. Vaughan drew on the 'Annals' and other chronicles (including the works of Powel and the Englishman Raphael Holinshed), combining them, it is thought, with lore current in his area. The care he put into gathering information is witnessed in Aberystwyth, NLW MS 13074D, in which in 1629 he copied extracts from late fifteenth-century texts,[11] and in marginalia which he wrote in a copy of Powel's *Historie* (which were copied into Aberystwyth, NLW Panton MS 11 in the eighteenth century). Most of Vaughan's compiled account is neutral, but Vaughan accused Glyndŵr of cruelty and covetousness and faulted him for not having joined in the battle at Shrewsbury. Vaughan's history became the accepted authority on which other scholars based their works. Thomas Ellis's *Memoirs of Owen Glendower*, also written in the 1660s, is essentially the same as Panton MS 53. (In fact, J.E. Lloyd believes the work was actually written by Ellis's friend Vaughan.) Edward Lhuyd used Vaughan's work when adding notes to William Camden's *Britannia* in 1695, and William Wynne of Garthewin based his 1697 work *History of Wales* on Powel and Vaughan. The next major development in histories of Glyndŵr came with Thomas Pennant, who added a discussion of Glyndŵr to his 1778 *Tours in Wales*. Pennant gathered material from all possible sources, including poetry, Welsh and English chronicles, and songs and stories in oral circulation, and tried to evaluate them afresh rather than simply accepting them or relying on previous interpretations. He also took into consideration a wide variety of political and social factors affecting Wales and England in Glyndŵr's period. His work became the new authority for subsequent historians and was not superseded in that role until J. E. Lloyd's carefully researched and balanced study *Owen Glendower in 1931*.

Amongst the chronicles useful in studying Glyndŵr are also certain English-oriented ones, beginning with *Chronicon Adae de Usk*, an extension of Ranulf Higden's extremely popular and influential *Polychronicon* (a universal history composed *c*.1320), covering the dates 1377–1421 and written some time before 1430. Adam of Usk was a Welshman, contemporary with Glyndŵr, but he was so strongly aligned with Henry IV that, despite his having taken refuge with Glyndŵr while in temporary disfavour with the king, his chronicles of the events in his lifetime reflect primarily English views. Glyndŵr is mentioned in basically all English chronicles of Henry IV, but perhaps the most influential is Raphael Holinshed's *Chronicles of England, Scotland, and Ireland* (1577), which served as a source for Shakespeare and for both Welsh and English historians.

The abundance of texts on Glyndŵr in itself indicates the importance assigned to him over the centuries. In the fifteenth century alone, several texts, written as special additions or as marginalia, show a strong interest in Glyndŵr. An unidentified author, after translating into English Higden's *Polychronicon*, updated it, concluding with an extended passage on Glyndŵr.[12] In a similar situation, in which the annals *Brenhinedd y Saesson* (Kings of the Saxons; for the years 683–1197) were extended to the year 1461 in the Black Book of Basingwerk (Aberystwyth, NLW MS 7006D), the annal for 1400 reports Glyndŵr burning Rhuthun and capturing Grey and Mortimer.[13] A single folio of the mid-fifteenth-century manuscript Aberystyth, NLW Peniarth MS 52, bound in with a thirteenth-century manuscript of *Brut y Brenhinedd* (Chronicle of the Kings, in Aberystwyth, NLW Peniarth MS 44), contains one paragraph on Glyndŵr:

> Pan goronet harri vrenin y pedwerydd oet yr Iessv m cccc excepto
> duo anno. y gwannwyn nessa i llosget aber conwy. y vlwyddyn
> nessa i kyvodes Ywain ap Gruff tridiev kyn gwyl vathev ar gwyl

vathev hwnnw i llosges ef Ruthyn Duw gwener nessa ar hyny i bv
y lladdva yny Vyrnwy mcccc iiij pan losges ywain ddinbech. Anno
m cccc vj ar dduw kalan mai i llosges y sayson ysgopty llanelwy.[14]

(When King Henry the Fourth was crowned in the age of Jesus 1400
except two years [i.e., 1398]. The next spring Aberconwy was burnt.
The next year, Owain ap Gruffudd rose up, three days before St
Matthew's Day. On that St Matthew's Day he burned Rhuthun. The
next Friday after that was the slaughter in Vyrnwy. 1404 when
Owain burned Denbigh. The year 1406 on the calends [first] of May
the English burned the bishophouse of St Asaph.)

This passage was recopied on the following folio by the
antiquarian William Maurice in 1660. One fragment of verse in
praise of Glyndŵr appears as marginalia on folio 151v of BL MS
Cotton Caligula A iii.[15] These last two items, like the Black Book
of Basingwerk, may have been associated with monasteries,[16]
which may in turn indicate that monasteries were relatively safe
places in which to show an interest in Glyndŵr so soon after the
uprising. Whether or not these texts demonstrate monastic
concern, they, taken with similar texts from later centuries, do
indicate a certain fascination with Glyndŵr.

When using these chronicles, both Welsh and English, many of
them interrelated, careful attention must be paid to the
culturally-based assumptions and political objectives which
affected their authors' choices in selecting from the available
written texts and oral traditions. The interplay of narrative and
political sensibility can be seen, for example, in the various
reports on the origin of hostilities between Owain Glyndŵr and
King Henry IV. The first account occurs in Peniarth MS 135,
compiled around 1422. For the year 1400 it simply states:

yddaeth Hari i prydein a llu mawr gidac ef a phan ytoedd ef ar
wastad yno y dywawt un or arglwyddi wrthaw yddoedd reidach
iddaw vod diwydwyr iddaw ynghymru a dywedyd y kyfodai
Owain ap Gruff i ryfelu yn i erbyn ac oddiyno i danvoned
arglwydd Talbod ac arglwydd grei o rruthyn i vod yn ddiogel o
ywain a hwynt ai kymerassant arnaddynt eisioes y gwr a
ddiangawdd ir koed [17]

(Henry went to Scotland and a great host with him. And when he
was at rest one of the lords said to him he needed to have faithful

men in Wales and said that Owen ap Gruff would rise to war against him. Therefore, he sent Lord Talbot and Lord Grey of Rhuthun to make sure of Owen and they took it upon themselves; however, the man escaped to the woods.)

No explanation is given as to why Glyndŵr might wage war, as indeed he did not until after King Henry took action against him. The next text, composed by Adam of Usk, a Welshman who served the English kings Richard II and Henry IV, though tempered by some sympathy for the Welsh, clearly presents an English point of view. Adam reports King Henry returning from Scotland to England,

> and hearing at Leicester how Owen, lord of Glendower, along with the Northern Welsh who had raised him up to their prince had broken out into rebellion and had seized many castles, and how he had burned on all sides the towns wherein the English dwelt amongst them, pillaging them and driving out the English, he gathered together the flower of his troops, and marched his array into North Wales. And the Welsh being subdued and driven away, their prince with seven others lay hid for a year among rocks and caves.[18]

Again no explanation for the uprising is given, but this time the Welsh break out into chaotic rebellion, which a peace-bringing Henry must subdue.

The next narrative development clearly depicts Glyndŵr as an innocent victim of the machinations of his neighbour Lord Grey of Rhuthun. The story, as mentioned earlier, is that Henry wrote Glyndŵr letters asking him to join him on his Scottish campaign. Unfortunately, he sent the letters with Grey, who did not deliver them until the day before the expedition. When Glyndŵr responded that he had neither sufficient time nor money to gather his men and prepare at such short notice, Grey reported back to the credulous king that Glyndŵr, despising his letters, had refused to obey. So when the king returned from Scotland, he went to Wales and, failing to capture Glyndŵr, gave his lands to Grey. But as the texts say, 'the grant of that land caused great trouble and hurt',[19] and, 'that caused great affliction between Wales and England'.[20] The first record of this account appears in BL MS Harleian 2261 in the extension of the second translation of

Higden's *Polychronicon*, compiled between 1432 and 1450 by an unknown author. The second time the story appears is in a fifteenth-century paper-copy, made by Gutun Owain of *Brenhinedd y Saesson* from the Black Book of Basingwerk. This paper manuscript has disappeared but excerpts from it, including the Owain Glyndŵr story, were copied by the antiquarian Robert Vaughan, in the course of collating the two manuscripts, in 1629 in Aberystwyth, NLW 13074D.[21] Vaughan was obviously intrigued by this account for he wrote it also in the margins of David Powel's *Historie of Cambria* (copied by Evan Evans in Panton MS 11) and included it in his own 'History of Owen Glyndŵr' (Panton MS 53), whence it entered all subsequent histories.

We cannot be certain that this story was picked up from oral tradition (though the texts discussed so far were all compiled within roughly fifty years of the events) or when it might have entered the oral tradition, but it does show a Welsh sensibility, or at least sensitivity. Basingwerk was a Cistercian monastery in North Wales, and the Cistercians were noted for writing chronicles, patronizing poets, and supporting the Welsh princes. They sided with Owain Glyndŵr, so it is not surprising that their copy of *Brenhinedd y Saesson* contains an account so supportive of him. Possibly, the unknown translator of the *Polychronicon* who first recorded the story and who refers to Glyndŵr as an 'esquier of great fame',[22] was himself from North Wales and may even have been at Basingwerk.

The next text chronologically is Elis Gruffydd's account in Mostyn MS 158, written *c.*1548. Gruffydd does not go into much detail, simply stating that the dams of the old enmity and jealousy which long stood between Glyndŵr and Grey finally broke in 1400. He includes examples indicating Welsh sympathy and pride, but his major comment on Glyndŵr appears to be one neither of support nor of condemnation – but rather of disappointment: after relating the story of Glyndŵr's disappearance from Y Berwyn and presenting several possible explanations of it, Gruffydd goes on to say that it does not matter in the least why he disappeared. The fact is that he did, and that because of that, the people were left without a leader and so abandoned the field – and thus ended the battle.

Adam of Usk and Elis Gruffydd were both undoubtedly

affected by English views, but their slight criticisms are nothing compared to those of the Englishmen. Raphael Holinshed writing in 1577 and relying heavily on Walsingham, reports that while Henry was in Scotland, 'the Welshmen tooke occasion to rebell vnder the conduct of their capteine Owen Glendower, doing what mischeefe they could deuise, vnto their English neighbours',[23] and that when Glyndŵr's suit against Grey over land did not go well, 'he first made warre against the said Lord Greie, wasting his lands and possessions with fire and sword, cruellie killing his seruants and tenants'.[24] It is not so much in the events as in the words used to describe them that one sees the English bias (except when it comes to Glyndŵr's cruelty, a point on which the English writers insist, as discussed in Chapter 4).

English views began to affect the Welsh (who, moreover, also began recording the histories in English) leading to very mixed reports. David Powel, writing in 1584, for example, though strongly supporting Wales, seems reluctant to accept Glyndŵr totally. Nevertheless, he introduces to the chronicles another account which shows Grey as the instigator of open hostilities. The two men had long been in conflict over common land lying between their territories but, during Richard II's reign, Glyndŵr was too powerful for Grey to attack. However, finding himself better favoured under Henry IV, Grey entered the common. Glyndŵr responded with force and in battle took Grey prisoner. 'This was the verie begining and the cause of Owens rising and attempts.'[25] Though he recognizes the provocation, Powel goes on to criticize Glyndŵr for not properly weighing the consequences of his misguided uprising, 'of which stirre and rebellion there insued much mischiefe to the Welshmen'.[26]

All of these narrative threads – Grey's machinations with the letter of summons; Grey, emboldened by his improved status under the new king, seizing Glyndŵr's lands and Glyndŵr responding; King Henry in Scotland, apprised of Glyndŵr's show of force, sending Lords Talbot and Grey to take him – come together in Robert Vaughan's seventeenth-century history of Owain Glyndŵr and remain entwined in subsequent chronicles including those of William Wynne, Thomas Ellis and Thomas Pennant. Not until the nineteenth century, when Glyndŵr's motivation becomes significant, does the story take on a new twist (see Chapter 5).

The various chronicles include oral traditions (both consciously and unconsciously on the compilers' part), but a richer written source for local traditions about Glyndŵr is the more general collections made by antiquarians. Some of these are in manuscript form, such as Aberystwyth, NLW MS 39B ('Survey of Harlech Castle, Poetry, &c'), which was compiled at the end of the eighteenth century and which includes several traditions from Glyndŵr's home area.[27] Other collections appear in published form, with travellers' journals being amongst the most useful in providing scattered but important pieces of information. Thomas Evans's *Cambrian Itinerary* (1801) and Richard Fenton's *Tours in Wales (1804–1813)* are two examples. Local histories and topographical dictionaries also provide valuable information. In the nineteenth century, a number of nationalist journals were created which made a point of reporting local lore (these are discussed in Chapter 5). Legends about Glyndŵr, naturally, also appear in works specifically concerned with folklore, such as John Rhŷs's *Celtic Folklore*.

There are many written sources (in both manuscript and published form) for traditions about Glyndŵr, but the lore about him does not belong only to the past. He is very much the subject of current folklore in Wales. Some of the materials for this study were obtained from the Welsh Folk Museum (now the Museum of Welsh Life), where Robin Gwyndaf and Trefor M. Owen gave me free access to their archives. Cledwyn Fychan of the National Library of Wales also allowed me to use legends which he had collected in the Pumlumon area. Nevertheless, most of the contemporary traditions used in this study come from my own fieldwork.

This book reflects the traditions and the attitudes of people with whom I spoke. To provide the statistical sampling of a sociological study was never its goal; nor would such have been appropriate even if possible. This study deals not with the quantitative but with the qualitative. (Nor is this meant as an encyclopaedic study containing every known reference to Owain Glyndŵr.) I went into the field looking for the ways in which Glyndŵr is viewed today, for any continuities in tradition, and for people's awareness of him. I do not present all views held in Wales, only those held by the individuals with whom I had contact, a sample which was affected both by who I am and by the subject. As a Welsh speaker, I had greater entrée than I would have had speaking only in English, but as an American I was always an outsider. I also tended to concentrate on the less-Anglicized areas of Wales. Moreover, it was the people concerned with nationalism and interested in folklore (and thus more alert to local traditions) who were more often brought to my attention and who were most willing to take the time to speak with me.

I carried out my fieldwork on Glyndŵr in Wales mainly during 1982, updating it on occasional return visits, particularly in 1992. I was based in Aberystwyth, which is the site of both the University College of Wales and the National Library of Wales, where I had made friends and acquaintances in previous years, but my plan was to collect in every part of Wales and from as many different types of people as possible. Due to a number of factors, including time, money, weather, transportation and accessibility, I was not able to travel to every area. I did, however, manage to speak with individuals from most areas.

I began with contacts I knew in Aberystwyth but who had come from all over Wales, and after refining the types of questions I wished to ask, ventured into other areas. I was also able to interview people from different areas at the National Eisteddfod, a week-long celebration of Welsh culture, which in 1982 was held in Swansea but which is attended by people from every part of Wales. I interviewed individuals of many occupations: shopkeepers, shop assistants, teachers, students, clergymen, cemetery workers, farmers, bus drivers, secretaries, the retired and children. I interviewed both complete strangers, whom I approached in the street and in shops, and people to whom I was introduced by mutual acquaintances. Each technique had advantages and hazards. Welsh society is generally very close-knit; each person has a place, and newly-met people take the time to establish the network of identity through discussing home area, chapel and friends. I, however, had no place in the network and was obviously foreign even to the most casual observer. I had hoped that my being American and Welsh-speaking would protect me from the distrust given to an English person asking peculiar questions, and although it did to a certain extent, I remained always an intruder. Since my questions about Glyndŵr were on the verge of politically sensitive matter, certain people were wary of speaking with me, while others were plainly afraid. (These reactions are discussed in Chapter 5.) Nevertheless, from those who were forthcoming, I received valuable information; even from those who were too frightened to speak or who expressed unwillingness, I learned a lot about Glyndŵr's power as a symbol. Generally, I had more success with individuals to whom I was introduced or had been vouched for in some way. This was true even when the person introducing me was also a stranger to the person being approached; it was as if just the fact of the intermediary's being Welsh testified to the safety of conversing with me. Nevertheless, the people acting as my guides often created other difficulties. One guide, as she introduced me to each person and explained why I was there, pointed out that there was, of course, no longer any folklore about Glyndŵr. Another helper kept agreeing with the person being interviewed that I should go and look in the books where I would find much more accurate information. Both these attitudes repeatedly plagued my fieldwork. Welsh society is highly literate and generally holds the mistaken attitudes (well-known to folklorists) that folklore is a thing only of the past or of remote, slightly-backward areas and that books are the authoritative sources. Even certain friends whom I thought I had trained better welcomed me back to Wales and declared my research project excellent though, of course, I would not find anything. However, I found quite a lot; I found that in certain areas of Wales, Glyndŵr is an important local hero and that in many parts of Wales he carries associations which make him a vibrant symbol of nationalist hopes.

Redeemer-heroes

Though Glyndŵr himself has received little attention from folklorists, some of his legends belong to a richly studied international complex of heroic narrative. The redeemer-hero has received the most attention, beginning in the nineteenth century with comparativists noting analogues throughout Europe. Thus, for example, Edwin Sidney Hartland, examines the sleeping hero in *The Science of Fairy Tales*.[28] In most studies, the primary example from the British Isles is Arthur, and he is compared with

Prince Marko, Holger Danske, Charlemagne and Frederick Barbarossa. Scholars of the nineteenth and early twentieth centuries included interpretations of the myth of the returning hero with attempts to understand other heroic patterns. These scholars argued over whether the legends were secularized tales of gods come to earth or reports of partially-euhemerized historical figures.

In more recent years, scholarly interest has focused more on what these heroes reveal about the culture in which they are remembered. The legends about these heroes are now being examined as 'usable myth', for as Albert B. Friedman points out, 'Myth certainly informs part of our political ideology. History may not unintelligently be read . . . as a subtle system of mythology.'[29] It is in this vein that Laurence A. Schneider examines the Chinese hero Ch'ü Yüan.[30] Questions of the origin for the myth of the returning-hero in general and of the actual history of specific heroes are still treated by scholars, but there is growing interest in the hero's relation to nationalist concerns.[31] Redeemer-heroes have also been studied in relation to millenialism, in such diverse ways as Mircea Eliade's examination of eschatology and cosmogony and Norman Cohn's examination of the interaction of social movements and economic conditions.[32]

Glyndŵr, in addition to being a redeemer-hero, functions as a trickster and a social bandit, as discussed in Chapter 4. The trickster, with his position on the margins of society and his cleverness, shown in impudent pranks and escapes, has been treated in such examinations as Paul Radin's *The Trickster*, Barbara Babcock-Abrahams's ' "A Tolerated Margin of Mess": The Trickster and His Tales Reconsidered', and Orrin E. Klapp's 'The Clever Hero'. The social bandit in general has been studied by scholars such as Eric Hobsbawm, and the pattern applied to specific figures in studies such as Kent Steckmesser's article 'Robin Hood and the American Outlaw', which explores the relationship between the patterns of the trickster and the outlaw. Several major studies, particularly those by Claude Levi-Strauss, Maurice Keen, Joseph Falaky Nagy and John W. Roberts, while each using different approaches, have all examined tricksters and outlaws as expressions of specific cultural concerns and values.[33]

The redeemer-hero in Welsh culture has received a great deal of attention from Welsh literary scholars. The figure of *y mab darogan* (the son of prophecy) is central to Welsh vaticination, which forms a substantial portion of Welsh literature and especially verse. The most thorough study of the vaticinatory materials is Margaret Enid Griffiths's *Early Vaticination in Welsh* (1937), but almost every scholar who deals with prophecy must take into consideration *y mab darogan*. Furthermore, prophecy and hopes for *y mab darogan* are so strongly and intimately bound with the political history of Wales that they must often all be discussed together, as in, for example, Glanmor Williams's 'Prophecy, Poetry, and Politics in Medieval and Tudor Wales'. Glyndŵr is so very clearly a redeemer-hero that literary discussions of the theme include him, while historical discussions about Glyndŵr include the theme of the redeemer. Modern histories and nationalist tracts often discuss the power of Glyndŵr's role as *y mab darogan*. Nevertheless, while studies of Welsh nationalism recognize the myth of the redeemer-hero and are aware of the political use of it, they do not deal with the question of an underlying patterning or with the use of traditional lore in maintaining nationalist sentiment.[34]

The redeemer-hero proves a rich subject for a folklore examination. Shaped by a deep-rooted pattern which emerges repeatedly around the world, the individual hero also reflects the specific conditions and needs of the community to whom he represents hope. Offering the dream of a world set right, he functions on many levels: the international pattern, the deep myth of a people's world before history, the legendry of a nation struggling for freedom, and the local legends told by individuals proud of their home territories and yearning for a better world. Some of the range of the redeemer-hero's effectiveness is indicated by Günter Lanczkowski who, in describing the hero's arising in times of need, suffering, and oppression, explains:

> It must be understood that the return of the hidden redeemer, above all when it deals with absent kings, is not awaited solely for national independence or in the hope of the restoration of the lost greatness of a kingdom, but also for the restoration of order, for a normative effect, which is ascribed to the former times of the sacred king.[35]

By concentrating on one redeemer, going beyond generalizations to examine the individual in the full context of his tradition and the world in which he is invoked, one can gain valuable insights into both how folklore functions and the concerns of the specific culture. Owain Glyndŵr stands out amongst Welsh historical figures as one of the most intriguing and heroic. He has a special quality that gives him great importance; he is not just another soldier who lost a war. From the traditions that have accumulated around Glyndŵr, it may be possible to discern what gives him his significance and what he signifies. This type of study also provides an opportunity for examining the interaction of traditional expectations and conceptions of what should be, with perceptions of characters and events. The effects of this interaction on tradition reveal themselves in the patterns running through historical, literary and traditional accounts. Through these materials, Welsh culture is also revealed. As Bruce A. Rosenberg explains, 'The hero is the vessel into whom the ethos of a culture or sub-culture is projected as a dramatic symbol of its aspirations.'[36] A study of Glyndŵr enables both understanding of how a single hero functions in his culture and recognition of the hopes and dreams of a nation.

2

The Pattern of the Redeemer-hero

A major aspect of Owain Glyndŵr's significance in Welsh tradition lies in his role as a redeemer-hero. In order to appreciate this, however, one must first understand something of that role in Wales and also of Glyndŵr's place amongst other Welsh redeemer-heroes. Glyndŵr is part of a pattern which was shaped long before he came on the scene and which must be discerned in order to comprehend his position.

I use the term redeemer-hero for the hero who has never really died, but who, either in sleep or in a distant land, awaits the time when his people will need him, when he will return and restore the land to its former glory (or in some cases to an unprecedented future glory). This type of hero, a familiar figure quickly recognized, has appeared in many cultures and many lands. In each case, throughout his varied manifestations, the redeemer-hero's development has been precipitated by the occurrence of two necessary conditions: the first, that a group has a sense of itself as a people, distinct from all others, and the second, that its members believe themselves to be oppressed by an outside group.

In Europe, where nationalism arose relatively late, the early redeemer-heroes were looked to as defenders of embattled Christianity against the oppression of heathendom, Islam or an unscrupulous clergy. Such a defender was seen in the person of Charlemagne, who in the eleventh century was believed to have led a successful crusade to Jerusalem and then to be sleeping until the time for his return. He, like other Christian redeemers viewed in the light of Christian eschatology, was looked to as the one who would establish the period of peace before the coming of the Antichrist and then the Last Judgment.[1] Sometimes the political situation combined with the religious to cause a community to look for the return of a king, as happened when the lands of Flanders and Hainut came under French domination after the death of Baldwin IX, count of Flanders and, for a short time, emperor of Constantinople. So eager were people in Flanders to see Baldwin return and restore a better world for both Flanders and Christianity, that in 1224 they accepted a hermit as the returned Baldwin and followed him in civil war.[2] Similarly, in Germany, where there was great political turmoil at the end of the thirteenth century, longing for the return of Frederick II was temporarily met by the appearance of a hermit who claimed to be Frederick. By the mid-fourteenth century, Frederick was looked to as the messiah of the poor.[3] For a while in Europe, the oppressors against whom the sleeping kings were to provide defence were the lords, burghers, clerics and various non-Christians. Eventually, with the development of national-ism, the oppressors became another nation and it was the whole people, the whole nation, not just the poor or the approved form of Christian, who could look for salvation. Thus Frederick Barbarossa in Germany, Holger in Denmark and Marko in Hungary, Serbia and Bulgaria, among a host of other leaders, came to be looked on as national redeemers.

In Wales, however, due to early confrontations of the Britons with first the Romans, then the Angles and Saxons, and eventually with the Normans, the need for a national redeemer was felt very early. In noting this, we need not entangle ourselves in the arguments over the definitions of nationalism and nationhood. As the historian R.R. Davies points out for the thirteenth century, but certainly with far wider application, a sense of national identity is not dependent on people sharing the systems and institutions of unitary governance. 'For national identity, like class, is a matter of perception as much as of institutions.'[4] Unlike the case in mainland Europe, where, in the ever-changing tides of conquest and domination, the oppressor usually lived next door and frequently shared (at least to some extent) the language and culture of the people oppressed, the

Britons were faced with totally alien foes. Their opponents came from over the sea, bringing with them unrelated languages and cultures, which, no matter how divided the Britons might have been in their own government, could not help but leave the Britons aware of their own fellowship. Most importantly, the Welsh shared a sense of history and communal myth, a point to which this discussion will return. Sometimes, non-nationalist concerns also contribute to the feelings of immediate need of a redeemer. Plague, drought and social upheaval combine with the economic hardships of subjection and heighten the yearnings for freedom from domination which give rise to the development of a national redeemer. In any case, nourished by whatever combination of factors, the need for a national redeemer developed early in Wales, and so powerful is the legend that it was played out over and over, as desperate individuals perceived certain leaders and events according to the pattern that betokened hope, and various leaders assumed the role and tried to act out the expected pattern. Each instance further validated and strengthened the legend. Over the centuries, at least eight redeemer-heroes came into prominence in Wales, with a number of other figures also occasionally being touted as the promised deliverer.[5] These heroes are Hiriell, Cynan, Cadwaladr, Arthur, Owain, Owain Lawgoch, Owain Glyndŵr and Henry Tudor.

These eight heroes, or rather the roles they play, are integral to the Welsh historical mythology. The national historical myth rests upon a few basic concepts, perhaps the most fundamental of which is that of the unity of Britain, according to which the whole island was once, and should be again, under one governance, by the Britons, the proper rulers of the island. The governance of the island, often symbolized by the crown of London, was lost to the Saxons. Thus the coming of the Saxons and their usurpation of authority reverberates down the centuries as a major trauma, unmatched until the trauma of 1282 with the death of the last native prince of Wales and the loss of Welsh independence.

Early historians tried to make sense of the Saxon victories. Gildas, in his *De Excidio Britanniae*, *c*.540, interpreted the Saxons as the instrument of God's punishment on the Britons for their sins. Because the Britons turned from God and invited the pagan Saxons to defend their island, they went into decline and lost their honour as a people.[6] When 'Nennius' wrote his *Historia Britonum, c.*840, he shifted the focus of interpretation so that while the Saxon conquest was still God's will, the Britons were overwhelmed not because of their sinfulness but because of their thoughtless naïveté in welcoming the foreigners.[7] 'Nennius' also provided hope for future relief from their oppressors, as for example when the fatherless boy Emrys defuses King Vortigern's plans to sacrifice him on the foundation of a stronghold whose building materials repeatedly disappear. Emrys discloses that the problem lies not with a need for his blood but rather with two worms (*vermes*) which lie wrapped in a cloth at the bottom of a lake beneath the foundation. Once uncovered, the worms fight each other and Emrys explains their actions:

> Regni tui figura tentorium est; duo vermes duo dracones sunt; vermis rufus draco tuus est; et stagnum figura hujus mundi est. At ille albus draco illius gentis, quae occupavit gentes et regiones plurimas in Brittannia, et paene a mari usque ad mare tenebunt, et postea gens nostra surget, et gentem Anglorum trans mare viriliter deiciet.

> (The cloth represents your kingdom, and the two worms are two dragons. The red worm is your dragon, and the lake represents the world. But the white one is the dragon of the people who have seized many people and countries in Britain, and will reach almost from sea to sea; but later our people will arise, and will valiantly throw the English people across the sea.)[8]

This hope underlies another of the concepts basic to Welsh historical mythology – that a deliverer will come to re-establish the golden age and to regain the crown of London.

These themes and others, such as the descent of the British from Brutus, grandson of Aeneas, and the glory of having been part of the Roman Empire, were picked up and expanded by Geoffrey of Monmouth in his *Historia Regum Britanniae, c.*1136. Geoffrey gave these themes, especially the theme of the loss of Britain, a shape and validation which took over the medieval historical imagination, not only of the Welsh but also of the Anglo-Normans, and extended even to other Europeans. Geoffrey provided a well-developed and coherent history which, in tracing the story of the British over a period of approximately two thousand years, from the fall of Troy to the death of Cadwaladr and loss of sovereignty to the Saxons in 689 CE, managed to satisfy the varied needs of his audience. For the Normans, he filled in the past, giving them knowledge of their new domain and a sense of continuity in taking their place in the long line of rulers over the land. For the Welsh, he confirmed their inherent worth by showing them their honourable and often glorious past and by indicating hope for the future. Geoffrey also gave new shape and added importance to the figure of Arthur, who eventually became one of the most renowned of redeemer-heroes. Indeed, Geoffrey is largely responsible for making the legendary King Arthur the model of the redeemer-hero. So well did Geoffrey's creative history suit the needs of the Welsh, that they not only accepted it but effectively adopted it as their official history, a position which, despite occasional challenges, it did not lose until the nineteenth century.[9] The *Historia*'s popularity and the importance of its impact on Wales is indicated even in the number of translations of the text into Welsh – three times in the thirteenth century, with copies of the Welsh versions carried in almost twenty manuscripts by 1400 and in over seventy by 1900.[10]

In addition to the *Historia*, Geoffrey also wrote the *Prophetia Merlini*, which was included in the middle of the *Historia*, and *Vita Merlini*, c.1150, which contains prophecies ascribed to Merlin (Myrddin) and the sixth-century poet Taliesin. Both of these works, and particularly the latter, derive from the Welsh tradition of prophecy. It is quite clear that while Geoffrey may have been instrumental in giving literary shape to the concept of the loss of Britain, he was not responsible for the prophecy itself, which was already well established, especially in verse. The early prophecies deal with a variety of topics – astrology, meteorology, even religion occasionally – but their main thrust is political. A major concern in the vaticinatory poetry is the coming of *y mab darogan* (the son of prophecy) and his ridding the land of alien forces. We do not know how early *y mab darogan* appeared in Welsh vatication, or even how early the vaticinations began. Constance Bullock-Davies, however, has shown that belief in a promised deliverer was established among the Britons at least by the third century when the Roman leader Carausius, rejecting the authority of Diocletian, crossed from Gaul to Britain, and declared himself emperor of his new, independent realm. He imprinted his coins with the statement, 'Exspectate, veni' (Long awaited, I come).[11] He was apparently playing on Latin literary references as well as on the Britons' need for relief from a series of invaders, but the coins would have had no meaning had not the expectation of a deliverer already existed.

In any case, judging by the earliest poetic evidence preserved, expectation of a deliverer was apparently well established in Welsh culture by the ninth century. Vaticinatory poetry is generally the richest source for information on *y mab darogan*, so it is mainly through the poetry that I will examine in the following pages the development of the pattern of the redeemer-hero. Welsh vaticinatory poetry divides into four main stages or periods,[12] each of which is characterized not only by its own poetic forms, but also by its themes, the pattern elements stressed in it, its prevalent heroes and the socio-political context which shapes it. Discussion of each of these periods in turn will permit examination not only of the pattern but also of the ways in which it is expressed and used, with the periods before Glyndŵr setting the background against which he was viewed in his own time, and the periods after Glyndŵr completing the background against which he must now be viewed.

The Pattern before 1200

The first stage of the vaticinatory poetry contains the pre-thirteenth-century verse which, though probably written in the ninth through thirteenth centuries, is generally ascribed to the sixth-century Myrddin and Taliesin. The earliest prophecies are recorded in *Llyfr Du Caerfyrddin* (Black Book of Carmarthen) and *Llyfr Taliesin* (Book of Taliesin), which are dated to around the middle of the thirteenth and the early fourteenth centuries respectively. In these, the earliest work is *Armes Prydein* (Prophecy of Britain), which appears in *Llyfr Taliesin* and is dated c.930.

In this earliest poetry, the heroes awaited are long-gone historical figures, mainly Cadwaladr, Cynan, Owain and Hiriell. Of these, Hiriell, about whom we know very little, is the least noted. Indeed, there are only a couple of clear references to him, prophesying that he will defend Gwynedd. Because his name became a common noun signifying hero or lord, it is often difficult to determine whether references are to Hiriell or simply to a hero, but from those found between 1200 and 1500 – sometimes to *hil Hiriell* (his race) or *bro Hiriell* (his region) – we do know that he was associated with Anglesey and Gwynedd. Thus, in a prophecy enumerating battles in which the northern hero Cadwaladr recovers the South, one line reads, 'fflemychawt hirell ty uch hafren'[13] (Hiriell will be causing flames/flaming out above the Severn). Ifor Williams considers that Hiriell was a local hero of whom memories faded early and who thus never took on the national stature of other heroes though playing the same role of redeemer.[14]

Cadwaladr was king of Gwynedd in the middle of the seventh century. His death, attributed to multiple causes, sometimes by violence and sometimes by plague, is recorded as having occurred at various times, with 664, the date of the great plague, being the most accepted. His career, however, has been little noted, and it is thought that he derives his role as a redeemer not from his own deeds but from being the son of his father, Cadwallon, who was noted for his victories over the Saxons. Cadwallon drove Edwin of Northumbria from North Wales and, following him into his home territory, defeated and killed him in 632. He died the next year, however, and all the hopes which had focused on him devolved to his son. It is quite likely that father and son became confused in folk memory, a fusion enhanced by Cadwaladr, whose name is a compound meaning 'battle-leader', also having assumed his father's epithet Bendigaid (Blessed). His names, his heritage and whatever military and political actions he took to maintain his kingdom kept alive the hope of him as a prophesied deliverer. He was well established as such before Geoffrey of Monmouth wrote of him in his *Historia* as the last Welsh king and rewrote the end of his life. According to Geoffrey, Cadwaladr flees the plague in Britain by going to Brittany, whence he is encouraged by an angelic voice to travel to Rome, where he dies in 689.[15] In this, Geoffrey was apparently combining Cadwaladr with the Wessex king Caedwalla, who did die as a pilgrim in Rome in 689.[16] While Cadwaladr is often invoked on his own, he is also sometimes paired with another hero, Cynan.

Cynan of the prophecies has been identified with Cynan Meiriadoc. This is Conanus Meriadocus who, according to

Geoffrey, helped Maximian (Maxen Wledic) conquer Gaul and who, as reward, was given Brittany.[17] In the Welsh version of the story recorded in *Breudwyt Maxen*, however, Cynan and his brother Gadeon conquer Rome and return it to its deposed emperor Maxen; only then does Cynan conquer Brittany, where he decides to remain.[18] Rachel Bromwich traces both of these stories to major migrations of Britons to Brittany around 400 CE. She further suggests that Cynan was adopted as one of the promised deliverers because of this very connection with Brittany, noting that, when *Armes Prydein* was being composed as a call to arms in response to very specific political needs in the tenth century, the poet made special point of including the Bretons in the pan-Celtic alliance which he was urging. Therefore, due to these specific pressures which were increased because certain Breton nobles had taken refuge in England, the poet ascribed to Cynan the attributes of a redeemer. Bromwich further points out that, if the Cynan invoked by the poet is the Cynan who founded Brittany, the tradition existed at least two centuries before Geoffrey and *Breudwyt Maxen*.[19]

Owain is very different from the other three redeemer-heroes thus far discussed, or is at least several degrees further removed in our knowledge of him. The Owain of the prophecies is not identifiable as any particular historical or literary Owain, though there are enough heroic Owains from which to choose. Nor can he even be associated with a particular area, as can Hiriell. Scholars often refer to him as the Owain of tradition, apparently trusting that more traditions about him once existed. As he appears in the vaticinatory poetry, he functions just as do the other deliverers, and in the later centuries he seems to be almost the generic redeemer-hero. (If you need a redeemer-hero, call on Owain.) Frequently heroes are called on to be an Owain, as in 'ac owein auyd . . .'[20] (and he will be Owain . . .).

While for none of the four heroes who predominate in the earliest poetry do the texts provide any background, the early vaticinations do show what is expected of a redeemer-hero. First, of course, the redeemer must come, but from where? The long sleep which characterizes Arthur, Owain Lawgoch and Owain Glyndŵr in later periods is not yet prevalent, and is suggested only for Hiriell.

> Rydibit div maurth dit guithlonet.
> Kywrug glyu powis a chlas guinet.
> A chivod hirell oe hir orwet.
> y amvin ae elin terwin gwinet.[21]

(A Tuesday will come, a day of wrath, between the warriors of Powys and the tribe of Gwynedd. And Hiriell will rise from his long sleep, to fight with his enemy for the border of Gwynedd.)

The hero may come from across the sea, as in this verse in which the princes are thought to be Cynan and Cadwaladr,

> Teernet dros mor a dav dyv. llun.
> Guin ev bid ve kymri or arowun.[22]

(Kings across a sea will come on Monday. Blessed will the Welsh be from that attack.)

or as in these verses on Cadwaladr,

> ardyrched katwaladyr lluch allachar.
> arwyneb bydinawr brooed ynyal.
> Yn wir dymbi dydranoneu.
> gofunet dysgogan yg kynechreu.[23]

(Splendour of Cadwaladr, shining and bright, defence of armies in desolate places. Truly, he will come across the waves (?), the promise of the prophecy in the beginning.)

Although in *Armes Prydein* it is understood that Cynan represents the Bretons, it is not specified that he is coming from Brittany. This is made clear, however, in the *Vita Merlini* where Merlin foretells,

> . . . Britones ut nobile regnum
> temporibus multis amittant debilitate,
> donec ab Armorica veniet temone Conanus
> et Cadualadrus Cambrorum dux venerandus

(. . . that the British shall be without their kingdom for many years and remain weak, until Conan in his chariot arrive from Brittany, and that revered leader of the Welsh, Cadwalader.)[24]

Sometimes the hero is said to rise from concealment, without any further specification, as in the following examples:

> Gwr o gud parawchrud wythuer adaw ylywyaw y lawer.
> hwnn abeir dechryn pan dechreuer torr terwynrwyd duw
> gwener.[25]

(A man from concealment . . . will come to govern many; he will cause terror when is begun the fierce break (?) on Friday.)

> Dyrchauawt unic o gud.
> nyt a chatuo ydeurud.
> Kynan ykwn kymry bieiuyd.[26]

(A single/lone man will rise from concealment. Not one who will defend his honour. Cynan of the hounds, the Kymry will possess him.)

> Dydaw gwr o gwd / awna kyfamrud /achat ygynhon.
> Arall adyfyd / pellenawc y luyd / llewenyd y vrython.[27]

(A man will come from concealment who will cause slaughter and battle to the foreign nations. Another will come, and his hosts attacking afar – joy to the Britons.)

Occasionally, the deliverer is said to come from the South, but whether this implies Cynan who, as will be seen later, is identified with the South, is not certain.

> Dyrchafaud maban inadvan y dehev.[28]

(A youth will arise in a region of the south.)

By far the most common prophecy of the redeemer's coming is simply that he will come, without particulars concerning the place from which he is to come.

> Dygogan awen dygobryssyn.

(The *Awen* [poetic inspiration] foretells, they [Cynan and Cadwaladr] will hasten.)[29]

Atporyn uyd Brython pan dyorfyn.
Pell dygoganher amser dybydyn.
Teyrned a bonhed eu gorescyn.

(The Britons will rise again (?) when they prevail (?), for long was (?) prophesied the time when they [Cynan and Cadwaladr] will come, as rulers whose possession is by [the right of] descent.)[30]

Yn wir dymbi teithiawc mon.
ffaw dreic diffreidyat y popyl brython.[31]

(Truly, the rightful one of Anglesey will come. Celebrated lord, defender to the Briton people.)

pan del katwaladyr . . . [32]

(When Cadwaladr comes . . .)

iny del kadwaladir oe kinadil.[33]

(Until Cadwaladr may come to his meeting place)

Pandisgynno kadwaladyr . . . [34]

(When Cadwaladr attacks . . .)

These redeemer-heroes are warriors. It is not simply their presence which will make everything turn right; it is their military prowess.

y kynnif Katwaladyr clot lathyr leu.[35]

(In battle Cadwaladr will be famous and shining his praise.)

Kynan a Chatwaladyr kadyr yn lluyd.
Etmyccawr hyt vrawt ffawt ae deubyd.
Deu vnben degyn dwys eu kussyl.
deu orsegyn Saesson o pleit Dofyd.
deu hael deu gedawl gwlat warthegyd.
deu diarchar barawt vnffawt vn ffyd.
deu erchwynawc Prydein mirein luyd.
deu arth nys gwna gwarth kyfarth beunyd.

(Cynan and Cadwaladr, with splendid hosts, will be honoured till Judgement Day: success will be theirs. Two overpowering lords of profound counsel; two conquerors of the Saxons, in the cause of God; two generous lords, two noble raiders of a country's cattle; two ready fearless ones, one in fortune and in faith; two defenders of Britain, with splendid hosts; two bears to whom daily fighting brings no shame.)[36]

The point is that the coming of the redeemer-hero precipitates violent battles. The prophecies describe these battles in great detail, apparently revelling in their bloodiness and destruction. Here are a few limited and isolated examples; the full impact of the gruesome battles is achieved within the fully developed poem.

> ygkymry yd erhy gwraged gweddawt.
> Rac baran kynan tan tardawt.
> katwaladyr ae cwyn.
> briwhawt bre a brwyn.
> Gwellt atho tei. ty tandawt.[37]

(In Wales, women will remain in widowhood. Before Cynan's wrath, fire will erupt. Cadwaladr will be tormenting them; he will destroy the highland and the rushes, grass and house roofs flaming.)

> Yn wir dymbi romani kar.
> Odit o vab dyn arall y par.
> Racdaw ryglywhawr maw gyfagar.
> abydin agwaetlin aryescar.
> Athriganed kyrn agwerin trygar.
> rythrychynt rygyrchynt yg cledyfar.
> brein ac eryron gollychant wyar.
> ar llwybyr gwrit arch gwrys diarchar.[38]

(Truly a kinsman of the Romans will come, a rarity of a son, (?)lively his spear. Great crying out is heard before him; and an army, a flood of blood on his enemies. And sound of horns, and people (?). Some hewing those who were attacking with swords. Crows and eagles craving blood, on the path of battle, a bear invincible in his wrath.)

> A mi discoganau e. kad coed lluiuein.
> a geloraur rution rac ruthir Owein.[39]

(I will prophesy a battle at Coed Llwyfain, and red biers before the rush/onslaught of Owain.)

> naw vgein canhwr y discynnant.
> mawr watwar namyn petwar nyt atcorant.
> dyhed y eu gwraged a dywedant.
> eu crysseu yn llawn creu a orolchant.

(Nine score hundred men, they (will) attack – What a mockery! only four (hundred) will return. They will tell the disastrous tale to their wives; they will wash their shirts full of blood.)[40]

> Kynan yn racwan ym pop discyn.
> Saesson rac Brython gwae a genyn.
> Katwaladyr yn baladyr gan y unbyn.
> trwy synhwyr yn llwyr yn eu dichlyn.
> Pan syrthwynt eu clas dros eu herchwyn.
> yg custud a chreu rud ar rud allmyn.

(Cynan striking foremost in every attack; the Saxons will sing their lamentation before the Britons, Cadwaladr will be a shaft of defence with his chieftains, skilfully and thoroughly seeking them out, when their people will fall for their defender (?) in affliction, with red blood on the foreigners' cheeks.)[41]

> Dychyrchwynt gyfarth mal arth o vynyd.
> y talu gwynyeith gwaet eu hennyd.
> Atvi peleitral dyfal dillyd.
> nyt arbettwy car corff y gilyd.
> Atui pen gaflaw heb emennyd.
> Atui gwraged gwedw a meirch gweilyd.
> Atui obein vthyr rac ruthyr ketwyr.
> A lliaws llaw amhar kyn gwascar lluyd.
> Kennadeu agheu dychyferwyd.
> pan safhwynt galaned wrth eu hennyd.

(They [the Welsh] will rush into battle like a bear from the mountain to avenge the bloodshed of their fellows; there will be spear-thrusts in a ceaseless flood, no friend [of ours(?)] will have pity for (?) the body of his opponent. There will be heads split open without brains, women will be widowed, and horses riderless, there will be terrible wailing before the rush of warriors, many wounded by hand; before the hosts separate the messengers of death will meet when corpses stand up, supporting each other.)[42]

gorvolet y gimry goruaur gadev.
In amuin kyminaud clefytaud clev.
Aer o saesson. ar onn verev.
A guarwyaur pelre ac ev pennev.[43]

(Great joy (?)will come to the Welsh with their mighty hosts,
fighting at/defending Cyminawd with soft swordstrokes. Slaughter
of the Saxons, with the ash spears. And playing ball with their heads.)

Of course, the point of all the battles is to get rid of the Saxons
and whatever other aliens may be intruding on Wales.

Ban gunelhont meiriev datlev bichein.
Anudon a brad gulad veibonin.
A phan del kadualadir y orescin mon
dileaur saeson o tirion prydein.[44]

(When stewards hold their little courts. Perjury and treachery of
the sons of the land. And when Cadwaladr comes to conquer
Anglesey the Saxons will be destroyed from the land of Britain.)

Gwaethyl gwyr hyt Gaer Weir gwasgarawt allmyn.
gwnahawnt goruoled gwedy gwehyn.

(The warriors will scatter the foreigners as far as Caer Weir – they
will rejoice after the devastation.)[45]

ef gyrhawt allmyn y alltuded.
nys arhaedwy neb nys dioes dayar.

(The foreigners will be driven into exile: no one will receive them,
they have no land.)[46]

treis ar eigyl a hynt o alltuted.
trwy vor llithrant eu heissilled.[47]

([(?)causing] oppression on the Angles and a path of exile, their
descendants will slip away through the sea.)

Carannawc uabon ymbronn gwaret.
kyuarwyd yw duw ymdamunet.
allmyn argychwyn gochwed dyghet.[48]

(Crowned son (?)in the breast of deliverance. God is familiar with
my wish. The foreigners about to begin the [(?)fated] slaughter.)

One of the characteristics of this cataclysmic period is that for a while all norms are upset and the proper world overturned. This theme, seen also in eschatological prophecies, seems to suggest that before order can be established total chaos must be achieved. The land itself is affected:

> erti heb medi ym bid dyhetauc.
> guell bet. no buhet pop yghenauc.[49]

(Ploughing without reaping in a bellicose world, better a grave than life for every needy one.)

But more significant, the social norms are set askew, resulting in all sorts of strange behaviour.

> Atvyd ryfedawt.
> gwr gan verch y vrawt.[50]

(There will be a wonder: a man with his brother's daughter.)

> Jeuhawt gwreic gan y gwas.[51]

(The wife will be yoked with her servant.)

> Morynion moelon. guraget revit.
> karant ny pharchant eu kerenhit.[52]

(Maidens bared, women wanton, kin who do not respect/care for their kindred.)

> Escyp agkyueith diffeith difid.[53]

(Bishops of strange language, wicked, without faith.)

and possibly worst of all:

> Kertorion allan heb ran teithi.
> kyn safont in y drvs tlus nys deupi.[54]

(Musicians outside without a rightful position; though they stand in the door, (?)no reward comes to them.)

Part of the cure for the turmoil and chaos is that Wales should be united. The different factions and realms must work together before they can rid the land of the oppressor. This unification is sometimes seen in the prophecy that Cadwaladr, who is primarily a northern hero, will come not only to North Wales, but also to the South. This appears, for example, in the following verses:

> Pandisgynno kadwaladyr allu llydan gantaw kymwed.
> duw merchyr yamwyn gwyr gwyned.
> . . .
> Pandisgynno kadwaladyr yndyffryn tywi.[55]

(When Cadwaladr attacks, and an extensive host with him [(?)in] joy, Wednesday, to deliver the men of Gwynedd . . . // When Cadwaladr attacks in Dyffryn Tywi, . . .)

Again the northern Cadwaladr is to go to the South:

> iny del kadwaladir oe kinadil. kadwaon.
> y erir tywi ateiwi affon.[56]

(until Cadwaladr may come to his meeting, [with] warriors, to the region of Tywi and Teifi river.)

A few lines later, Cadwaladr is to meet Cynan at a ford before they jointly attack the Saxons.

> yny del kadwaladir oe kinadyl. Rid Reon.
> Kinan in y erbin ef kychwin ar saesson.[57]

(until Cadwaladr may come to his meeting [to] Rhyd Rheon. Cynan opposite him, rising against the Saxons.)

Since Cynan appears to be the representative of the South just as Cadwaladr is of the North, their repeated association in the prophecies may reflect the need to unify Wales. This unity is more fundamental than urging an alliance of the Bretons with the Welsh through invoking their founder Cynan. Cynan and Cadwaladr, the deliverers of South and North, must work together because the land must be made whole before it can be healed. Order must come out of unity, not out of the chaos of division. The importance of the unity to be achieved by an alliance between Cynan and Cadwaladr is suggested in these verses:

Kynan kadwaladir. Kymri penbaladir.
bitaud ev kinatil a edmyccaur.[58]

(Cynan, Cadwaladr. Wales completely. Their meeting will be praised.)

Geoffrey reaffirms the link between Cynan and Cadwaladr, as seen in his *Prophetia Merlini*:

Cadualadrus uocabit conanum. & albaniam in societatem accipiet.
Tunc erit strages alienigenarum. tunc flumina sanguine manabunt.

(Cadwallader shall summon Conanus and shall make an alliance with Albany. Then the foreigners shall be slaughtered and the rivers will run with blood.)[59]

The aim of all the activity, indeed of the redeemer's coming, is peace and the establishment of a golden age. The prophecies remind of the promise. One poet, after bewailing the horrors of the time, declares,

gwir ydaw gwaret.
drwyrdyn damunet.
. . .
kymry vngyffret.
eullu alluchet.
coeluein euguaret.[60]

(Truly salvation will come through the longed for/desired man. // Wales one society, their host gleaming, their deliverance a gift/glad tidings.)

The dream is to rid the land of the aliens and to restore a proper society.

A chiureithau gulad. a chistutia gwad.
a llv a lled[ ] divahaur.
An bi ni inaeth guared guyd[ ]aeth.
Neb o haelonaeth ni didolaur.[61]

(And the country will be ruled by establishing law and chastising betrayal. And a host and theft will be destroyed. We shall have then deliverance after evil. None of generosity will be banished.)

Hope is held out, and there are descriptions of the peace to come.

> maraned a meued a hed genhyn.
> A phennaeth ehelaeth a ffraeth vnbyn.
> A gwedy dyhed anhed ym pop mehyn.[62]

(We shall have wealth and property and peace, and wide dominion, and ready leaders; [and] after commotion, settlement in every place.)

> Arbenygaul mon ae. guledychuy.
> Guraget dan y gint. Guir yg kystvy.
> Dedwytach no mi ae harhowe.
> Amser kadwaladir. kert a ganhwi.[63]

(The lord of Anglesey will govern it. Women under the (?)pagan people. Men in affliction/punishment/chastisement. More fortunate than I the one who may await him. The time of Cadwaladr. May he sing a song.)

> Kimry a orvit kein bid eu dragon.
> kaffaud paub y teithi. llauen vi bri. brython.
> Kenhittor kirrn eluch. kathil hetuch a hinon.[64]

(The Welsh will triumph, excellent will be their leader. Everybody will get their rights. Joy will be the honour of the Britons. Horns of rejoicing will be sounded, a song of peace and fair weather.)

In *Vita Merlini*, Merlin prophesies:

> hostibus expulsis renovato tempore Bruti,
> tractabuntque suas sacratis legibus urbes.

(The enemy will be driven out and the time of Brutus will be back once more. The natives will administer their own cities by the time-hallowed laws.)[65]

As can be seen from these early examples, while no biographical pattern emerges for these redeemer-heroes, their traditional role is well established. Clearly, a deliverer is awaited, and when he comes, whether from sleep, hiding or across the sea, he will, through blood and terrible battles, rid the land of the hated alien presence, and then restore peace, prosperity and justice to a united Welsh people. The pattern revealed in this early poetry remains essentially the same basic pattern for the nature of the redeemer-hero; in later periods, changes appear in the hero and in the expression of longing for him to fulfil the promise.

Of the heroes appearing in the earliest vaticinations, Cadwaladr appears to have the strongest tradition as a redeemer, with his sometime co-saviour Cynan sharing in the honour. Apparently, the tradition concerning these two was strong enough that not only did Geoffrey of Monmouth hear of it, but he also gave them precedence over Arthur as redeemers of Britain. This is particularly significant because it was Geoffrey who gave Arthur fame as a redeemer-hero. In *Vita Merlini*, Taliesin recounts how, after the battle at Camlan, Arthur was taken to the Island of Apples where he was left to be healed in the care of Morgen. Upon hearing of the tribulations in Britain, he suggests sending for Arthur so that he can vanquish the enemy and restore peace. Merlin, however, rejects the suggestion, saying that the British must continue to suffer until Cynan and Cadwaladr come.[66]

Arthur's lesser role as a saviour is demonstrated by the fact that he does not even appear in the early vaticinatory poetry. He appears elsewhere in early Welsh poetry,[67] but not in the vaticinations and not as a redeemer-hero. In other aspects of his character, however, Arthur is seen firmly rooted in tradition from an early period. He appears to have been a hero of North Britain whose legends, along with those of other such heroes, were relocalized to Wales. Nevertheless, the earliest references do show him in the North and, furthermore, show him as a man of prowess. In the *Gododdin* (preserved in a version possibly from the ninth century in a thirteenth-century manuscript), one of the warriors is reported doing great deeds, 'ceni bei ef arthur'[68] (although he was not Arthur). Arthur's victories in twelve battles against the Saxons are described by 'Nennius', also in the ninth century.[69] Arthur apparently had the qualifications to be a national redeemer; he had demonstrated military prowess in general and success in fighting the Saxons in particular. Though we do not know when he came to be viewed in that role, it is clear that by the early twelfth century he was well established in tradition as a deliverer. Nevertheless, the only indication in the early poetry that he might have been considered a deliverer is in one line in a series of verses called *Englynion y Beddau* (Stanzas of the Graves).

> Bet y march. bet y guythur.
> bet y gugaun cletyfrut.
> Anoeth bid bet y arthur.[70]

(A grave for March, a grave for Gwythur, a grave for Gwgawn of the red sword; (?)difficult of finding in the world/(?)a wonder of the world is a grave for Arthur.)

The unknown grave, a motif which we shall see repeated with Owain Glyndŵr, carries with it the suggestion that Arthur is not dead. This association of ideas is presented even more clearly by William of Malmesbury, an Englishman writing *c.*1125, when he notes, 'Sed Arturis sepulchrum nusquam visitur, unde antiquitatis naeniarum adhuc eum venturum fabulatur'[71] (But Arthur's tomb is nowhere to be seen, whence the ancient sorrowful songs tell the story that he is yet to come). Then in 1139, Henry of Huntingdon wrote in a letter about Arthur that, although Arthur fell on the battlefield from numerous wounds, 'parentes sui Britones mortuum fore denegent, et venturum adhuc sollenniter expectent'[72] (his own kinsmen the Britons deny that he died and solemnly expect even now that he will come). Though this letter was written in connection with Geoffrey's *Historia*, it was written so soon after that work that it surely reflects genuine current tradition as yet uninfluenced by Geoffrey. It is of particular significance that these two examples of belief come from English sources; the belief in Wales must have been widespread and strong indeed for the English to have noticed it. Moreover, we have further indication of the power of that belief in that it created a force which intrigued and possibly threatened Henry II. Twelfth-century Wales, as resentful as ever of Anglo-Norman domination, was enjoying successful leaders such as Owain Gwynedd, and tensions were high. The poets were reminding both the community and the leaders of the prophecies and urging them to action. Possibly responding to these circumstances, in an attempt to prove that Arthur would not return to their aid because he had indeed died, Henry II passed on information he had learned from a Breton singer about the location of Arthur's grave. Following his directions, in 1191 the monks of Glastonbury Abbey exhumed two bodies which they claimed to be Arthur and Guinevere. Details of the exhumation are recorded by Giraldus Cambrensis, who visited the site a year later, and who, in ridiculing the Arthurian legends, adds valuable information about the beliefs extant at the time.

> Hujus autem corpus, quod quasi phantasticum in fine, et tanquam per spiritus ad longinqua translatum, neque morti obnoxium fabulae confinxerant, his nostris diebus apud Glastoniam . . . est inventum . . .

> (In our own lifetime Arthur's body was discovered at Glastonbury, although the legends had always encouraged us to believe that there was something otherworldly about his ending, that he had resisted death and had been spirited away to some far-distant spot.)[73]

> Porro quoniam de rege Arthuro et ejus exitu dubio multa referri solent et fabulae confingi, Britonum populis ipsum adhuc vivere fatue contendentibus . . .

> (Many tales are told and many legends have been invented about King Arthur and his mysterious ending. In their stupidity the British people maintain that he is still alive.)[74]

> Quae [vulnera] cum sanata fuerint, redibit rex fortis et potens, ad Britones regendum, ut ducunt [Britones], sicut solet; propter quod, ipsum expectant adhuc venturum sicut Judaei Messiam suum, majori etiam fatuitate et infelicitate, simul ac infidelitate decepti.

> (According to them [the Britons], once he has recovered from his wounds this strong and all-powerful King will return to rule over the Britons in the normal way. The result of all this is that they really expect him to come back, just as the Jews, led astray by even greater stupidity, misfortune and misplaced faith, really expect their Messiah to return [to come to this place].)[75]

There are conflicting traditions in Wales, such as one preserved in one of the Triads, which includes a description of the battle of Camlan and the wounds inflicted on each other by Medrawd and Arthur.

> Ac o hynny y bu uarv. Ac y myvn plas yn Ynys Auallach y cladvyt.

(And from that [wound] he died, and was buried in a hall on the Island of Afallach.)[76]

Nevertheless, the dominant belief appears to have been in Arthur's survival so that he might eventually return. The belief in Wales was noted by a variety of people in both England and on the continent for at least several centuries,[77] and eventually became evident in the later vaticinatory poetry in Wales.

Developments from 1200 to 1400

In the meantime, however, in the period from 1200 to 1400, which is considered the second stage of development in vaticinatory poetry, Owain came to the fore as the most frequently invoked deliverer. He, too, is expected to come, take part in great battles, and rid the land of the Saxons.

> Mabon bronn breiskerdd mebyt yny ddewredd
> a wledych wladedd.
> A digwymp teyrnedd. o von hyt vannedd.
> ny cheis tagneuedd o ddechreu hyt ddiwedd
> ysgelwir hwnnw Owein. ysgwyt brwyt brydein[78]

(A youth of (?)powerful breast, a youth in his prime who will rule lands and kingdoms without fall from Anglesey to the peaks. He will not seek peace from the beginning to end. That one is called Owain, a shattered shield of Britain.)

> Ef a ddaw byd anhyffryd i saesson
> rhag maint ei gallu ni allant fuddion
> er hyd for coed cadarn nys cuddion
> na dym nis bydd wrth i boddion
> cyfyd o gudd gwr a wna bydd iw obeithion
> ag ywein fydd i henw honaid gyfrangon
> llew gloew a glowir ei adchwelon[79]

(He will come, an unpleasant state for the Saxons, (?) in spite of the immensity of their strength they will not succeed, on the expanse of the sea strong wood will not hide them, nor will anything be to their satisfaction. There will arise from concealment a man who will do advantage for his hopes, and Owain will be his name, of famous battles, a shining lion, whose return is heard/felt.)

> Owain i galwant pan gyrchwynt gyrch ar ddiuieu
> ac yna yn wir y daroganeu
> Bit lawen beirth a heirth gogau.[80]

(They will call on Owain when they attack, an assault on Thursday, and then, in truth, the prophecies. Joyful will be poets as fair cuckoos.)

The idea that he will be crowned is additionally included:

> etto benn llew a goronir
> Ywein Beli ywein holion i gyd
> ywein gwedi biau kymry Cymro hyfryd[81]

(Again the lion's head will be crowned, Owain of Beli, Owain of all claims, Owain then will possess Wales, fine Welshman.)

and in the prose-ending to a poem:

> Ac yna y gossodant oethydd [oed dydd] batel yn ol hono ac y kaffant y ddeuddydd yn un yrothy batel y syberwyd lloegr. Yna y gorvydd bweill llechlin a gwewyr ywerddon a bwae y brytanyeit ar syberwyd lloegr. Ac yna y kyrchant y dynas kaer lindein. Yna y gosodant wr a elwir Owein yn vrenhin ar ynys y brytanieid.[82]

(And then they will appoint a day of battle after that and they will get two days in one to give battle to the pride of England. Then the battle-axes of Norway and the spears of Ireland and bows of the Britons will prevail over the pride of England. And then they will attack the city of London. Then they will place/raise a man named Owain as king on the island of the Britons.)

Moreover, there seems to be an added vehemence as in the following emphatic statement:

> Ywain a fu ag ywein a fydd ag etto
> Ywain a rydd gwared i frython[83]

(Owain was and Owain will be and again Owain will give deliverance to Britain.)

In this late medieval period, the prophecies are attributed to poets such as Adda Fras, Goronwy Ddu, Y Bergam, Y Bardd Cwsg and Rhys Fardd, as well as to Myrddin and Taliesin.

Determination of authorship and date is virtually impossible, however, because any one poem may be ascribed to more than one poet, and with the poems referring to events ranging over several centuries, there is neither sufficient internal nor external evidence. Furthermore, the poets have sometimes taken older works and interpolated their own verses.[84] While Owain was foremost of the traditional redeemers, the poets looked not only to heroes from the past, but also to contemporary leaders. Owain Gwynedd, Llywelyn y Llyw Olaf and Owain Lawgoch, amongst others, were called on to fulfil the prophecies. However, since these heroes were referred to simply as Llywelyn, Owain, Rhys or Gruffudd and were implored to be another Owain or Cynan, it is rarely possible to determine which particular leader is being exhorted to save the Welsh and drive out the Saxons (or Anglo-Normans, as the traditional enemy had by then become). Interpretation of references is further complicated by the use of a few animals, such as bear, wolf, lion and boar, as symbols for the individuals under discussion, and by the practice of referring to past events as if in the future, in order to give credence to the prophecies. Another difference in this period is that while the earlier vaticinations dealt with the general conflict and enmity between Britons and Saxons, the works produced in the thirteenth and fourteenth centuries were concerned with the specific problems faced by the Welsh princes dealing with intrusions across their borders and, even when not concerned with invasion in particular, with the sense of deprivation in post-conquest Wales.[85]

After 1282, the need for a deliverer became profound and added to the immediacy of the vaticinations. Llywelyn ap Gruffydd, prince of Wales (also known as Llywelyn II, Llywelyn ein Llyw Olaf [our Last Leader], or simply yr Olaf [the Last]), rebuilding and expanding the work of his grandfather Llywelyn Fawr (the Great), had unified North Wales and brought most of the other Welsh princes to pay homage to him rather than to the English king, Henry III. He had achieved statehood for Wales, but then Edward I came to the throne and relations worsened. Llywelyn did not act the proper vassal and Edward did not observe all the treaties. In 1282, Llywelyn's brother Dafydd precipitated a war, and on 11 December of that year, Llywelyn was killed in an ambush. Although the war continued for a short while, Llywelyn's death signalled the end of Welsh political independence. Nevertheless, the shock of defeat and loss of independence only increased the longing for a national redeemer. The poets pushed individual leaders harder than ever to assume this role.

The way in which the poets use the promise of the redeemer-hero and apply it to their own political circumstances reveals that the redeemer is a figure of intense political immediacy rather than mere mythological romanticism. Belief in the redeemer seems to exist not simply on a symbolic level, but to be rather firmly and literally held. Indeed vaticinatory poetry can be seen as realistic in that it uses the myth of the redeemer in specific contexts. Even the manipulations by individual poets of the prophecy in favour of their own patrons shows acceptance of the underlying faith in the promise of the prophecy.

It should be remembered that the Welsh poets played an active part in their society. They were not simply recording with fine words the valorous deeds of the princes, the bounty of their courts or the sorrow at their deaths. They were also reminding those princes of their duties and obligations both to the community and to tradition. Court poets were actually officials of the court, with both their duties and their privileges set by law. They sang for their patrons, but they acted for society. Through their eulogies and elegies, they reinforced the values of the society, and through their use and preservation of history and genealogy, they validated both the prince's and the people's claim to their land and their heritage. Guardians of the past, they were also ensurers of the future, using their knowledge and training for society's sake. As Eurys I. Rowlands explains,

> . . . the bards were not simple dreamers and immature politicians. They were the most politically aware element in Welsh society, fanatical perhaps, but both intelligent and knowledgeable, by vocation closely connected with the centres of political power in Wales, by aptitude theorists and thinkers, by training the guardians of the traditions and culture of the Welsh as a Brythonic people.[86]

Well-versed in politics, they used their work to advise and to urge actions necessary to the welfare of the land. They constantly held up the glass of tradition to give perspective on current as well as past events. In other words, they helped interpret the world in the light of traditional understanding.[87]

Thus, when Owain Lawgoch emerged in the 1360s, the poets eagerly worked to spread the news that the prophesied deliverer was come, showing that he was *y mab darogan* and urging support for him. Owain Lawgoch has been identified as Owain ap Thomas ap Rhodri,[88] great-great-grandson of Llywelyn Fawr and great-nephew of Llywelyn y Llyw Olaf. Known also as Yevain de Galles, he seems to have spent most of his life in France, where he served the French king as a mercenary. He was, however, aware of his lineal descent from the Llywelyns and his rights as heir to succeed them. With the support of the French, who undoubtedly were more interested in discomfiting England than in helping Wales, Owain prepared to invade Wales and re-establish its independence. The Welsh, encouraged by the prophecies, looked forward to his coming. However, he got only as far as Guernsey, whence he and his fleet were recalled to deal with other matters. Before he could resume his plans, he was assassinated in 1378 at the siege of Montagne-sur-Mer by one John Lamb, who, while pretending sympathy with Owain's cause, was in the pay of the English.

Owain Lawgoch's role remained the same as that of the earlier redeemers – to rid the land of the Saxons, as is seen in the following verses, which also contain the recurring motif of alliance with the Norse.

> Pan vo rrvdd rredyn
> pan vo koch kelyn   } ai bwiall awchliw
> y daw gwyr Llychlyn
>
> Gidag Owain Lowgoch
> Ai baladr rryddgoch   } Ynghors Vochno[89]
> i gyro Sayson val moch

(When the bracken will be red, when the holly will be red, the men of Norway will come with their sharp battle-axes// With Owain Lawgoch and his red spear to drive the Saxons like pigs in Cors Fochno.)

Two poems in particular give us an indication of contemporary attitudes towards Owain Lawgoch. In one, which says the hero's name contains a Y, an N, an I and a double U, we see how the coming of the deliverer from over the sea is made especially relevant for this particular hero, who must come from France.

> Ni wybyddir, o hirynt,
> Ar fôr gwyrddlas, gwynias gwynt,
> Oni ddêl tarw rhyfel taer
> Ym mysg Eingl, ymwasg anghlaer
> Trwy Gymry, lle try llew trin,
> Yno bydd y naw byddin.
> Myrdd ar fôr gwyrdd a fwrw gwynt,
> Lwgr ddeffro, i Loegr ddyffrynt
> A chanddo fwyell Ellmin,
> Llychlynnig llwybr tremig trin.
> I Fynyw dir neu Fôn y daw,
> Leder ar bobl o Lydaw,
> A chanthaw, er blinaw'r blaid,
> Llynges o naw can llongaid.
> Llong a ddaw gerllaw ffawydd,
> Llyngesawg o farchawg fydd;
> A llong fraith a lleng Frython,
> A llynges gar mynwes Môn.[90]

(It will not be known, from a long course, on a green sea, white-hot wind, until a bull of ardent war comes in the midst of Angles, wretched throng, through the Welsh, where will turn the lion of battle, then will be the nine armies. A myriad on a green sea will be blown by the wind foul awakening, to England's valley, and battle-axe for the Anglo-Normans with him, Norse path, contempt of battle. To the land of Mynyw or Anglesey, he'll come, leader of the people of Brittany, and with him, despite tiring of the party, a fleet of nine hundred ships. A ship will come near beech trees, sailor of a knight he will be; and a speckled ship and Briton legion, and a fleet near Anglesey's breast.)

The poem also shows that the expectation was that this would happen not in some distant time but at that time – *this* is the year for Wales's (the red dragon's) victory.

> Mae yn ei fryd, wryd aer,
> Rhuthro Eingl rhethri anghlaer.
> Morgenau, nid amheuir,
> Y morol flaidd hoywwraidd hir.
> Blwyddyn yw hon, gron gryno,

> I'r ddraig wen roi'i phen ar ffo,
> A'r ddraig goch, lwybr wrthgroch lid,
> A'i hamlwg ffagl a'i hymlid.[91]

(It is in his mind, bravery of battle, to rush the Angles, grievous spears, sea cub, it is not doubted, the sea wolf, agile-valiant, tall one. This is the year, concise circle, for the white dragon to put her head to flight, and the red dragon, angry, sullen path, and her visible flame will pursue her.)

The other poem appears to have been written soon after Llawgoch's assassination; in recording the dashing of hopes, it shows just how powerful the dream had been. Alerted by the prophecies to watch for Owain's arrival, many of the Welsh readied themselves with horses and arms for the coming battle, but then Owain was killed. The necessary portents had not occurred this time, but one day Owain would come and achieve the mission of his rightful heritage. The dream still lived.

> Adda Fras goweithas gain
> Byrgwd ffals y bergain
> A ddysgodd ini ddisgwyl
> Beunydd bwy gilidd bob gwyl
> Gwiliaw traethau yn ieufank
> Gorllanw ffrwyth gorllwyn Ffraink
> Prynu meirch glud hybarch glod
> Ac arfau ar fedr gorfod
> Yn ol oiri yr aeth ini
> Er edrych am wyr Rodri
> Llyna och ym lle ni chawdd
> Lleddid a diawl ai lladdawdd . . .
>
> Y Mab or Berffro ym Mon
> Ni ddoeth diben ych penyd
> Ni ddaw byth oni ddel byd
> O llas Owain gain gwynedd
> Fab Tomas ffureiddwas y ffydd
> Mae gan Grist gyfiawn wisgall
> Awen aer Owain arall
> Ni ladd dur ruw natur rus
> Nowtawdd pryd ystin atus . . .
>
> Ni syrthiodd y seren bengrech
> Ir llawr mae Owain yn llech

Pan ddel o drais i geisiaw
Owain o dre Rufain draw
Aur dalaith ar daith i daid
O randir i orhendaid
Di argel fydd ryfel rrwy
O Lyn Kain i Lan Konwy.[92]

(Adda Fras of fair retinue/company, the false (?) of Y Bergain, taught us to expect daily each feast day, to watch the shore, in our youth, fruit of the high tide, to await the French, buying horses, diligent, of honourable praise, and arms ready for attack ... despite looking for Rhodri's grandson. He was killed and a devil slew him ... Lo! our wailing where he does not rent his anger, the son from Aberffraw in Anglesey, the end of your penance has not come. It will never come until (?)the world will come. If Owain was killed, noble of Gwynedd, son of Thomas, strong servant of the faith, Christ has a just (?). (?)Awen, an heir of another Owain, steel will not kill an ardent nature, predestined protector . . . The curled comet did not fall. Owain is in concealment. When he will come from oppression to attack, Owain yonder from Rome, gold crown on his grandfather's mission. From the region of his great-great-grandfather, unconcealed will he be, war leader, from Glyn Cain to Glan Conwy.)

Glyndŵr's Period, 1400–1500

With Owain Lawgoch lost to them, people turned to the next Owain – Owain Glyndŵr. Glyndŵr, too, had the qualifications to redeem a united Wales: in him were joined the royal lines of Wales. Although he was not a direct descendant of the Llywelyns and therefore could not, unlike Owain Lawgoch, claim to be prince of Wales by that right, he did have claim to the country through its separate pieces. His immediate inheritance was the barony of Glyndyfrdwy and Cynllaith Owain (Sycharth), but through his father he was also heir to the then-dismantled kingdom of Powys in the North and through his mother to the similarly shattered kingdom of Deheubarth in the South. Furthermore, although the relationship was distant, he did have, after Owain Lawgoch's death, one of the best claims to Gwynedd. Thus, he did indeed have the technical right to style himself prince of Wales, a right which was confirmed by the acceptance of his position by other Welsh nobles[93] (though, of course, yet others rejected the claim). The times, too, were right for the coming of a redeemer; conditions demanded one. The Welsh were not suffering from outside domination alone. The whole socio-economic system was collapsing. Both the free and the unfree were overwhelmed by new and excessive financial burdens, and on top of all this, there were outbreaks of the plague.[94] All over Europe similar problems were creating peasant revolts. In Wales, Glyndŵr was welcomed as a national redeemer, a role discussed in the following chapter. He led the Welsh in long-awaited war but he, too, lost and once again they were left waiting for their deliverer.

The miserable pre-rebellion conditions in Wales grew even worse after 1400, when yet more restrictive laws were introduced. Apparently commenting on his own times in the early 1400s, though placing it in an earlier historical context, the scribe of Hopcyn ap Tomas's copy of *Brut y Brenhinedd* wrote a note at the end of the text about 'y rei yssyd yn godef poen ac achenoctit ac alltuded yn eu ganedic dayar'[95] (those who suffer pain and want and oppression/exile in their native land). Set against that misery is the strength of belief in a future deliverer, seen in the calm assumption of a *cywydd* composed probably 1420–40 by Siôn Cent, where the poet traces the legendary history of Wales (as established by Geoffrey of Monmouth) from biblical and Trojan antecedents through encounters with the Anglo-Saxons and Normans, and after each stage repeats his refrain, 'Gobeithiaw a ddaw yddwyf' (My hope lies in what is to come). He makes no reference to Owain Glyndŵr or any other particular deliverer, but he confidently assumes one is coming. In the last stanza, he writes of awaiting 'geni'r daroganwr' (the birth of one who is prophesied):

> Awr py awr, Gymru fawr fu,
> Disgwyl ydd ŷm, a dysgu,
> Dydd py gilydd y gwelwyf,
> Gobeithiaw a ddaw ydd wyf.[96]

(From hour to hour we await, and learn, Wales formerly so great, from day to day may I see, my hope lies in what is to come.)

The deliverer was still awaited. This time, however, the poets shifted their tactics. Most realized that the hope for an independent state was gone. The country was far too exhausted after Glyndŵr's uprising even to consider another for awhile. While enmity for the English, exacerbated by tyrannous penal laws, was, if possible, stronger than ever, the politically alert realized that the best way to achieve their rights, equality with the English and control, was to work within the English political system. Thus the poets urged people such as William Herbert and Henry VI's half-brothers Edmund and Jasper Tudor to seize power.[97] In this third period of vaticinatory poetry the prophecies became even more cryptic, as under a delayed influence from Geoffrey of Monmouth, animal names proliferated and, under increased political tension, caution became even more necessary.

Prophecy and the Tudors

The second half of the fifteenth century begins the pre-Tudor and Tudor stage in the development of vaticinatory poetry. By this time, a new form, the *cywydd brud* (cywydd of prophecy) had come to the fore. Iolo Goch had begun to turn the *cywydd* form to political uses towards the end of the fourteenth century and, by the second half of the fifteenth century, a type of *cywydd* devoted to prophecy had been developed. These *cywyddau brud* enumerated battles and omens and made particular use of symbolic animal names. Scores of such names exist for both heroes and enemies.[98] Acting on the belief that the crown of London should be Welsh, and on the understanding that victory was to be gained only through the established English system, the poets determined that the next Welsh deliverer should wear the crown. Thus they turned to the Welsh-born Henry Tudor, supporting his efforts in the Wars of the Roses because he was the new *mab darogan* and, when he gained the throne, glorying in the rewon crown of London and the start of a new golden age.[99]

The following lines are taken from a *cywydd* which wonders where Henry is and calls for him to come and do battle.

> Tyred, ŵr a draeturiwyd,
> O Fanaw dir, f'enaid wyd . . .

Dyred i'n gwlad dur dân gledd,
Deyrnaswr drwy ynysedd . . .

Dir y gwnei, darogan oedd,
Fyd teilwng o fateloedd.
Gwna frwydr a gwaith grwydr [yn] groch,
Eurllew mawr, iôr, lle mynnoch.
Gwaith dy law a ddaw yn ddig,
Gwŷr meirw a geir ym Merwig . . .

Deigr Cadwaladr fendigaid,
Dyred a dwg dir dy daid.
Dyga ran dy garennydd,
Dwg ni o'n rhwym dygn yn rhydd.[100]

(Come, man who was betrayed, from the land of Man; you are my life/soul . . . Come to our land, sword of tempered steel, ruler through the islands . . . Certain will you, it was a prophecy, make a world worthy of battles. Make battle and widespread strife fiercely, great gold lion/noble lord, lord, where you wish. Work of your hand will come angrily, dead men will be had in Berwick . . . Tear of Cadwaladr Bendigaid, come and take the land of your grandfather. Take your kinsmen's portion, make us free from our severe bondage.)

In the following lines of a *cywydd brud* to Henry and his uncle Jasper, we see both how thoroughly Geoffrey of Monmouth's *Historia* had been accepted and also how Henry was linked with the lineage of that other redeemer, Cadwaladr, from whom he even claimed descent in the twenty-second degree. The association with Anglesey which is mentioned in the poem is also traditional for the Tudors, based on the fact that they came originally from Penmynydd, Anglesey.

Cadwaladr a ddaw adref
Wythryw dawn o'i weithred ef . . .

Siasbar a fag in ddragwn,
Gwaed Brutus hapus yw hwn . . .

Tarw o Fôn yn digoni,—
Hwn yw gobaith ein iaith ni.
Mawr yw'r gras eni Siasber
Hil Cadwaladr paladr pêr.

Hors a Hengestr oedd estron
I Frud Groeg ac i'r Ford Gron;
Gwrtheyrn a wnaeth gwarth â ni,
Rhoi rhan o'n tir i'r rheini.
Siasbar in a ddarparwyd,
Yntau'n rhydd a'n tyn o'r rhwyd.[101]

(Cadwaladr will come home, eight kinds of gift from his deed . . .
Jasper will raise for us a dragon, blood of Brutus, happy is he . . . A
bull from Anglesey labouring— He is the hope of our nation. Great is
the grace that Jasper is born, lineage of Cadwaladr of sweet spear.
Hors and Hengest were strangers to the Prophecy of Greece and the
Round Table; Vortigern made shame for us, giving part of our land to
those. Jasper was prepared for us, he will drag us free from the net.)

Henry Tudor seemed the ideal representative of Wales. Born
and raised for a period in Pembrokeshire, he was descended
from Welsh royal families through his grandfather Owain
Tudur. Through his mother, he held the Lancastrian claim to the
throne. Thus he could claim both the right to lead the Welsh and
the right to rule the English. After the Lancastrian defeat in 1471,
Henry fled to Brittany, but in 1485 he returned, landing at
Milford Haven and marching through Wales, all the time
gathering Welsh troops under the banner of the red dragon. He
drew the Welsh to him not only with the claim of his lineage but
also with the announced objectives of his campaign: to gain for
himself the English Crown, to overthrow Richard III, to restore
England to its former state of honour and prosperity and, most
important for the Welsh, to regain for the Welsh all their rights
and privileges and to remove the oppression under which they
suffered. Delighted with their deliverer, the Welsh helped Henry
to victory at Bosworth and thus to the throne as Henry VII. For a
while, the Welsh felt that the prophecies had been fulfilled – a
Welshman wore the crown of London. Henry furthered this
perception by using the red dragon of Cadwaladr on his
standard, through marrying Elizabeth of York, a lineal
descendant of Llywelyn Fawr, and by naming his first son
Arthur.[102] Although Henry did not usher in a golden age for
Wales, so great was the joy in having a Welshman wear the
crown of London, that it was many years before the Welsh
realized that the prophecies had not yet been fulfilled and that
they were still in need of a redeemer.

Throughout these centuries of awaiting a redeemer, the historical myth had shaped Welsh perceptions and thus history itself. Not only were events of the past interpreted in accordance with the historical pattern believed to exist, but the present also was viewed in this way. With a lost island to be regained and the promise of a prophesied hero to help win it, political plans and actions could be given traditionally acceptable shape and justification. One scholar explains,

> Men fought and died for such futilities in Wales because there was a long tradition, an intense national culture at the back of it all . . . Whether vaticination is nonsense or not, the Welsh were actually fighting for the crown of Cadwaladr, and they did not care so much who should wear it, so long as he was supposed to be of Welsh blood.[103]

The conception of how things should be affected perception of what was, and actions were structured accordingly. Though we cannot see this effect directly for the earliest heroes, whose lives are almost prehistorical, we can see how they are drawn into the pattern which then directly affected the later heroes. The strength of the myth and its influence on people and events are shown by Henry II trying to disprove Arthur's survival by digging up bones, by men selling their property to buy horses and arms in preparation for Owain Lawgoch's coming, and by Welshmen uniting in Henry Tudor's cause because he was a Welshman who would wear the crown. It is against this background, as part of the pattern of hope and expectation, that Owain Glyndŵr should be viewed.[104]

3

Legends of Glyndŵr the Redeemer

Owain Glyndŵr comes seventh in the line of eight redeemer-heroes who arose in Wales. His role as such a hero is well established in medieval vaticinatory poetry, in historical accounts written soon after his time, and in the narrative tradition which grew up around him.

In the poetry contemporaneous with Glyndŵr, there is almost no reference to him as *y mab darogan*; the major poems concerning Glyndŵr appear to have been written in the years before his war. Of the three *cywyddau* composed for him by Iolo Goch, one outlines his lineage, one describes him as a warrior in the Scottish campaign of 1385, and one describes his home at Sycharth.[1] Gruffudd Llwyd also composed a *cywydd* describing Glyndŵr's feats in Scotland.[2] There is, however, no indication yet that Glyndŵr might be the next deliverer. Iolo Goch's mention of Hiriell in his *cywydd* on the Scottish campaign[3] appears to be simply evocation of a great hero rather than direct assertion about Glyndŵr's role. In a second *cywydd* by Gruffudd Llwyd, which has been dated 1383–7,[4] however, the bard does seem to be moving closer to a view of Glyndŵr as a redeemer. He describes the pitiful state into which Wales has fallen and contrasts it with the glorious days under three emperors: Brân brawd Beli, Cystennin ap Constant and Arthur. He bemoans the lack of honour in Wales and the fact that of two men rewarded with knighthood, one is dead; then he asks who will be that man's successor.

Pa un weithion, pan ethyw,
Piau'r swydd ? parhäus yw:
Owain, mael ni wn i mwy,
Iôr Glyn daeardor Dyfrdwy;
Arglwyddfab o ryw gwleddfawr
Sycharth caduarth ced fawr.[5]

(Which one, now that he [Sir Hywel y Fwyall] has gone, will have
his office ? continuous is it: Owain, a prince, I do not know more,
Lord of the Glyn of the cleft of Dyfrdwy; lord's son of some great
feast of Sycharth, battle-yard of great bounty.)

The bard seems to be pushing Glyndŵr to be a real leader and a
lord amongst lords. Even so, this is only the gentlest of
suggestions for a potential saviour and could well be
conventional. Despite these early, pre-uprising poems praising
and encouraging Glyndŵr, we have none composed for him
during his war. Certain poems which were at one time believed
to belong to this period have, through more recent scholarship,
been determined to belong neither to Glyndŵr nor to the period,
but rather to another leader in another time. Other poems which
are actually to Glyndŵr are now recognized as having been
composed long after the event.[6]

Various social and political pressures on the contemporary
poets may account for both the mildness of the early poetry and
the lack of rebellion-era texts. As Dafydd Johnston suggests, the
bardic calls for a redeemer may have been muted by the
complexity of fourteenth-century Welsh–English relations,
including the poets' dependence on a new set of patrons, the
uchelwyr (gentry) who, while upholding Welsh cultural tradition,
also supported English rule and law. Individual poets may
themselves have preferred the social stability maintained under
English rule; others may have chosen not to upset their patrons,
particularly those in the Marches and with newly forged English
ties.[7] On the other hand, strong calls for Glyndŵr specifically
may have been unwarranted until right before the uprising. We
have no indication that there was any reason to perceive
Glyndŵr as the next potential redeemer before he claimed that
role. He does not seem to have stood out from other men of
similar estate until forced by circumstance and when the time
was ripe. Nevertheless, once the uprising started, one would

expect the poets to have joined in the widespread support for Glyndŵr, and yet we lack extant *cywyddau* composed during the war period. Ifor Williams suggests that this lack can be explained by factors of the bards' lives and the nature of the times. The bards were wanderers, travelling from court to court. Their compositions were preserved primarily in their memories and sometimes in manuscripts which either they or their patrons might keep. Although this was not peculiar to Glyndŵr's period and is part of the reason why, for all periods, chance determines whether any particular work will survive, it is particularly pertinent in Glyndŵr's time. Glyndŵr's war was very bitter in Wales, sometimes pitting brother against brother, and almost always destructive of life and property on both sides. After things quietened down in 1415, the bards found themselves in a very awkward position. They certainly could not sing in praise of Glyndŵr to the victors, those who had opposed him, but no more could they praise him to the defeated, his supporters who were living precariously with their newly received royal pardons and, presumably, the desire to forget. So they would not sing the old *cywyddau* and they would destroy any manuscript copies as damning evidence. Mention of Glyndŵr and the war appears for a time to have become taboo, and any existing *cywyddau* were lost.[8]

During this period of public silence, when people weary and weakened from war suppressed open discussion of Glyndŵr (even invoking his name could carry the danger of a call to action), interest in Glyndŵr may have been forced into the safer channels of more intimately transmitted narratives, laying a strong foundation of legendry about Glyndŵr. The legends themselves might contain politically dangerous material, but the narrators have greater control over the context of their transmission, and the narratives themselves, told in informal conversational style, with no set text and open to debate, are more readily deniable. Eventually, at a safe enough distance in time, when Glyndŵr had lost the immediacy of his danger-ousness, the bards once again invoked him, adding him to the line of other redeemers. Indeed, as early as the work of Ieuan ap Rhydderch (*fl.* 1430–70), slight references began appearing, as in a line in a *cywydd brud* addressed probably to Jasper Tudur telling him, 'Na weinia gledd Owain Glyn' (Do not sheathe the sword of Owain Glyn), i.e. do not sheathe the sword, end the struggle, loosed by Glyndŵr.[9]

Prophecy

The prophecies, or rather the belief in prophecies and the use of them in the development of Glyndŵr's campaign, is brought to light not only in poetry but also in the early histories. This is nowhere clearer than in Glyndŵr's own words, in letters written to the kings of France and Scotland and the lords of Ireland. In a letter taken from captured messengers and recorded by Glyndŵr's contemporary Adam of Usk in his *Chronicle* (*c.*1420–30), Glyndŵr, before asking for support with arms and men, reminds the king of Scotland of their common descent from Brutus, his own direct descent from Cadwaladr, and the suffering of the people under Saxon tyranny. Then, drawing on the old prophecies in which the Saxons are driven out by the united forces of Wales, Scotland, Ireland, Brittany and Norway, he points out:

> Des quex oppressions et bondages le prophecie dit que je serray delivere par eid et socour de vostre dit roial mageste.

> (And from this tyranny and bondage the prophecy saith that I shall be delivered by the aid and succour of your royal majesty.)[10]

Similarly, in a letter to the Irish lords, after describing the war with their common enemy, the Saxons, Glyndŵr writes:

> Sed, quia vulgariter dicitur per propheciam quod, antequam nos altiorem manum in hac parte haberemus, quod vos [et] vestri carissimi consanguinei in Hibernea ad hoc manus porrigetis adjutrices . . .

> (But, seeing that it is commonly reported by the prophecy that, before we can have the upper hand in this behalf, you and yours, our well-beloved cousins in Ireland, must stretch forth hereto a helping hand . . .)[11]

Glyndŵr is not only claiming his own actions to be part of the prophecy, with himself as the awaited deliverer of fitting lineage, but is also instructing these foreign lords to fulfil their part of the prophecy.

Other evidence of the use of prophecy is recorded in slightly later histories. In the late sixteenth century, David Powel explains that, when Glyndŵr took Lord Grey prisoner at the beginning of the war, some Welsh turned to him, believing he was still in great favour with the king, and others

> putting in his head, that now the time was come wherein the Brytaines through his meanes might recouer againe the honour and liberties of their ancestors. These things being laid before Owen by such as were verie cunning in Merlins prophesies and the interpretations of the same (for there were in those daies, as I feare there be now, some singular men which are deepelie ouerseene in those mysteries, and hope one daie to meete veluet upon London bridge with their bowes) brought him into such a fooles paradise, that he neuer waieng what title he might pretend nor what right he had, proceeded and made warre upon the Earle of March . . . [12]

A century later, William Wynne repeats the first sentence of the above passage, and then later goes on to write:

> This good Success over the Lord Gray, together with the numerous resort of the Welch to him, and the favourable interpretations of the Prophecies of Merdhyn, which some construed very advantagiously, made the swelling mind of Glyndŵr overflow its Banks, and gave him some hopes of restoring this Island back to the Britains.[13]

Although considering hopes of reclaiming Wales to be foolish, both of these men recognize the importance of the Welsh dream of independence and the role of the prophecies in keeping it alive. Both also suggest that Glyndŵr was egged on and to some extent manipulated by the prophecies. Pennant however, writing in 1778, indicates that Glyndŵr himself used the prophecy to incite the Welsh in his support.

> It was on this occasion that *Owen*, to animate his countrymen, called up the antient prophecy, which predicted the destruction of *Henry*, under the name of the *Moldwarp, cursed of* God's *own mouth.*

Himself he styled the *dragon*; a name he assumed in imitation of *Uther*, whose victories over the *Saxons* were foretold by the appearance of a star with a dragon beneath, which *Uther* used as his badge; and on that account it bacame a favourite one with the *Welsh*. On *Percy* he bestowed the title of *lion*, from the crest of the family; on *Mortimer*; that of the *wolf*, probably from a similar reason. And these three were to divide the realm between them.[14]

It is apparently to these same prophecies that Shakespeare, following Holinshed, refers when Hotspur in *Henry IV*, Part I, mocks Glyndŵr.

> . . . Sometime he angers me
> With telling me of the moldwarp and the ant,
> Of the dreamer Merlin and his prophecies,
> And of a dragon and a finless fish,
> A clip-winged griffin and a moulten raven,
> A couching lion and a ramping cat,
> And such a deal of skimble-skamble stuff
> As puts me from my faith.[15]

Glyndŵr's interest in prophecy is further illustrated by his having had a personal prophet, Crach y Ffinant, who interpreted signs for him and urged him to rise in revolt. Nevertheless, the one example we have of Glyndŵr's actions being specifically affected by prophecy is in the tradition that Hopcyn ap Tomas ab Einion, a scholar of prophecy (*brud*), warned Glyndŵr that somewhere between Carmarthen and Gower he would be captured under a black banner. It is said that Glyndŵr defeated the prophecy by avoiding that area.[16] The point in all this is not so much whether Glyndŵr used the prophecies or was controlled by them, since it is doubtful that the truth, which is probably a combination of the two, could ever be precisely determined, but rather that the ancient hopes and prophecies were working on the imaginations of the Welsh and affecting both their perceptions and their actions.

Further 'divine' support for Glyndŵr was also perceived in the appearance of a comet in 1402, as recorded in a seventeenth-century text: 'A.D. 1402 a blazing starr appeared which flattering Bards made to portend all good to Owen.'[17] Pennant, in the eighteenth century, concurs with this interpretation of the comet's appearance.

This year was ushered in with a comet, or blazing-star; which the bards interpreted as an omen favorable to the cause of *Glyndwr* . . . It served to infuse spirit into the minds of a superstitious people: the first success of their chieftain confirmed their belief, and gave new vigor to their actions.[18]

A much earlier reference to the comet by Elis Gruffydd in 1548, however, indicates that the comet was taken to portend war in general rather than Glyndŵr's victory specifically.

Ac ynn drydedd vlwydd o wladychiad y brenin hari y pydwerydd ir ymddangoses seren ddisglair ar y ffurauen yr hon a alwai yr ysgolheigion sdela kometta ne gomett yr hon medd yr asdronimers ar brudwyr nid ymddengys onid ynn erbyn hryuel ne laddua ar ddynion.[19]

(And in the third year of the reign of king Henry IV, there appeared a shining star in the firmament which the scholars called Sdela Kometta or comet, which the astrologers and prophets say does not appear except against war and killing of men.)

This interpretation, the only one to concern itself with war rather than with victory, may be a reflection of Gruffydd's having been a soldier, and thus more than aware of the horrors of war and the slaughter required to achieve the desired victory. The association of the comet with Glyndŵr was apparently so strong that it misled people into interpreting poems which mentioned the comet or a special star as referring to Glyndŵr. This is what happened, for example, with 'Cywydd y Seren a Welwyd Uwchben Sir Fôn' (*Cywydd* of the Star which was Seen above Anglesey), which the copyist assumed to refer to the 1402 comet and thus to Glyndŵr. Even as recently as Charles Ashton's 1896 edition of *Gweithiau Iolo Goch* this assumption was maintained.[20] Only more recent, closer readings have led scholars to assign a different time and subject to the poem.[21]

For a while, especially in 1404 and 1405, at the height of Glyndŵr's powers, it must have appeared as if the people's hopes were about to be realized and Glyndŵr would indeed restore Wales's golden age. This golden age was most clearly expressed in Glyndŵr's three-part plan for an independent nation. The first part was the establishment of a parliament. In

1404 he summoned four representatives from every commote to the first parliament in Machynlleth, where he also had himself officially crowned prince of Wales. The second part was the establishment of an independent Welsh Church. For centuries, Welsh churchmen had resented being under the control of Canterbury and having English bishops in the Welsh dioceses. Glyndŵr hoped to free the Welsh Church of English domination and to create St David's as the metropolitan see. Following the lead of his new Scottish and French allies, Glyndŵr decided to reject the Roman pope and to support the rival pope at Avignon instead. The third part of Glyndŵr's plan was the establishment of an educational system with universities in North and South Wales. Unfortunately, he was never able to put into effect any part of his educational plan. The other parts of the plan also withered with Glyndŵr's eventual defeat, but for a short while they recalled the golden ages of Arthur, with its peace, order and cultural pursuits, and of yet earlier times before even Cadwaladr and Cynan were needed. Moreover, the brief glimmer of that golden age in the 1400s refuelled the hopes and dreams for another, more lasting one.

Disappearance of the Hero

The war of 1400–15 proved not to be the decisive one which would win Wales its independence from England, throwing out the foreigners and restoring Wales to its former glories. Nevertheless, Glyndŵr did not lose his role as national redeemer; it was the time that was wrong; he would simply have to wait. Therefore, expectations were transferred to a future date and Glyndŵr was perceived as never having died. Peniarth MS 135, a manuscript originally compiled shortly after 1422, only seven years after the end of Glyndŵr's rebellion, records:

> MCCCCxv y ddaeth Owain mewn difant y gwyl Vathe yn y kyn gayaf o hynny allan ni wybuwyd i ddifant rrann vawr a ddywaid i varw y brudwyr a ddywedant na bu.[22]

> (1415 Owen went into disappearance on St Matthew's Day in harvest-time, and thereafter his [place of] disappearance was not known. A great many say that he died; the seers maintain he did not.)

In this passage we see that there are already two lines of thought – one that Glyndŵr must have died and the other that he never did. The early historians appear generally to adopt the rational attitude that he did die.

> Death put [an end] to Owen's life and misery upon the Eve of St. Mathew A.D. 1415 some say he died at his daughter Scudamore's others at his daughter Monnington's house both of them harboured him in his low forlorn condition, they say that he was fain to go up and down disguised in a shepherd's habit into his daughter and other friends houses.[23]

The above passage brings out two points that are taken up by tradition. One is that Glyndŵr died on the same day of the year as he began his war, bringing it to full circle.

> Canys noswyl Vathau nessaf at hynny y doeth Owain am ben tref Ruthun ai llosgi a lladd cymmaint a a gavas o wyr ynthi. Ac o hynny hyt ymhen y pumtheng mlynedd ir un Noswyl Vatheu ni bu heddwch gwastad ynghymru canys yna i bu varw Owain.[24]

> (Because on the next St Matthew's Eve, Owain came upon the town of Rhuthun and burned it and killed as many as he got of men in it. And from that until the end of fifteen years to the same St Matthew's Eve there was no peace the width of Wales since Owain died then.)

The other point is that Glyndŵr's last years were spent in hiding and in decline.

> After this [Battle of Huske], we hear little of Glyndwr, excepting that he continued and persisted to vex and plague the English upon the Marches, to the tenth year of King Henry's reign, when he miserably ended his life; being as Holingshed reporteth, towards his latter days driven to that extremity, that despairing of all comfort, he fled and lurked in Caves and other the most solitary places, fearing to shew his face to any Creature, till at length being starved for hunger and lack of sustenance, he miserably ended his life.[25]

Pennant takes all of this information and assesses it:

It is probable that it [treaty negotiations with Henry] was interrupted by the death of our hero, which happened on the 20th of *September*, on the eve of St. *Matthew*, in the sixty-first year of his age, at the house of one of his daughters; whether that of his daughter *Scudamore* or *Monnington*, is uncertain; but, according to the tradition of the county of *Hereford*, it may be supposed to have been at that of the last. It is said, that he was buried in the church-yard of *Monnington*; but there is no monument, nor any memorial of the spot that contains his remains.

Both the printed histories, and the manuscript accounts, represent his latter end to have been miserable; they state that he wandered from place to place in the habit of a shepherd, in a low and forlorn condition; and that he was even forced to take shelter in caves and desert places, from the fury of his enemies. This does not wear the face of probability; for, had his situation been so deplorable, majesty would never have condescended to propose terms to such a scourge as *Glyndwr* had been to his kingdom. His retreat, and the distresses he underwent, were probably after the battle of *Pwll Melyn* in 1405, from which he quickly emerged. Death alone deprived *Owen* of the glory of accepting an offered accommodation . . . Our chieftain died unsubdued; unfortunate only in foreseeing a second subjugation of his country, after the loss of the great supporter of its independency.[26]

There is some variation in the year given for Glyndŵr's death,[27] ranging from 1414 to 1417, but an *englyn* noted in 1820 sets it as 1415.

> Mil, a phedwar-cant, nid mwy—cof ydyw
> Cyfodiad Glyndyfrdwy;
> A phymtheg, praff ei saffwy,
> Bu Owain hen byw yn hwy.[28]

(A thousand, and four hundred, not more—[the] memory [of] the rising of Glyndyfrdwy; And fifteen, stout his staff, did old Owain live thereafter.)

Adam of Usk, Glyndŵr's contemporary, also gives 1415 as the date of his death. In his note on Glyndŵr's death, he brings in two other points as well – one that he had been in hiding for the years preceding his death, and the other that his grave was kept secret on purpose to protect it from his enemies.

> Died Owen Glendower, after that during four years he had lain hidden from the face of the king and the realm; and in the night

season he was buried by his followers. But his burial having been discovered by his adversaries, he was laid in the grave a second time; and where his body was bestowed may no man know.[29]

The site of the grave becomes a subject of some importance because, faced with the rationalist assumption that Glyndŵr did actually die, the question becomes where and under what circumstances. The solution to this mystery becomes a matter of local tradition, with each place putting forth its own suggestion. In Hereford, tradition claims that Glyndŵr died at Monnington and is buried either there or at Kentchurch.[30] According to one record, an unmarked but well-made grave, supposed to be that of Glyndŵr, was discovered and opened c.1680, but was closed again after two days during which everything crumbled to ashes.[31] Another tradition in the area suggests that John Kent (Siôn Cent), a bard and priest patronized by the Scudamores, flourishing around 1400, was actually Owain Glyndŵr in hiding. This man also attracted other traditions such as that he was a magician, that his horses flew through the air and that he lived to the age of 120.[32] The nationalist journals of the late nineteenth and early twentieth centuries record the Hereford traditions of the Wye valley, but support the claims of Corwen and the Dee valley.

> Ni ŵyr neb i sicrwydd pa le mae ei fedd. Dywed un traddodiad mai yn Nyffryn Gwy y mae; ond y tebygolrwydd ydyw mai yn rhywle yn Nyffryn Dyfrdwy y gorwedd, ym mynwent Corwen feallai.[33]

> (No one knows for sure where his grave is. One tradition says it is in the Wye valley; but the likelihood is that he lies somewhere in the Dee valley, in Corwen graveyard perhaps.)

Yet another suggestion, found in an eighteenth-century manuscript, is that Glyndŵr was buried at Llanfair Caereinion in Montgomeryshire.[34] A tomb in the south aisle of Bangor Cathedral is also said to be that of Glyndŵr but, in each case where this tradition is recorded, the antiquarian involved immediately suggests that it is more likely to be the tomb of Owain Gwynedd.[35]

Those few people whom I met in the field who said that Glyndŵr was dead rather than asleep, placed the site of his death, or at least his disappearance, on Y Berwyn, though they all agreed that the grave site remains unknown. One man, in answer to my question as to whether he had heard any stories about Glyndŵr hiding in a cave, replied,

> Wel, na chlywes i ddim byd ond bod nw'n deud bod o 'di marw mewn ogof yn rwle, yn ble ond Duw a ŵyr. Glywes i ddweud bod o 'di, wedi marw mewn ogof ar Y Berwyn 'ma rwle, ond y lle Duw a ŵyr, does neb yn gwbod, nag oes. Ond dyna be dw i 'di glwad sawl gwaith. Ond pw' sy'n gwbod, do's na neb wedi dod o hyd i'w fangre ola' fo, do's na neb yn gwbod, ond dw i wedi clwad ne wedi darllen yn rhwle bod o wedi'i gladdu yn ym, yn ym ar Y Berwyn 'ma rwle. Ma'n hawdd gynna'i gredu hynny 'de. Ond damcaniaeth hollol 'di hynny 'de. Do's na ddim, os na 'llwch chi brofi, dydi'r haneswyr 'ma hyd 'n oed ddim yn gallu lleoli 'i farwolaeth o, o gwbl ynde. Ne ma 'na ddigon o ogofeydd yn y cyffiniau.[36]

> (Well, no I didn't hear anything but that they say he died in a cave somewhere, where only God knows. I heard it said that he had, had died in a cave on Y Berwyn here somewhere, but where God knows, nobody knows, no. But that's what I've heard many times. But who knows, there's no one who's found his last place; there's no one who knows, but I've heard or read somewhere that he was buried in um, in um, on Y Berwyn here somewhere. It's easy for me to believe that. But that's completely hypothesis. There's nothing, if you couldn't prove it, these historians can't even place his death, at all. There are enough caves in the vicinity.)

All of these contradictory reports, including the conjectures that Glyndŵr died at his daughter's home, may be manifestations not only of the uncertainties surrounding Glyndŵr's death, but also of the conflict set up between logic and the more gratifying belief that Glyndŵr never died. It is as if all the attempts to determine the facts of how he died, in providing counterpoint to the deeper and more basic belief that he did not, merely serve to reinforce the tradition of his survival. One schoolboy told me that Glyndŵr was buried on Y Berwyn, but when asked for more information said, 'I ysbryd e dal yn fyw'[37] (His spirit keeps on living). He then continued, 'Ie, yn ogof – cysgu yn y mynydd o, ie, efo'i filwyr – ie' (Yes, in a cave – sleeping in the mountain – oh, yes, with his soldiers, yes), and went on to tell a story about a boy finding the cave which is full of jewels and other treasures. This boy's transition from a slightly dull fact to an intriguing story may be a minor reflection of what is happening on a larger scale in the tradition. Another informant shows how uncertainty about Glyndŵr's death contributes to his role as *y mab darogan* who has temporarily disappeared.

> Hefyd, wrth gwrs, ydi, mai fe oedd y mab darogan ac ma'r ffordd nath o ddiflannu a neb yn gwbod lle buo fo farw na lle ma'i fedd o. Dyna oedd – ydi'r elfen chwedlonol yn Owain Glyndŵr ydi y ffaith 'i fod o wedi diflannu i'r gwyll uwchben Llangollen . . . [38]

> (Also, of course, he is, that he was *y mab darogan* and the way he disappeared and nobody knowing where he died or where his grave is. That was – is the mythological element in Owain Glyndŵr, is the fact that he disappeared into the darkness above Llangollen . . .)

The unknown grave leaves open possibilities for the hero. If the grave cannot be found, perhaps the hero does not need one. As was noted in the previous chapter, Arthur's grave, too, was undisclosed.

The folk community (as opposed to the historians) accepts the possibility that Glyndŵr never died. So strong are the longings and dreams which keep him alive, that even academic historians must take note of them, as in the following two passages from twentieth-century works. The first is from a children's history of great heroes, and the second is from an author's reminiscences of his schoolteacher's lessons.

> It is not known where he died, though it is inferred that he died in 1416. In Gwent they say that he did not die. They say that he and his men sit sleeping in Ogov y Ddinas, buckled in their armour, their spears leaning against their shoulders, their swords across their knees. There they are waiting till the day comes for them to sally forth and fight for the land again.[39]

> He carried the death of a nation upon his back. He fashioned for his soul a unique torment. Is it any wonder then that he did not completely die, that he waits even now beneath a friendly and lightly poised rock for the moment of recall. He may be lying at Ogof y Ddinas, a cave well to the west of here . . . [40]

These two examples only hint at the multitude of cave legends involving Glyndŵr, which will be discussed in the next section. The point here is that tradition basically recognizes only that Glyndŵr disappeared. The conjectures and proposed grave sites only serve to underscore the fact that there is no record of his death or burial. Even if the claim that Glyndŵr had never died was, as of 1422, being presented mainly by the seers, it is a claim which was taken up by the rest of the community as well.

Awaiting the Hero's Return

Owain Glyndŵr is *y mab darogan*, son of the prophecy. He is awaited, if not always in body, then at least in spirit. Although Glyndŵr's years of rule were all years of war, as pointed out earlier, they were also years of attempting to establish Wales as an independent state with its own parliament, a national system of education, and an independent Welsh Church – all of which are cited when people recall the golden age of Glyndŵr's hopes. It is this which gives so much power to him as one of the primary symbols of modern Welsh nationalism. This matter is discussed in Chapter 5; here it is enough to point out that his name is not simply invoked by politicians and protest singers; it carries a true weight of meaning. A few examples taken from fieldwork demonstrate clearly the way in which Glyndŵr's return is looked to as a solution to society's problems today. One man when asked whether he had ever heard of Owain Glyndŵr referred to as *y mab darogan* before a recent rock opera of that name, replied,

> Naddo. Ddim mwy na bod yr hen ddarogan sy'n bod, yndê, pan fydda Cymru mewn angen y dôi Owain Glyndŵr yn 'i ôl. Pryd glywis i hynna gynta o'dd yn amsar rhyfel 1914–1918.[41]

> (No. No more than the old prophecy which is when Wales would be in need, Owain Glyndŵr would come back. When I heard this first was in the time of the 1914–1918 war.)

That this man first heard of Glyndŵr's prophesied return during war points up the way redeemer-heroes tend to rise in national awareness, becoming more common and important in folkloric narratives and expresssions, when a culture is under stress. This same man, remembering attitudes held during World War I, goes on to recall,

> Ma'r hen draddodiad bod Owain Glyndŵr yn dod yn ôl pan eith hi'n ddrwg ar Gymru. Mae o'n wir heddiw. Mae Lloyd George wedi dwad a mae Lloyd George yn mynd i ennill y rhyfal.[42]

> (There's the old tradition that Owain Glyndŵr will come back when Wales is in trouble. It's true today. Lloyd George has come and Lloyd George is going to win the war.)

A contrasting view of Lloyd George, but with the same attitude towards Glyndŵr, is expressed by the same teacher whose lessons are recalled in the passage quoted earlier on Ogof y Ddinas. 'But he'll be back. He'll be back to twit the local councillors . . . He'll be back to censor Lloyd George . . .'[43] Another time, the man who gave the positive view of Lloyd George described a very heated fight with the Forestry Commission, during which one of the men, Robin y Bara, commented to my informant, 'Damn it, . . . we are losing the battle. I wish that Glyndŵr came in here this afternoon.'[44] Again, this same person explained about Glyndŵr:

> A mae o'n ffigur cenedlaethol, ydi a fel hyn mae 'na fawr edmygedd ohono fo a rhywun 'dan ni'n 'i gymryd o fel arwr ac yn hawdd iawn ganddon ni sôn amdano fo pan fyddan ni'n teimlo'n bod ni'n cal yn gwasgu run fath ag oedd Robin y Bara yn cal 'i wasgu yn y pwyllgor 'na ddoe.[45]

> (He's a national figure, he is, and as such there is a lot of admiration for him, someone we can take as a hero and it is very easy for us to invoke him when we're feeling pressed, the same way as when Robin y Bara was being pressured in the committee yesterday.)

Gwynfor Evans, a former Member of Parliament and president of Plaid Cymru (the Welsh Nationalist Party) for thirty-six years (and, incidentally, one of the prime invokers of Glyndŵr's name), in response to a question on Glyndŵr as *y mab darogan*, replied:

> O ie, o ie, ma hwnna – mae e'n cymryd 'i le fel mab darogan. O'dd 'na fwy nag un wrth gwrs, o'dd sawl un. Un o'i flaen e o'dd Owain

– Owain arall, Owain Lawgoch. Ro'dd y beirdd yn 'u canu brud wedi bod yn rhagweld rhyw waredwr a fydde'n dod wrth gwrs. Ac – Owain a gyflawnodd y freuddwyd yna lawna.[46]

(Oh yes, yes, there's that – he's taken his place as a *mab darogan*. There was more than one, of course, there were a number. One before him was Owain – another Owain. Owain Lawgoch. The bards in their prophecies had foreseen a saviour who would come, of course. And – Owain fulfilled the dream most fully.)

Glyndŵr is awaited, and in a way, the theme of waiting, of awaiting the right moment to accomplish the dream is at the heart of all the legendry about redeemer-heroes. One of the legends which most clearly brings out this point is one commonly told as evidence that Owain Glyndŵr *is* a redeemer-hero. The basic story is that one morning Glyndŵr was walking in the hills where he met an abbot, to whom he said, 'Good morning, father; you're up early.' The abbot replied, 'No, Glyndŵr, it is you who is up early, a hundred years too early.' In the variants of this, people sometimes point out that the meeting took place on Y Berwyn or that the abbot was from Glyn-y-groes Abbey (also known as Glynegwestl or Valle Crucis). Usually, the story is told as an indication that Glyndŵr will return. Moreover, it is often told as if the encounter takes place not during Glyndŵr's life proper, but rather a few hundred years later, on one of the breaks from his sleep. All the variants, regardless of the narrators' particular interpretation and emphasis, make the same point – that the time must be right for a return.

The first report we have of this legend, recorded in 1548 by Elis Gruffydd, uses the story to explain Glyndŵr's disappearance from the battlefield at Mynydd Berwyn.

Or man megis ac J mae llyure kymru yn dangos J diulanodd ef o uysc J bobyl oherwydd serttein o o eirriau a ddyuod abaad glynn Egwysdyr wrtho ef ar voreg-waith yr hwn a oedd wedi kyuodi o hir vore ac ynn kerdded ar hydd llethyr bron ac ynn dywedud J blygain yr hwn a gyuaruu ac ywain yr hwn a ddyuod a syr abaad chychwi o godasogh ynhryuore. nag e hebyr yr abad chychwi a gyuodes ynhryuore o gan mhlynedd Je hebyr Owain Ac ynnol opiniwn hraii or kymru yvo a golles ac a ddiulannodd ymaith o uysg J bobyl hrag kaffel kywilidd kanis wrth ymadrodd yr abaad yvo a ydnabu nad y vo ydoedd yr ywainn ir ydoedd ef ynn ymkanv J vod Jr hwn Jr ydoedd y brudiau yn addo dwyn koron loygyr . . . [47]

(From this place, as the books of Wales show, he disappeared from the midst of the people because of certain words the abbot of Glyn Egwysdyr said to him. One morning he had risen in early morning and was walking along the slope of a hill saying his matins when he met Owain who said, 'O Sir Abbot, you have risen too early.' 'No', answered the abbot, 'it is you who has risen too early by a hundred years.' 'Yes,' answered Owain. And according to the opinion of some of the Welsh he vanished and disappeared away from amidst the people lest he get shame, since from the abbot's words he recognized that he was not the Owain he intended to be, who the prophecies were promising to take the crown of England.)

When Glyndŵr realized that he was not *the* Owain, that this was not the prophesied time, he was too ashamed to continue. Gruffydd, with a soldier's eye for essentials, adds as an alternative explanation for his disappearance that he did not have enough money to pay his troops.

In a tale which is similar to Gruffydd's in that the abbot's words caused Glyndŵr to recognize that the time was wrong, one person related:

. . . mae stori amdano fo yn ochrau Llangollen, Abaty Glyn-y-groes, yn cerdded allan yn gynnar rhyw fore, a gweld abad o'r abaty. A'r abad yn deud wrtho fo, ne'n gofyn iddo fo, 'Be w't ti da allan adeg yma o'r dydd Glyndŵr? Mae'n rhy gynnar i ti.' Mae Glyndŵr yn cymryd hyn i olygu nad nid yr adeg honno oedd yr amser i godi gwrthryfel.[48]

(. . . there's a story about him around Llangollen, Glyn-y-groes Abbey, walking out early some morning, and seeing the abbot from the abbey. And the abbot said to him, or asked him, 'What are you doing out this time of the day Glyndŵr? It's too early for you.' Glyndŵr took this to mean that that period was not the time to raise a rebellion.)

An interesting variation in interpretation appears in a twentieth-century poem when Glyndŵr rejects the advice to come back in one hundred years because his people are suffering and cannot wait.

> Cwrdd ag Abad Glyn Egwestl
> Ar y Berwyn fore claer,
> 'Tyrd yn ôl mewn canrif eto,
> Owain', oedd ei neges daer,
> 'Canrif eto i fy ngwerin
> Ymdrybaeddu yn y llaid?
> Na! mae'r 'sgrifen ar y pared
> Trechu'r gelyn 'nawr sydd raid.'[49]

(He met the Abbot of Glyn Egwestl on Y Berwyn on a fine morning. 'Come back in another hundred years, Owain,' was his earnest message. 'A century yet for my people wallowing in the mire? No, the writing is on the wall; it's necessary to overcome the enemy now.')

With wistfulness for unaccomplished dreams, a retired schoolmaster, who a few minutes earlier had been describing Glyndŵr as a man of great vision, gives the abbot's reply to Glyndŵr's comment that he is up early as: 'Ddim mor fore â chi . . . Godsoch chi cyn ych amser ac oherwydd hynny ddaru'ch fethu sylweddoli ych breuddwydion.'[50] (Not as early as you. You rose before your time, and because of that you have failed to realize your dreams.) Another retired man told the story with Glyndŵr and the abbot meeting outside the abbey at Glyn-y-groes to discuss Glyndŵr's plans:

> . . . mi o'dd gan Owain Glyndŵr tair delfryd, yndê, llywodraeth i Gymru, prifysgol i Gymru a Eglwys Rydd, eglwys i Gymru, yndê. Ma'n rhaid i bod nw wedi mynd i sôn am 'i ddelfryde, a'r abad yn troi rownd yno a deud wrtho fo i fod o 'di codi can mlynedd rhy fuan de. A man before his time, yntê. Dyna be sy tu ôl i'r stori bod o yn ddyn o flaen ei oes ynde.[51]

(. . . Owain Glyndŵr had three ideals, government for Wales, a university for Wales, and a Free Church, a church for Wales. They must have gone to discuss his ideals, and the abbot turned around there and said to him that he had risen a hundred years too early. A man before his time, isn't it. That's what's behind the story, that he's a man before his time.)

The same point about being before his time ('Chwi sydd o flaen eich oes' – It is you who is before your time) is made in an earlier twentieth-century poem by T. Gwynn Jones, but one with a very different tone – a cross between a ghost story and a prayer. The abbot is thinking about the cruel troubles in Wales and about Glyndŵr's disappearance, when Glyndŵr's spirit rises out of the mist and then melts back into it after their short conversation.[52] This poem seems to assume previous knowledge of the legend, suggesting that the poem may have served more as a reminder than as a purveyor of tradition. Another variant comes from a member of Cofiwn (meaning 'We [will] remember'), a group trying to educate the Welsh towards action by increasing their awareness of their history and the richness of their past. In a story first heard from this young man's father, the abbot asks Glyndŵr who he is and, upon hearing the name, answers, 'O ie, Owain Glyndŵr, dach chi 'di dod i Gymru llawer ynghynt na ddyle chi fod wedi dod.'[53] (Oh yes, Owain Glyndŵr, you have come to Wales much sooner than you should have come.) The informant then goes on to explain,

> Ac falle dyna beth o'dd un o'r rhesyme am 'i methiant e, 'chos bod e 'di dod, ac wedyn do'dd y Cymry ddim yn barod i ymladd. Efalle os bydd pethe wedi digwydd yn dwy ganrif ar ôl hynny fydde pethe wedi bod yn well a bydde Cymru'n wlad rydd erbyn heddi.[54]

> (And perhaps thát was one of the reasons for his failure, because he had come, and after all the Welsh weren't ready to fight. Perhaps if things had happened two centuries after that things would have been better and Wales would be a free nation by today.)

According to the prevalent tradition, Glyndŵr awaits the proper hour asleep in a cave. Owain Glyndŵr is repeatedly associated with caves. In some he rested or hid while awaiting the moment to continue battle, and in others he sleeps while awaiting the right time to renew the struggle. There are two major periods when he is supposed to have lived in caves. The first is around 1405, in the middle years of the war, when he was having some temporary reversals. Adam of Usk describes this period thus: 'Owen, with his only remaining son Meredith, miserably lay in hiding in the open country, and in caves, and in the thickets of the mountains.'[55] This is the period sometimes referred to as *difancoll* (disappearance). As was seen with the tradition about the appearance of a star or comet, the strength of the tradition about a period during which Glyndŵr vanished is indicated by the way in which certain poetry is interpreted.

Poems which contain no reference to the period of *difancoll* were nevertheless assumed to do so because knowledge of the particular tradition seemed to outweigh all other possibilities. Only relatively recent scholarship has revealed the actual references. The best known case is the *cywydd* beginning with the line, 'Y gŵr hir a gâr Harri', and sometimes titled 'I Owain Glyndŵr ar ddifancoll' (To Owain Glyndŵr on disappearance). Since even the first line is problematic (and its interpretation an important part of the argument for reascribing the *cywydd*), rather than providing the current reading I will quote from an 1881 translation, which will show more clearly the interpretation previously put on the verse.

> Tall man, thou mark for Harry's hate,
> Art living still? is past thy fate?
> If thus it be, with fiery spear
> Come, show thy shield, say, 'I am here!'[56]

The legendry of this period shows many similarities to the legendry of Robert the Bruce who, a century earlier, after being crowned Robert I of Scotland, was forced to take to the woods and caves, where he developed his techniques of guerilla warfare.[57]

The second period of Glyndŵr's living in caves is dated between 1411 and 1415, when his forces were very weakened. As was previously explained, many of the early historians claim that during his last years Glyndŵr went about in the guise of a shepherd and had to live in caves in order to avoid King Henry's wrath. Later historians dispute this, saying that all his hiding in caves was done during the middle period. His situation is described by a nineteenth-century, nationalist antiquarian thus:

> Gwelwyd ef [Owain Glyndŵr], pan oedd aflwyddiant yn gwgu arno, yn grwydryn ar hyd y wlad, weithiau yn gwisgo fel bugail, bryd arall yn ffoi oddiwrth y naill gyfaill at y llall i gael lloches a thamaid o fwyd: – ei fywyd mewn cymaint o berygl weithiau, fel nad oedd yn ddyogel iddo aros mewn tŷ na chastell, ac felly ceisiai loches mewn ogofeydd; a'i wely yn fynych fyddai y graig galed a llaith.[58]

> (He [Owain Glyndŵr] was seen, when misfortune was pressing on him, wandering about the land, sometimes dressing as a shepherd,

another time fleeing from one friend to another to get shelter and a bit of food: – his life in so much danger at times, that it was not safe for him to stay in house or castle, and thus he sought shelter in caves; and his bed often was the hard and damp rock.)

In any case, oral tradition records his having stayed in caves all over Wales. Sometimes he was not hiding, but simply sleeping there before a battle or retreating there with his men as part of his guerilla tactics. For example, one man in Corwen recalled a place above Dyffryn Hyddgen, near Pumlumon, where: 'ma 'na ogof hefyd neu beth tebyg i ogof lle ro'dd e i fod wedi treulio'r noson cyn y frwydr'[59] (there's a cave also or something like a cave where he was supposed to have spent the night before the battle). The following information, which may describe the same place, was collected in the 1960s from a Mr Pugh concerning Siambr Traws Fynydd, a cleft in the rock near Hyddgen.

> Clywodd gan ei dad mai yno y cysgai milwyr Owain Glyndwr pan ddaeth y Saeson ar eu gwaethaf a bod llawer ohonyn nhw wedi eu claddu ar y mynydd gerllaw. Dywedodd Mr Pugh fod yr hen bobl yn arfer adrodd y stori hon fel pe baent yn ei chredu yn wirioneddol ac nid fel rhai o'r traddodiadau eraill.[60]

> (He heard from his father that that was where Owain Glyndŵr's soldiers slept when the English came at their worst/upon them and that many of them were buried on the mountain nearby. Mr Pugh said that the old people used to tell this story as if they truly believed it and not like some of the other traditions.)

Often, however, the caves are described as hiding, rather than just resting, places. On several occasions, Glyndŵr made fabulous and very narrow escapes when he fled to the woods and hid in a cave. One time, when he was almost captured while dining with a friend, he swam across a tidal river and climbed a previously impassable cliff face, including a rock chimney. He then hid in a cave on the rock face and was supplied with provisions by the prior of a nearby abbey.[61] In some variants, he is said to have been there for six months and the abbey is specified as being at Beddgelert. Knowledge of a local cave as the one used by Glyndŵr appears to persist, even when divorced from the escape narrative. This is helped, of course, by the fact that maps show the name Ogof Owain Glyndŵr, but the following examples from print and oral sources show there is more to the tradition than just the name.

> West of the village [Beddgelert] also rises, with great grandeur, Moel Hebog, or the hill of the hawk. In a deep hollow on this mountain Owen Glendwr, upon one of his expeditions to harass the English forces, was fain to shelter himself from his enemies.[62]

> Ond ma 'na un [stori] dw i wedi clywad am ogof Glyndŵr sy yn Meddgelert, sydd ddim ymhell o Feddgelert, a ma nw'n deud bod o'n medru cuddio fanno am hanner blwyddyn tra roedd y bradwyr yn chwilio amdano fo. Ac mae'n bosib ymweld â'r ogof 'ma ond rhaid i chi fod yn ddringwr da am fod o braidd yn beryglus.[63]

> (But there's one [story] I've heard about Glyndŵr's cave, which is in Beddgelert, which isn't far from Beddgelert, and they say that he was able to hide there for half a year while the traitors were looking for him. And it's possible to visit this cave but you must be a good climber because it's fairly dangerous.)

Another time when misfortune was against him, Glyndŵr hid in a cave on the shore near Tywyn (cited as near Llangelynin or Llanegryn), where he was provisioned by Ednyfed ab Aron, whose name is almost always noted in association with this cave. As Pennant notes,

> [1405] . . . he was obliged to seek protection from a few trusty partizans; and often to conceal himself in caves and desert places. A cavern near the sea-side, in the parish of *Llangelynin*, in the county of *Meirioneth*, is still called *Ogof Owain*, in which he was secretly supported by *Ednyfed ap Aaron*, of the tribe of *Ednowain ap Bradwen*.[64]

The role of provisioner remains a source of pride to ab Aron's descendants, who note it in the official family history. The genealogy of the Peniarth family, under Ednyfed ab Aron of Peniarth, contains the note that, 'He concealed Glyndyfrdwy in a cave by the sea-shore, in the parish of Llanegryn, still called Ogof Owain.'[65] Such a role is an important and cherished one. An 1894 newspaper reports in the obituary for a Mrs Richards that she is the daughter of John Vaughan:

yn ddisgynydd mewn llinell uniawn o'r hen foneddwr gwladgarol Gruffydd Fychan, o'r Cefncamberth, yr hwn, fel y dywed hanes-wyr, a guddiodd y gwrol a'r gwladgarol Owain Glyndwr mewn ogof rhag dialedd y gwaedgwn Saesnig.[66]

(a descendant in direct line from the patriotic nobleman of yore Gruffydd Fychan from Cefncamberth, who, as the historians say, hid the brave and patriotic Owain Glyndŵr in a cave, for fear of revenge by the English bloodhounds.)

The association between Glyndŵr and caves is so strong that it seems as if any cave, of which there are plenty in Wales, may be connected with the hero, though sometimes the details are a little confused. In one such instance, a man standing with me in Corwen and looking across the valley to the hill on the other side with the ruin of its ancient fortification, Caer Drewyn, explained:

Mynydd y Gaer. In English it means Chester mountain [lit. Mountain of the Fort]. And Owain Glyndŵr – Oh, you can see all the Roman walls around the mountain there – supposed to be built by his band of men. And that's where he fought the English. It's, it's a good spot there, you see. Just lower down, there's some houses there. It's a council estate. That was his village, but he fled from there to the top when the English come. And to flee the English, he went straight through. There are caves on that mountain. You can only go so far in, you know, there's a wall . . . As the story goes in the history, local history books, he fled straight through and come out in Chester. That's how he fled the English. It was true, though. He did have a camp there, up there on top.[67]

This account also demonstrates what can happen in the development of a legend; one is the conflation of historical periods, here having the Romans, the English and Glyndŵr all coming together; the other is in justification of the name. In translating 'Caer' as the place-name 'Chester' rather than the common noun 'fort', the translator justifies inclusion of it in the name of the mountain by explaining that the caves run straight through from Corwen to Chester – a geographic impossibility.

Another person, an older woman in Carrog, began to tell me about Glyndŵr hiding in a cave in Llanarmon, in y Coed Cochion (the Red Wood), but was unsure from whom he was hiding.[68] Sometimes, Glyndŵr must share a cave with other traditions which have a claim on it. For example, the cave Ogof Coed Cochion brings to one informant's mind three separate traditions – one, that it is linked by an underground passage with another special cave at Pen y Bryn; two, that Owain Glyndŵr used it as a hiding-place 'when pursued by his enemies'; and three, that Ned Puw was seen entering the cave, 'never to return, piping the air "Ffarwel Ned Puw" when he escaped from his wife, an inveterate scold'.[69]

Apart from any caves in which Glyndŵr may have hidden towards the end of his natural life, there are the caves in which, sleeping, he awaits the proper hour for his return. As one informant says:

> ma' 'na chwedl 'i fod o'n cuddio ar lethr y Wyddfa rhwla mewn ogof, a 'dyn, pan fydd angen ar Gymru, bydd Glyndŵr yn codi unwaith eto ac yn ailgychwyn y gwrthryfel.[70]

> (There's a legend that he's hiding on the side of Snowdon somewhere in a cave, and after, when Wales will have need, Glyndŵr will rise once again and restart the rebellion.)

Amongst the many places (often anonymous or unspecified) in which Glyndŵr and his men are said to be sleeping are Craig Gwrtheyrn in Carmarthenshire,[71] on Mynydd yr Aran, beyond Llanuwchlyn,[72] and Ogof y Ddinas.[73]

In addition to the legends which simply state the presence of Glyndŵr and his men, there are more elaborate tales which recount finding the cave, and describe the sleepers and their surroundings. These more developed tales of finding Glyndŵr (or other sleeping Welsh redeemers) usually take one of two forms. The following tale exemplifies one of these types.

> There was a drover from near Llandegla, outside Mold, you see, and he was working with a big herd of cattle which were collecting from right across into Caernarvonshire and bringing them across the top, which is across the Denbigh moors and then Rhuthun way over the mountains near Mold and the Clwydian Range and coming along, avoiding toll-gates, of course, all the time, keeping to the old mountain tracts, staying the night here and there, and because he was just an ordinary labourer with the drovers, he hadn't got a horse to ride or anything like that as many of the assistants; he just walked. And when they got near a place outside

Mold called Llanarmon-yn-Iâl, he cut a fresh stick from a hedge there to walk with because, obviously, as the roads were getting harder, the stick was wearing out pretty quickly and he just cut one when he needed it. And anyway they went across the top there and eventually came down outside Mold, a small town called Mold, Yr Wyddgrug in Welsh, where to prove the story true there's a pub called the Drover's Arms. And then they crossed from there, picking up more cattle, sheep all the way, and of course getting them shod because the roads were now harder, got to go through turnpikes, that sort of thing, until eventually weeks later they get up for the Barnet Fair just outside London where there are enormous amounts of Welsh cattle taken. And he'd been there before. Well now the custom was after they'd got rid of the cattle for the heads of the drovers, the bosses to remain behind because they had banking to do, they had lots of things to do for people in Wales, but for the ordinary sorts of assistants to start out, to walk back home. And when he got to London he noticed that a very strange thing had happened. This stick which he'd cut hadn't wore out. It was still as good as it was before. So he thought, 'Before I go back to Wales, I may as well have a look at London.' So he went walking with this stick to the centre of London and eventually he came to one of the bridges over the Thames. 'Well now,' he thought, 'I'd better say I've crossed the river Thames.' So he started to walk across and as he was going across he was stopped by a very tall, a complete stranger to him, a man very well dressed, a complete stranger. And he didn't want to speak to the man at first, but anyway the man spoke to him, in English, and asked him, 'Where did you get that stick?' And he said, 'Oh, I cut it by a little place near Llanarmon-yn-Iâl, which you would never have heard of.' And the stranger said to him, 'Well now, when are you going back?' And he said, 'Well, I'm going to go back to Wales soon.' The man said, 'Well, do you mind if I come with you?' The Welshman said, 'No.' So all the way back to Wales he had the company of this man, and the man insisted that they went back the same way, no short cuts, but the same route as they travelled to London. And then eventually they got through Mold again, the same old way and got up by Llanarmon-yn-Iâl, where the limestone is, and then when they got there the stranger said to him, 'I want you to show me *exactly* the copse or the thicket where you cut this stick.' So, the chap was able to show it him and he showed him the very spot where the mark of the knife was still there. So the stranger said to him, 'Well now, you watch.' So he started to pull up this thing. And then the whole clump came away from the ground. There was the entrance, you see. And so they both went down. The Welshman by then was wishing he'd kept a bit further away from all this. And they go into a huge cave all brilliantly lighted up which is in the limestone rocks by Llanarmon. And there in the cave were a huge number of men, all sleeping. In the middle of the men was a huge pile of armour. They'd taken their armour off and piled it up. And they were all sleeping there. And hanging from the roof of the cave, quite pulled down was an enormous silver bell. And the stranger told the Welshman quite quietly, 'Don't do anything to wake these men or they'll, they may knock you about because these are Glyndŵr's men and that man sleeping over there in the middle is Glyndŵr himself. And one day when Wales needs them, the bell will be rung and they all will come out and go out of the cave, but in the meantime, you'll notice that there's a great deal of treasure in the cave, of money, of gold and silver. Now you can take some of that when you leave here, but you must be terribly careful not to touch that bell or you'll wake them. But you can take some money and you can come again and take more.' So anyway, this chap was very excited and he took, not too much, but he took a certain amount of money and he went out, replaced the sort of bush at the mouth of the cave, said goodbye to the stranger and went off home, and was very pleased about it. And then after a while he went back to the cave and he took some more, still very careful, till eventually he got over-confident and also a little bit greedy, so he goes in there now very, very confident, bold, loads himself up with far too much stuff so he can hardly walk, slips, touches the bell and, of course, the whole issue starts to wake up. Well, of course, he has to drop the stuff and get out of the cave as fast as his legs will carry him, put the thing over the front, and, of course, he went back there many times, but he could never find the entrance to the cave again.[74]

There are, naturally, a number of variants to this tale. One element which is not present in this example, but which is specified in almost every other version, is that the staff which the drover cut is hazel. The bridge on which the drover meets the stranger is most often named as London Bridge. Other variations are that the stranger may promise the drover treasure if he will lead him to the hazel tree, and that entrance to the cave is gained by digging or moving a stone. More attention is usually given to the leader of the sleeping men, who is generally described as a particularly splendid warrior sleeping in the centre of the room, either on a raised platform or sitting at a table with his hand grasping his sword. The men usually sleep in their armour. On the floor are heaps of treasure – gold, silver, pearls. The drover is told he may take as much as he likes as long as he observes some condition, such as that he may take only what he can carry in his hands or that he may not mix the different kinds of treasure. Although warned not to touch the bell hanging in the entrance, the drover is told that if he does, the warriors will wake up and ask, 'A yw hi yn ddydd?' (Is it day?), and he must answer, 'Nac ydyw, cysgwch' (No, sleep on). Most often the tale concludes with the drover accidentally hitting the bell but, in his fright at the ensuing clamour, forgetting the appropriate response. The warriors throttle him and throw him out of the cave. Never again can he find the entrance. Nor does he ever again have a healthy day.

The other basic form of the legend begins with a shepherd who, in trying to rescue a lost sheep, clambers along precipices and down to a narrow shelf and thereby finds the cave entrance.[75] The rest of the legend – with the treasure, the warriors and the bell – proceeds as in the previous tale. These legends clearly have international analogues, as can be seen even from Thompson's motif number D1960.2 ('Kyffhäuser. King asleep in mountain [Barberossa, King Marko, Holger Danske, etc.] will awake one day to succor his people') and Baughman's D1960.2.2 ('Man gains entrance into cavern where a king, his warriors, dogs and horses lie asleep. The man sees articles [a sword, garter, bugle, etc.] on a table before the king. He partly unsheathes the sword or the like; and the men and animals begin to awake. He sheathes the sword again and they go back to sleep . . .'). Arnold Van Gennep suggests that the cycle of legends dealing with kings asleep in mountains, which he calls 'légendes impériales', reflects the convergence of two independent themes, that of the person who has not died but who will return some day to help his friends and undo his enemies and that of the hero enclosed in a cave or a mountain.[76] I do not know that this fusion, which Van Gennep dates to the fifteenth century, has any special significance; indeed, it seems a natural association of ideas, but there are some interesting connections with other aspects of legendry to be noted. Both the Welsh legends and their European analogues are obviously closely related to certain types of treasure tales in which, under special circumstances, treasures are discovered in a cave or underground and are then abruptly lost through a broken taboo. The treasures in such cases are often fairy hoards. The connection between the treasure surrounding the sleeping king and fairy treasure is further marked by the common motif of the only occasionally visible opening in a hillside as an entrance into the fairy otherworld. This shows even more clearly in European variants of the legend where the person who enters the sleepers' cave loses years rather than the minutes or hours he supposes, just as mortals commonly do when they enter the otherworld.[77] In the Welsh variants, the major link to fairy treasure appears in the persistently recurring motif of the hazel staff cut by the drover, since in Welsh tradition the hazel tree is associated with the otherworld.

Another of the persistently recurring motifs in the Welsh legends, the meeting on London Bridge, brings to mind another form of treasure tale, AT 1645 The Treasure at Home, Motif N531.1 (Dream of treasure on the bridge). In this tale, a poor villager dreams that he will find treasure if he goes to a certain big city bridge. When he goes there, he learns from a scoffer at superstitions, who had had a similar dream about travelling to a small village, that the treasure is buried at his own cottage.

Nevertheless, despite interesting connections with treasure tales, the main issue of these Welsh legends is the sleeping warrior. The central warrior, the leader of the sleeping men, is identified as one of three men – Arthur, Owain Lawgoch or Owain Glyndŵr – all three of whom are established as Welsh national redeemers. I have taken the time to discuss the 'hazel rod' and the 'lost sheep' cave-finding legends, not simply because they are well developed and have interesting analogues, but more particularly because I wish to establish how readily any of these three redeemers can assume the role of the central warrior. This is not to say that Arthur, Owain Lawgoch and Glyndŵr are completely interchangeable in these legends. Actually, in the versions which I have encountered either in print or in the field, Arthur and Owain Lawgoch figure more frequently than does Glyndŵr.[78] The whole field of Welsh legends about sleeping heroes (rather than just those which describe finding the cave), however, names Arthur, Owain Lawgoch and Glyndŵr in fairly equal numbers.

As to the identity of that sleeper, whether in simple statements of belief or in the more extended narratives, much depends on where the legend is being told. The location may affect not only the choice of hero but also the variations in associated legendry. For example, in south-west Wales, the cave at Craig y Dinas near Llandybïe[79] is usually associated with Owain Lawgoch. In the area there is also a lake, Llyn Llech Owen (Lake of Owen's Slab), which is said to have been created when Owain forgot to recover a well, which then overflowed until Owain bounded it by riding his horse around the flood. The two legends often become connected, and it is related that when Owain rode back to where his men were waiting on a neighbouring hill and told them about the lake, they fell asleep and have stayed that way since.[80]

In another example, in the Snowdon area, there is a cave called Ogof Llanciau Eryri (Cave of the Lads of Snowdon), which is almost always said to have been discovered by a shepherd following his lost sheep. This cave is always associated with Arthur, though, curiously, he does *not* lie in it. Mention of the cave is most often accompanied by mention of Bwlch y Saethau, the mountain pass where Arthur is said to have been shot with an arrow and killed. The lads in their cave are said to be awaiting Arthur's second coming, when he will regain the crown of Britain.[81] The purpose of the sleeping youths is further kept alive by a saying in the area, 'Llanciau Eryri a'u gwyn gyll a'i hennill hi' (The lads of Snowdon, with their white hazels, will win it) – 'it' being the crown of Britain. Reports indicate that this phrase served as a general rallying cry in the last century.[82]

One of the major factors affecting the telling of the cave legends is whether they are being told as part of national or as part of local tradition. (This distinction, which I have found clearly defined in lore about Glyndŵr, is further discussed in Chapter 5.) In this case, everybody in Wales seems to know that there is supposed to be somebody sleeping in a cave somewhere. When that is all they know, there is, perhaps, a tendency to name Arthur. On occasion, however, a chance experience may have provided more definite knowledge. For example, one woman who could recall almost nothing about Glyndŵr except that he *is* a national hero, was able to tell me that he had been in a particular cave (Ogof Glyndŵr near Beddgelert), because she happened to have gone on a college walking-trip to this cave, which bore Glyndŵr's name.[83] On the local level, however, when individuals tell about a local hero in a local cave, there is potentially more elaboration. People tend to tell much fuller narratives, put in more local detail, and often name the slope on which the cave is to be found. The legend may be localized, as happens in the 'hazel rod' legend already quoted in full, in which the narrator tracks the drover's route through North Wales. Or the legend may become even more localized, as in a couple of renditions of the 'hazel rod' legend I collected from people in Glyndŵr's home area of Corwen. Instead of the drover's taking his herd to market in London, he drives them to Bala, the major market town in that part of the country, only a few miles down the road from Corwen.[84] However, with a local legend about a local hero, the opposite may also occur. Instead of giving the full story of finding the cave or many details about it, people to whom the existence of the cave and its sleeper is familiar and obvious may make only passing reference to the sleeper.

Let me return now to the point of why these Welsh heroes are sleeping in their caves, that is, they are awaiting the proper time for their return. The cave legends clearly express the redeemer's long wait for the proper hour of true need, and in this, the sleepers, whether Arthur, Owain Lawgoch or Glyndŵr, do seem interchangeable. The redeemer, whoever he may be, is waiting. One person, in relating the 'hazel rod' legend, recounted:

> . . . dyna'r dyn diarth 'na'n deud wrth yr hogyn ifanc ma hwn o'dd Owain Lawgoch, a bod o wedi bod yn arwr, a bod o wedi brwydro dros Gymru ac ati, ac ati, a bod o wedi diflannu ar ôl ryw frwydr a bod o'n cysgu yn yr ogof yna a wedyn pan ma'r dydd yn dod, pan o'dd angen y dyn a help Owain Lawgoch ar y Cymry fysa fo'n deffro a wedyn fysa popeth yn iawn.[85]

> (. . . then the stranger said to the young lad that that was Owain Lawgoch, and that he had been a hero, and had fought on behalf of Wales, etc., etc., and that he had disappeared after some battle, and that he's sleeping in that cave, and afterwards, when the day comes, when the Welsh need the man and Owain Lawgoch's help, he would awaken, and afterwards, everything would be all right.)

Sometimes, when recorded in antiquarians' reports, the legend takes on a slightly nineteenth-century, romantic flavour, but the same basic information is provided. For example, some of the records of the legend in which Arthur is the sleeper tell of his awaiting the hour when the Black Eagle and the Golden Eagle will go to battle and the clamour of their battle will shake the earth, in turn causing the bell in the cave to ring, so that Arthur and his men will awaken and repossess the Island, re-establishing his court at Caerleon and his rule, so that there will be peace for the British until the end of time.[86] Nevertheless, no matter how it is expressed, the point is that the hero is expected to return. When I asked an informant, who had been telling me about Owain Lawgoch's sleeping in a cave, whether the hero was expected to return some day, he appeared taken aback at the stupidity of my question, and said, 'Wel, ie, wrth gwrs, dyna pam mae e'n cysgu, yndê?'[87] (Well, yes, of course, that's why he's sleeping, isn't it?).

Perhaps the most significant of the recurring motifs in these legends is the warning that if the bell hanging in the cave is rung, the warriors will awake and ask, 'Is it day?' to which the intruder must reply, 'It is not day. Sleep on.' It is not simply a matter of waking the redeemer, but rather of whether it is the proper time for his arousal. In this may lie a difference between the Welsh narratives and their international analogues. In other cultures, the redeemer may remain asleep because the intruder fails to do the right thing, such as draw a sword, sound a horn or pour water over the leader's outstretched hands; or he may remain asleep because he has not yet reached a set time, such as when his beard has grown to encircle three times the table on which he rests his head.[88] In Wales, on the other hand, the warrior remains asleep because the country's need is not at its greatest and the people are not yet ready to receive and follow the redeemer.

These legends dealing with the national redeemer, whether of the hero's meeting with the abbot, being found asleep in the cave or even temporarily hiding, and whether recorded in medieval histories, in nineteenth-century antiquarians' reports or in twentieth-century fieldwork, all seem to reiterate the same idea: both the hero and the people must wait until the hour is right. The hero seems to be as dependent on the time as the people are on the hero. As one of the sleepers in the cave is reported to say when awakened by the ringing of the bell and upon being told by the intruder to sleep on: 'My warriors, the day has not come when the Black Eagle and the Golden Eagle shall go to war. It is only a seeker after gold who has rung the bell. Sleep on, my warriors, the morn of Wales has not yet dawned.'[89]

The legends which grew up around Owain Glyndŵr,

depicting him as a redeemer-hero, are powerful statements of hope and expectation, carried from the past and projected on the future. They show Glyndŵr not only as the starting-point of new legends but also as the culmination of pre-existing legendry, as one moulded by the past. Prophecy and legendry both permitted and shaped perception of him as a redeemer, and then he gave new shape and impetus to the legend. He is both the shape and the shaper, the image formed and the formulating image.

4

The Multifaceted Character of Owain Glyndŵr

Owain Glyndŵr, as a figure of great importance in Welsh culture, has become the focus of a wealth of lore. The lore, showing him in a wide variety of ways, highlights different aspects of his traditional character. The foremost of these is his role as a redeemer-hero, but it is not his only heroic role. He also appears in legendry as a trickster, a social outlaw, the epitome of a Welsh noble and warrior, and the military leader of his particular, fierce and destructive war. These and other traditional views of Glyndŵr's character will be examined not only for the conditions giving rise to them and the traditions supporting each, but also for the ways in which they complement each other and reflect Glyndŵr's functions within Welsh culture.

Trickster

Glyndŵr's most prominent traditional role apart from that of the redeemer-hero is his role as a trickster. The focus remains on Glyndŵr's wars, but simultaneously demonstrated are his cunning and his ability to make fools of his enemies. His victories come not only through military prowess in proper battles, but also through his strategies and his skills in deception. His cunning and deceit are both essential for his survival and part of his triumph, as is the case with other medieval outlaws who play the trickster and with whom he shares many of his deceptions.

Glyndŵr's ruses, which he may use offensively to gain military advantages, defensively, such as in spectacular escapes, or quite simply to taunt his enemies, range widely in both their complexity and their nature. Probably the simplest trick occurs when Glyndŵr orders his blacksmith to turn his horse's shoes around, so that no one can tell from his tracks which way he has gone.[1] This internationally well-known motif (K534.1) also appears elsewhere in Welsh tradition, notably in connection with Llywelyn y Llyw Olaf, who, fleeing an English trap and unwilling to leave clear tracks in the snow, asked the blacksmith Madog Goch Fin Mawr (Red Madog of the Wide Mouth) to turn his horse's shoes. However, Madog betrayed Llywelyn, who was that day ambushed and killed.[2]

Another simple ruse with which Glyndŵr is credited involves dressing wooden poles in coats and caps so that at a distance they look like soldiers, a trick which in legendry has saved many a fort and garrison for the French Foreign Legion and the US Cavalry. All of the legends involving this motif appear to be centred on Glyndŵr's home area of Corwen. The first of these that I shall cite (though the most recently recorded) places the events at the 'field with the sewage works', but most give the location as the fields called Dôl Pennau (Meadow of the Heads).[3] A Corwen story which I heard in 1982 tells of the time Glyndŵr had to travel to another part of Wales, and Lord Grey, knowing that he was away from home, came to attack. But Glyndŵr had heard of Grey's plan and had set up in the field (the field with the sewage works) poles wearing coats and caps, so that when Grey arrived and saw the field full of soldiers he dared not attack.[4] A man from the neighbouring village of Cynwyd told the story thus:

> A ma nw'n deud, y stori glywes i, bydda fo [Iarll Grey] 'n gyrru'i sbiwyr i ben Bwlch Coch ynde i weld tybed oedd Owen Glyndŵr a'i filwyr yn digwydd bod gartre. Ol, rŵan dê, yn naturiol iawn fydde Owen Glyndŵr . . . fydde Owen Glyndŵr a'i filwyr mae'n debyg yn mynd i ben bob man de ond pan fydde fo i ffwrdd mi fydde milwyr a sbiwyr Iarll Grey yn ymosod ac yn dwyn i'w ddefaid a'i anifeiliaid o a'i geffyle fo a hambygio, llosgi'i ŷd o a llosgi'i wair o ac felly'n y blaen. Ol rŵan, be oedd Owen Glyndŵr yn 'i neud yn yr hafn 'ma yn y Dôl Beni, sydd yn syth, fedrwch chi'n weld o, o ben Bwlch Coch, oedd gwneud ffug filwyr

wyddoch chi. Wedyn fydde fo'n 'u gwisgo nw. Be oedd y deunydd dw'mbod – coed, gwair, gwellt, beth bynnag o'dd gynno fo. A rhoi gwisg milwyr amdanyn nw. Ac wedyn fydde fe'n i gosod nw fanno. Rhywun o dop Bwlch Coch yn naturiol o dipyn o bellter, bod y fyddin yno, bod Owen Glyndŵr yno. Ond mewn gwirionedd hwrach bod Owen Glyndŵr ugeinie o filltiroedd i fwrdd ylwch chi, 'ndê.[5]

(And they say, the story that I heard, he [Lord Grey] would send his spies to the top of Bwlch Coch to see whether Owain Glyndŵr and his soldiers happened to be at home. So now, very naturally Owain Glyndŵr would . . . Owain Glyndŵr and his men would likely go to the top of each place then, but when he was away, Lord Grey's soldiers and spies would attack and steal his sheep, and his animals, and his horses and plague him, burn his corn and burn his hay, and so on. So now then, what Owain Glyndŵr did in the hollow here in Dôl Beni, which is straight [on a line], you can see it, from the top of Bwlch Coch, was to make fake soldiers, you know. Then he would dress them. What the material was I don't know – wood, hay, straw, whatever he had. And he would put soldier's clothes on them. And then he would place them there. Someone on the top of Bwlch Coch naturally from a bit of a distance would suppose the army was there, that Owain Glyndŵr was there. But in fact, perhaps, Owain Glyndŵr would be scores of miles away, you see.)

A nineteenth-century antiquarian records another case, which shows a deeper stratagem to the ruse:

Yr ochr arall i'r afon, yn nghyfeiriad Llangollen, mae cae a elwir Dôl Penni, a'r traddodiad ydyw fod Owain unwaith wedi gosod nifer o bolion yn y maes hwn, a gwisgo pob un o honynt mewn gwisg filwraidd, er mwyn twyllo byddin y Saeson. Llwyddodd y ddyfais. Ymosodwyd yn ddi-drugaredd ar y milwyr pren, y rhai nad oeddynt fymryn gwaeth; ac wedi i'r gelyn ddarfod ei saethau, ymosodwyd arno gan Owain.[6]

(The other side of the river, in the direction of Llangollen, there is a field called Dôl Penni and the tradition is that Owain once set up a number of poles in this field and dressed each one of them in military dress, in order to trick the English army. The device succeeded. The wooden soldiers, who were none the worse, were attacked mercilessly and after the enemy had spent their arrows, they were attacked by Owain.)

Another report relates that 'the Welshmen decoyed their opponents into a bog by lying behind bushes and raising their headgear on poles to make it appear that the ground was firm'.[7] The *Atlas Meirionnydd* records even more simply under Dôl Penni, cae yng Nglyndyfrdwy (a field in Glyndyfrdwy), 'Traddodiad i Owain Glyndŵr roi gwisg milwyr am bolion er mwyn twyllo'r Saeson' (a tradition that Owain Glyndŵr put soldiers' garb on poles in order to trick the English).[8] While the ruse is simple, the manner in which it is used has varied, and there is even one story in which Glyndŵr becomes the victim rather than the perpetrator of the trick. A fifth story from the Corwen area, told in connection with a particular pathway, reports:

Dywedir mai rhodfa y Tywysog Owen oedd hwn, a'i fod yn codi yn fore, ac yn dyfod yma er mwyn cael golwg ar y dyffryn, rhag bod rhyw elyn wedi gwneud rhyfelgyrch iddo yn y nos; a dywedir iddo un bore weled cannoedd lawer o filwyr yn gorchuddio rhai o'r meusydd islaw y domen. Ystryw rhyw elyn neu fradwr a geisiai ei frawychu oedd hyn; oblegid ar ôl gwneuthur ymchwil briodol, cafwyd nad oedd yno ddim ond polion wedi eu gwisgo â chapiau a chotiau milwyr; ond ni chymerodd y Tywysog druan, yn ei fraw, amser i wneud ymchwiliad, ond credodd fod y meusydd yn llawn o filwyr yn meddu cnawd ac esgyrn gwroniaid. Gelwir un neu ddau o'r meusydd hyn Dolbeni hyd heddyw: a dywedir ar lafar gwlad mai o'r amgylchiad hwn y tarddodd yr enw.[9]

(It is said that this was Prince Owain's pathway, and he would rise early and come here in order to get a view of the valley, lest some enemy had laid siege to him in the night; and it is said that one morning he saw many hundreds of soldiers covering some of the fields below the mound. This was a trick by some enemy or traitor who sought to frighten him because after making a proper search, it was discovered there was nothing but poles dressed with soldiers' coats and caps; but the poor prince, in his fright, did not take time to make a search, but believed the fields full of soldiers of real flesh and bone. One or two of the fields are still called Dolbeni today: and it is said traditionally that the name derived from that circumstance.)

Another example of Glyndŵr's cunning use of disguise was told to me by a young inhabitant of Carrog (in the Corwen area). In this legend, when Glyndŵr attacked Lord Grey in his castle, he first sent a small band including someone dressed as himself. When Grey saw that it was only a small band, he left his castle and attacked. Glyndŵr, however, was waiting in the wood with more forces and was able to take Grey by surprise.[10]

These tricks are ones for which records appear in the nineteenth and twentieth centuries, but not earlier. There are, however, examples of Glyndŵr's cunning which are found much earlier. One such example is Glyndŵr's retaking of Aberystwyth Castle from Prince Henry. The earliest surviving record of this appears in Peniarth MS 135, a manuscript written by Gruffudd Hiraethog between 1556 and 1564, but whose original was compiled soon after 1422, and thus only a few years after Glyndŵr's defeat.

MCCCCVII y doeth y twysoc Sais a llu mawr gidac ef i osod sits ar gastell Aberystwyth ac nid aeth oddiwrtho oni kavas eddewid ar y kastell mewn oll tydd byrr a phedwar or goreugwyr mwyaf i gallu ar oedd o vewn yr kastell yn wystl drostaw o vewn i hynn myned Rrys di i Wynedd i ovyn kenad y Owain i roddi y kastell ir Saesson kadw o Owain Rys gidac ef yn i gavas y nerth attaw a myned i gida Rrys i Aberystwyth a gossod ar dorri pen Rrys oni cheffid y kastell ac ar hynt rroddi y Owain y kastell.[11]

(1407 The English prince with a great host came to lay seige to Aberystwyth castle and he did not go from there until he got a promise of the castle in a short time, and four of the best, most able men who were in the castle as pledge of this. Meanwhile, Rhys Ddu went to Gwynedd to ask Owain's permission to give the castle to the English. Owain kept Rhys with him until he gathered his strength and went with Rhys to Aberystwyth and threatened to cut off Rhys's head unless he got the castle, and at once he gave the castle to Owain.)

Even the English historians maintain the idea of Glyndŵr's cunning. In the late sixteenth century, Raphael Holinshed tells how Prince Henry successfully besieged the castle at Aberystwyth and set conditions for a truce:

but the prince was no sooner from thence departed, but that Owen Glendouer by subtill craft entered the castell, put out the keepers, and charging them with treason for concluding an agreement without his consent, placed other in that fortresse to defend it in his vse.[12]

A much less detailed account is given by Robert Vaughan of Hengwrt in his mid-seventeenth-century history of Owain Glyndŵr transcribed in Panton MS 53: 'Prince Henry came against the castle of Aberystwyth, and took it upon articles, but Owain took it again by stratagem soon after.'[13] Nevertheless, the essential element of Owain's (or his officer's) cunning remains. This element, however, is lost in William Wynne's late seventeenth-century *The History of Wales*, where it is recorded that the prince 'Took the Castle of Aberystwyth, which was quickly again retaken by Owen Glyndŵr, who thrust into it a strong Garrison of Welch.'[14]

Thomas Pennant appears to record a variant of the tradition in the section 'Of Owen Glyndwr' in his *Tours in Wales* (1778), when he places the events at Lampeter Castle, about twenty miles from Aberystwyth, and in the year 1405.

> After the defeat of *Gryffydd* son of *Glyndwr*, by *Henry* prince of *Wales*, that youthful warrior undertook the siege of *Llanbedr* castle, in the county of Cardigan. After some time, the governor placed there by Glyndwr agreed to give it up, in case it was not relieved between the 24th of *October* and the feast of *All Saints*. He was to surrender it in good condition . . . He took the sacrament in witness of his sincerity, and delivered hostages for the performance of his agreement. He probably relied on the assistance of the *French* for relief. *Henry* apprehended the same. But, in order to frustrate any attempts of that kind, he issued out a writ, dated from *Cawood* the 22d of *September*, to the lieutenants of *Devonshire*, and of other counties, to raise their forces, and to rendezvous at *Evesham* on the 10th of October. This caution took effect so far, as to oblige *Rees ap Gryffydd ap Shenkin*, alias *Rees ap Llewelyn*, to agree to the terms proposed; but seemingly without any design of preserving them; for, no sooner was the prince departed, than *Rees* permitted *Glyndwr* to turn him and his garrison out, under pretence that they had been guilty of treason in submitting without his consent.[15]

The variation may be at least in part due to English influence, for Pennant cites two English sources, which may also account for the less approving attitude towards the trickery.

The next case of Glyndŵr's skills in deception, while an excellent example of the type of narrative dealing with that aspect of Glyndŵr's character, does provide some difficulties concerning its provenance, as to whether or not it is truly traditional. The problem is that the earliest record of the story is in the *Iolo Manuscripts*, edited in 1848 by Taliesin Williams from the papers of his father Edward Williams, or Iolo Morganwg. Iolo (1747–1826) deeply loved his land, particularly Glamorgan, and was fascinated by its literature, history and traditions. He did much serious research and genuine fieldwork, but his Romanticism and his sense of history as it should have been often led him to manipulate his materials or to create new ones. Combining traditional materials, his reworkings of characters, places and events found in tradition, and his own inventions, Iolo shaped the legendry and other materials to suit his personal vision of Glamorgan's rich bardic past. The threads have become so entwined that it is now almost impossible to disentangle them, to distinguish between genuine tradition retold by Iolo and Iolo's creations put into traditional form. Moreover, Iolo's works took on great importance, and like those of Geoffrey of Monmouth before him, became an accepted standard. Held in high repute, they were cited by historians and antiquarians, and repeated frequently. In some cases, therefore, even when a story is to be found orally, if the first record of it is provided by Iolo, one cannot readily determine whether Iolo took the legend from oral tradition, rewrote it, invented it or initiated subsequent oral tradition.

In this story, found first in Iolo's papers, Glyndŵr, disguised as a Frenchman, stays in the home of his enemy, Lord Berkrolles, at Coety in Glamorgan.

> Pan oedd Owain Glyn Dwr yn Tramwy'r wlad ynghydfelydd Gwr bonheddig dierth a chydag ef ond un cyfaill cywir yn Rhith gwas iddaw, a'r ddau yn anarfog, achos nid diogel nebun Dan arfau yr amser hynny, a Thrammwy er deall edryn Gwyr y wlad ydoedd: felly myned at Gastell syr Lawrens Berclos, a gofyn Lletty noswaith yn ffrangeg iddaw ef ai was; cael hynny yn rwydd iawn, a chael groeso mawr, a goreuon a bob peth yn y Castell, a chan mor foddlon oedd Sir Lawrens idd ei ei gyfaill, bu'n daer arno aros rhai ddiwarnodau gydag ef a dywedyd ei fod yn disgwyl ar fyrr o ddyddiau gweled Owain Glyn Dwr yno am ei fod wedi danfon allan ei holl Ddeiladon ai weision, a llawer eraill o ffyddloniaid iddo, yng nghyrch pob rhan or wlad yn wyr twng iddo i gyd, i ddala Owain, yr hwn a glywsai fod wedi dyfod i'r rhannau hynny o Gymru, ai fod hefyd dan dwng ei hunan i roddi gobrwyon

anrhydeddus iddei wyr os nhwy a ddelaint ag Owain Glyn dwr
yno y naill neu yn fyw neu yn farw, Da iawn yn wir, ebe Owain y
byddai diogelu'r Gwr hwnnw, abod gallu yn rhyw rai i wneuthur
hynny, gwedi bod ynghastell Syr Lawrens bedwar diwarnod a
thair noswaith yn fawr ei barch ai roeso, meddylws Owain mai call
fyddai myned iddei ffordd, a chan rhoi ei Law yn llaw Syr
Lawrens, dywed wrtho fal hynn. 'Y mae Owain Glyn Dwr, yn gar
cywir, heb na digofaint na brad na thwyll yn ei galon, yn rhoi llaw
yn llaw Syr Lawrens Berclos, ag yn diolch iddo am y groso ar
caredigrwydd ar syberwyd bonheddigaidd a gafodd ef ai gyfaill yn
rhith gwas iddo, yn ei Gastell, a chan addaw ar lw Llaw yn Llaw a
Llaw ar Galon, na ddaw fyth ar feddwl iddaw ddial yr hynn a
feddyliodd Sir Lawrens Berclos iddo, ag nas goddefai i hynny fyw
ar ei gof, nag ar wybod iddo hyd y bai yn ei allu ym meddwl ag ar
gof nebun o'i geraint ai gymmhlaid,' ag ar hynny Owain ai was a
gyrchasant eu ffordd a myned ymaith. Ar hynny syrthwys Syr
Lawrens Berclos yn fud gan syndod, a phyth wedi hynny ni chafas
efe ei oddeg ag ni chlywyd gair byth wedi hynny oi benn.—(Llyfr
Mr. Lleison or Prysg, gan Ifan o'r fferm, yn Llanfleiddan fawr.)

(When Owen Glyndwr travelled about the country, in the guise
of a strange gentleman, attended by one faithful friend, in the habit
of a servant, and both being unarmed, [for no armed person was
secure at that time] and going about to ascertain the disposition of
the inhabitants, he went to the castle of Sir Lawrence Berkrolles,
and requested, in French, a night's reception for himself and
servant, which was readily granted, attended by a hearty welcome;
the best of every thing in the castle being laid before him; and so
pleased was Sir Lawrence with his friend, that he earnestly pressed
him to remain with him for some days; observing, that he soon
expected to see Owen Glyndwr there; for that he had dispatched all
his tenants and servants, with many other confidential persons,
under an oath of fidelity, through all parts of the country to seize
Owen, who, he was told, had come to that district of the
principality; and that he was, himself, sworn to give honourable
rewards to his men who should bring Owen Glyndwr there, either
alive or dead. 'It would be very well, indeed,' said Owen, 'to secure
that man, were any persons able to do so.' Having remained at Sir
Lawrence's castle for four days and three nights, Owen thought it
would be wise to go his way; therefore, giving his hand to Sir
Lawrence, he addressed him thus: 'Owen Glyndwr, as a sincere
friend, having neither hatred, treachery, nor deception in his heart,
gives his hand to Sir Lawrence Berkrolles, and thanks him for the
kindness and gentlemanly reception which he and his friend [in the
guise of a servant] experienced from him at his castle; and desires
to assure him, on oath, hand in hand, and hand on heart, that it will

never enter his mind to avenge the intentions of Sir Lawrence towards him; and that he will not, as far as he may, allow such desires to exist in his own knowledge and memory, nor in the minds of any of his relations and adherents:' and then he and his servant departed; but Sir Lawrence Berkrolles was struck dumb with astonishment, and never afterwards recovered his speech; no word, thenceforth, having ever escaped his lips. [The Book of Mr Lleison of Prysg, with Ifan from the farm in Llanfleiddan])[16]

The story is retold in the Welsh encyclopaedia *Y Gwyddoniadur Cymreig* in 1866 and Iolo's version is repeated almost exactly in the nationalist journals *Y Llenor Cymreig* in 1882 and *Y Geninen* in 1904.[17] J.Y.W. Lloyd also refers to it in his 1881 *History of Powys Fadog* and C.J. Evans in his *Story of Glamorgan* (1908).[18] The story was also turned into a ballad, 'Owain Glyn Dwr a Syr Lawrence',[19] published in the nineteenth century by the poet Ceiriog and in that form disseminated through the schools. Indeed, current knowledge of the story in North Wales appears, on admittedly limited evidence, to be based mainly on the ballad. One informant from the Llŷn peninsula in North Wales, recited bits of the poem that she had learned in school forty or fifty years earlier.[20] Another informant, from the Corwen area and quite knowledgeable about Glyndŵr legends in that area, also told of Glyndŵr's visit with Sir Lawrence, claiming to have learned it at school from the ballad and never to have heard it in general circulation.[21] In South Wales, however, in the area near Bridgend where the events of the narrative are located, the story of Glyndŵr's visit to Coety Castle does appear to be current in oral tradition. One version of the legend, collected from a man who had heard it as a child in the Bridgend area where 'everybody knows that story',[22] even has one gratifying change in motif, which would seem to offer evidence of at least this version's oral sources and independence from the printed tradition. In all of the printed sources, when Glyndŵr announces his true identity, Sir Lawrence is dumbfounded, literally struck dumb. In this version, however, the lord is struck blind. Another difference from the printed sources, and one which is shared by a version from an informant who believes he learned the story from a children's book on European heroes, has to do with the timing of the events within Glyndŵr's life.[23] The earlier materials all seem to indicate that Glyndŵr's incognito travels in the South take place at the height of his powers, when he is full of cunning and daring and greatly feared by his enemies. In these other two versions, however, the events occur when Glyndŵr's powers are waning and when he is fleeing his enemies.

The motif of moving freely and unrecognized amongst one's enemies occurs repeatedly in outlaw narratives. Hereward the Wake visited the enemy camp disguised as a potter; William Wallace presented himself variously as a woman, a potter and a monk; and Robin Hood, also in the guise of a potter, spent time in Nottingham and participated in an archery contest.[24] Hereward and Robin, like Glyndŵr, even discussed with their enemies the hoped-for capture and punishment of the outlaws. Hereward also shares with Glyndŵr the role of language as an element in disguise, though while Glyndŵr used French to hide his Welshness, Hereward pretended ignorance of French in playing a peasant in front of whom plans could be discussed safely in that language. Nor are these motifs of outlaw-trickster tradition peculiar to the British Isles. Non-British examples include such seemingly disparate characters as the tenth-century Icelandic hero Gisli, who lived for fourteen years as an outlaw alternately hidden by friends and relatives or, having escaped discovery, in the safety of the wilds, and who disguised himself in servants' clothes; and the seventeenth-century Turkish hero Kurroglou who, away from his mountain fastness, repeatedly entered enemy territory in the guise of a shepherd, mullah or singer, once even seizing the Sultan's daughter from the heart of Constantinople.[25]

Glyndŵr's declaration of his identity as he leaves his enemy's court hints at another characteristic which is at times associated with the prankster – taunting. The prankster's taunts may take various forms. The mocking of one's foes in their discomfiture is demonstrated in another incident, one which involves Dafydd Gam (presumably so named because of having only one eye although *cam* now more commonly means 'bent' or 'crooked'), who later distinguished himself at Agincourt. The basic story, for which the earliest records I was able to find begin in the 1650s, is that when Glyndŵr called a parliament in Machynlleth, Dafydd Gam attended with the aim of assassinating him. The plot was discovered and Dafydd Gam imprisoned. Glyndŵr's friends, however, convinced him to let Dafydd Gam go with promises of loyalty. Nevertheless, once returned safely to his own territory Dafydd Gam again began attacks against Glyndŵr and his allies. In retaliation, Owain Glyndŵr burned Dafydd Gam's home, and when doing so,

> called to him one of David's tenants, to whom he spoke thus merrily in verse.

> > o gweli di wr coch cam
> > yn ymofyn y Gernigwen
> > dywed ei bod hi dan y lan
> > a nod y glo ar ei phen.[26]

> (if you see a red-haired, one eyed man/ seeking the (?)fair troop/ say that it is under a bank/ and the mark of the coal on its head.)

A counterpart to the prankster's tricks is his ability to recognize a ruse and avoid its dangers. Indeed, in Elis Gruffydd's sixteenth-century account, Owain Glyndŵr states very clearly that he will not be tricked. He had demanded ransom for the lord of Rhuthun whom he had taken in battle but, when the messengers arrived with the gold, he discovered that a tenth of it was not true gold. Realizing that the lord's men had tried to deceive him, he sorted out the true gold and sent the rest back with a demand for twice the ransom and with an indignant message:

> nad ydwyf J am kenedlaeth mor ddi ssynwyr ac na vedrwn i ednabod aur oddiwrth mettel arall a deffol yr aur da o vysg yr hrai drwy Jr vy mod J am kennedlath yn dlawd o aur. Ac ynn gymaint ac J chwi vyngwattwar J ynn y modd hwn myui a dyngaf J dduw na ollyngaf J arglwydd h[r]uthun byth ynn vyw allan oi garchar nes yw gennedyl ef dalu J i mi ddau kymaint o aur batthol ynn arianswm drostaw ef.[27]

> (Neither I nor my people is so without sense that we cannot distinguish gold from another metal and choose the good gold from amongst these though I and my people are poor of gold. And as much as you have mocked me in this way I myself swear to God I will never release lord Rhuthun alive out of prison until his people pay me twice as much in minted gold as ransom for him.)

In another instance, Glyndŵr, prepared for treachery, saves himself from his cousin's villainous intent. Glyndŵr and his cousin Hywel Sele had been at odds, but were brought together for a reconciliation. While they were out walking, they saw a deer and Owain told Hywel, a fine archer, to try to shoot it. Hywel aimed but then turned his bow on Owain, who was only saved by the armour which he wore under his clothes.[28]

Master of Escape

Glyndŵr's escapes from death, and more generally from capture, demonstrate an aspect of his character, which if not part of the trickster role, is certainly correlative to it. Glyndŵr is an escape artist. He repeatedly makes narrow and dramatic escapes. One of the earliest such escapes, both in the records (*c*.1560) and in the chronology of Glyndŵr's life (1401), took place at Mynydd Hyddgant, where Owain Glyndŵr and his small band of 120 men were surrounded by 1,500 Flemings. Glyndŵr and his men decided to fight their way through, or die in the attempt. They attacked so fiercely that they put the enemy to flight, except for 200 who lay dead.[29] Another time, at Y Berwyn, he instructed his servant to treat one of the dead as if it were he so that he might escape the cordon.[30] Glyndŵr's skill in eluding his enemy's grasp is, however, perhaps best seen in the examples where he is staying with friends, receives warning at the last minute of the approaching enemy, and slips away. An early form of this escape from a surrounded house, appearing in a mid-seventeenth-century text transcribed in Panton MS 53 and repeated by Thomas Ellis and Pennant in the 1770s, tells of events immediately before Glyndŵr openly broke with the king and while he was still in his home.

> . . . he [King Henry] in his return sent the Lord Talbot and Grey to reduce Owein with part of his forces, and they came so unexpectedly about Owain's house, that he had much ado to make his escape into the woods.[31]

Glyndŵr's escapes more usually take place during the war period when Glyndŵr must effect his escape from the home of a friend. The most noted of these dramatic escapes is recorded thus:

Ryw dro, pan oedd ffawd yn pallu ar Owain Glyndwr, efe a ffodd at ei gyfaill a'i bleidiwr twymgalon, Rhys Goch, i'r Hafod Garegog, am nodded a chuddfa. Eithr ni bu yn hir heb i'w elynion ddod o hyd i'w hynt, a rhyw ddiwrnod daeth haid o weision boneddwr gelynol i Owain, hyd at yr Hafod i'w ddal, i'r dyben o'i drosglwyddo i'r brenin. Ond un o weision Rhys a'u canfyddodd mewn pryd, ac a redodd i'r ty i rybuddio Owen a Rhys o'u perygl. A hwy a ffoisant ymaith yn nillad eu gweision. Rhys i fyny trwy flaen Nanmor, ac Owain hyd lan y Traeth. A'r gelynion wedi canfod Owain yn ffoi yn llechwraidd, a ymlidiasant ar ei ol, a phan welodd efe hwynt, ymdaflodd i'r traeth; ac er ei bod y pryd hyny yn uchaf y llanw, efe a nofiodd i'r lan yn ddiogel yn ymyl Dinas Ddu, ac a aeth i fyny ar hyd Cwm Oerddwfr, yn cael ei ddilyn gan ei erlidwyr yn dyn, hyd i'r Foel. Esgynnodd Owain i fyny hyd i ymyl y *Simnai*; ond erbyn myned yno, yr oedd yn y perygl mwyaf; o blegid fod ei erlidwyr yn pwyso yn drwm arno, fel, os âi ym mlaen hyd i'r esgynfa gyffredin, y byddent sicr o'i oddiweddyd yn fuan. Edrychodd i fyny yr hafn serth, a gwelodd os gallai esgyn hwnw y caffai y blaen ar ei erlidwyr; ond yr oedd y graig yn noeth, serth, a diafael; os collai ei droed unwaith, nid oedd ond marwolaeth annocheladwy i'w ddysgwylyn y codwm. Eithr gwron oedd Owain, ac â meddwl a phenderfyniad gwron, dechreuodd esgyn i fyny y *Simnai*; a phan oedd ei erlidwyr wedi cyrhaedd hyd ati, yr oedd Owain yn cael y grib yn llwyddiannus! Nid oedd un o honynt a feiddiasai ei ddilyn y ffordd hono; felly gorfu arnynt fyned o gylch hyd i esgynfa hawddach. Yn y cyfamser rhedodd Owain yn anweledig iddynt hwy hyd uwch ben y *Diffwys*; a disgynnodd i lawr drwy ddanedd y dibyn ofnadwy hwnw, i ogof ëang. Aeth ei erlidwyr yn eu blaen i'r Pennant, gan dybio ei fod wedi myned y ffordd hono, ac felly hwy a'u collasant yn llwyr. Dywedir y bu Owain yn llechu yn ei ogof am chwe mis; ac yr oedd yn cael ei gynnal yno gan Brior Bedd Gelert. Aeth Rhys Goch yn ei flaen hyd i Nant y Benglog, a bu yntau yn llechu yno ryw hyd, mewn lle a elwir 'Twll Rhys Goch;' a'i fod yn cael ei gynnal gan un Meredydd ab Ifan.[32]

(One time, when fortune was failing Owain Glyndŵr, he fled to his friend and warm-hearted supporter Rhys Goch, at Hafod Garegog, for sanctuary and a hiding place. But it was not long before his enemies found his path, and one day a swarm of an enemy nobleman's servants came to Owain to Hafod to capture him, in order to hand him over to the king. But one of Rhys's servants discovered them in time, and ran to the house to warn Owain and Rhys of their danger. And they fled away in their servants' clothes, Rhys up through the front of Nanmor, and Owain along the shore.

And the enemies after discovering Owain stealthily fleeing, chased after him, and when he saw them, flung himself towards the beach; and although it was then high tide, he swam safely to the shore near Dinas Ddu, and he went up along Cwm Oerddwfr, followed closely by his pursuers, to the Moel [bare hill-top]. Owain went up it as far as the edge of the Simnai [Chimney]; but when he got there he was in the greatest danger; because his pursuers were pressing heavily on him so that if he went on to the usual ascent, they would be certain of overtaking him swiftly. He looked up the steep ravine, and saw that if he could climb that way he would get ahead of his pursuers; but the rock was bare, steep, and without any holds; if he lost his footing once, there was nothing but inescapable death to expect in the fall. But Owain was a hero, and with the mind and determination of a hero, he began the ascent up the Simnai; and when his pursuers had arrived at it, Owain was successfully reaching the summit! Not one of them dared follow him that way; thus they had to go around to an easier ascent. In the meantime, Owain ran unseen by them along above the Diffwys [steep slope]; he descended down through the teeth of that awful precipice, to a wide cave. His pursuers went on to Pennant, supposing he had gone that way, and thus they lost them completely. It is said that Owain was hiding in his cave for six months; and he was supported there by the Prior of Beddgelert. Rhys Goch went ahead to Nant y Benglog, and he was hiding there for some time, in a place called Twll Rhys Goch [Rhys Goch's hole]; and he was supported by one Meredydd ap Ifan.)

The climb, Simnai y Foel, is today listed in the mountaineering books as having first been made by Owain Glyndŵr.

Another tale draws in the poet Iolo Goch, who by a coded message in Welsh verse warned Glyndŵr that Lord Grey's men were treacherously approaching. The story, noted by seventeenth-century antiquarian Robert Vaughan, explains that when Dafydd ap Gruffudd, the brother of Llywelyn y Llyw Olaf, was executed in Shrewsbury in 1283, the executioner threw his heart on the fire but the heart leapt from the fire, striking the executioner in the eye and destroying it. About one hundred and twenty years later, Lord Grey, at the instigation of Henry IV, invited himself to dine at Owain Glyndŵr's:

. . . ac ir attebodd Owain i byddai groesaw wrthaw oni ddygai gydag ef uwch ben 30 wr, ac a ddoeth yr Arglwydd yn yr oed terfynedig ag ychydig gwmpeini gydag ef, a gallu mawr yn arfog tan lech yn dyfod ar ei ol. A phan aeth Owain i giniawa efe a osodai wersyll ar ben bryn i wersyllu tra fyddai Owain ar giniaw: a phan oed Owain ar ganol ciniaw nychaf i gwelynt y gwersyllwyr lonaid y ddol heb enni o wyr arfog ac i dywedassant i Iolo Goch i rybuddio Owain, ac yna i daeth Iolo i mewn, canys didyb oedd efe, ac i canodd ar ddameg yr englyn rhybudd yma ar ostec rhac tybied yr Arglwydd fod twyll ynddo: er bod yr Arg. yn deall traethawd Cymraec, nid oedd ef yn deall ein mydr ni:

> coffa benn a lleñ a llywenic lys
>   a las nos nadolic
> coffa golwyth* Amwythic   *sef calon Dd. ap Gr.
> o'r tan a neidiodd naid dic.
>   Iolo Goch ai cant.[33]

(. . . and Owain answered that he would be welcome, unless he brought more than thirty men, and the lord came at the set time, with only a small company, and a great force in arms under cover coming behind him. And when Owain went to dine he set a camp on top of a hill to encamp while Owain would be dining; and when Owain was in the middle of dinner, behold the encamped men saw the fill of the meadow without containment of armed men and they told Iolo Goch to warn Owain, and then Iolo came in, since he was undoubted, and he sang as a parable this verse of warning in public lest the lord think there be deceit in it; although the lord understood a Welsh treatise, he did not understand our metre:

> Remember a head and mantle and (?) court
> who was killed Christmas night
> remember the cutlet* of Shrewsbury
>   [*that is, D. ap Gr.'s heart]
> from the fire it leapt an angry leap.
>   Iolo Goch sang it.)

Most of Glyndŵr's escapes, however, result in his hiding in caves for a while.

The combination of cunning and hiding in caves brings Glyndŵr into line with some other Welsh tricksters, such as Twm Siôn Cati, a sixteenth-century antiquarian and poet better remembered as a prankster who lived at times in caves, or Dafydd ap Siencyn, a mid-fifteenth-century supporter of the Lancastrians and a declared outlaw. The legendry about Twm Siôn Cati shows him robbing people with great humour as well as cleverness. While distracting a shopkeeper by arguing over whether or not a pot has a hole (which turns out to be the opening), he steals all the other pots. He tricks a highwayman out of his horse, sells a bull back to the original owner from whom he had stolen it after convincing him that it is a different bull, and commiserates about all the rogues who frequent fairs with a woman from whom he himself has stolen cloth.[34] Dafydd ap Siencyn, in addition to being skilled at slipping in and out of enemy territory, was also an excellent shot with his bow. He is reported to have shot arrows through the caps of a whole band of king's men without even scratching their heads.[35] Another legend tells of a victory feast prepared by the English forces. As the soldiers were about to begin eating, an arrow came through the air and landed in the meat at the centre of the table. Another landed directly in the custard, and so on until there was one arrow in each dish. Dafydd ap Siencyn, having watched the festive preparations from his cave, had decided to put a stop to them.[36] One informant from Dyffryn Conwy remembered the story slightly differently.

> Wel dad oedd yn deud hon – do'dd dad ddim yn deud lot o sens chwaith – ond – bod na milwyr – milwyr Lloegr, yn y dyffryn ag yn iste allan yn yr awyr agored, yn bwyta – pwdin mawr, mawr – a bod Dafydd ap Siencyn yn saethwr mor dda bod o'n saethu o dop y mynydd, saeth ar ddarn o gortyn, a bod o wedi saethu'r pwdin nes bod y pwdin wedi fflio i fyny'r mynydd! – chi'n bod, di'o'n yn gneud lot o sens, ond – ![37]

> (Well, dad used to say this – dad didn't make a lot of sense either – but – that there were soldiers – English soldiers, in the valley and sitting out in the open air, eating – a great big pudding – and that Dafydd ap Siencyn was such a good marksman that he was shooting from the top of the mountain, an arrow on a piece of cord, and that he shot the pudding so that the pudding flew up the mountain! – you know, it doesn't make a lot of sense, but – !)

Dafydd ap Siencyn is also reported to have done such things as dress his men in green, so that they might be taken for fairies and left alone.[38]

Even apart from physical attributes which may be human, animal or an amorphous combination of the two, tricksters appear in various guises, not only from culture to culture, but even within one culture. As Stith Thompson recognized in his discussion of Native American tales, the trickster may appear as 'the beneficent Culture Hero, the clever deceiver, or the numskull'.[39] Frequently, as with Coyote in North America or Spider in West Africa, the trickster moves through a world in which boundaries are not yet set or understood, and may indeed, while still learning the boundaries between his own body and the rest of the world, treat the parts of his own body as separate self-acting beings (e.g. burning his own anus in punishment for not having kept proper watch over the day's catch while the trickster slept). Not all tricksters, however, require a body as resilient and malleable as that of a cartoon character; some rely on their wits alone in practising their impudent deceits.[40] Through playing the fool (both fooling and being fooled), the trickster refashions the world and establishes cultural norms, often providing important features of culture, such as fire and basic foods. Moreover by turning the world, or at least expectations, upside down, the trickster clarifies societal conditions, underscoring both the good and the oppressive.[41] Owain Glyndŵr, Twm Siôn Cati and Dafydd ap Siencyn, are the second type of trickster, not the one who plays with the laws of nature, like Coyote or Spider, but rather the one who, with daring and cunning, repeatedly confounds his enemies, taunting them even in their own fastnesses, and always slipping from their grasp, escaping to security in the wilds – heroes such as Robin Hood or the Turkish Kurroglou.

Social Outlaw

The similarities amongst these clever men, moreover, go beyond the cunning tricks and ability to slip in and out of danger in various guises. The similarities have also to do with Glyndŵr's relationship to society, both Welsh and English, for like Robin Hood and Kurroglou, he too, is a social outlaw.

Maurice Keen has shown that the medieval English outlaws, in addition to sharing narratives of daring and skill, disguise and escape, and life spent in the wilds, also share a struggle against a society gone out of kilter. Whether Hereward the Wake resisting the Norman invaders, Fulk Fitzwarin pushing King John to sign the Magna Carta, Gamelyn wresting his land and rights back from a corrupt legal system, or Robin Hood countering the Sheriff of Nottingham's greedy and unlawful acts, the heroes are upholders of a rigid code who, despite having been forced outside the law, fight for an ordered society and against the injustice and abuse which would destroy it.[42] The same concern with justice and re-establishing a properly ordered society appears as a recurring and unifying theme for other social outlaws, as can be seen in Eric Hobsbawm's studies of social bandits and rebels where he has determined nine points which are characteristic of the noble robber in both literature and history.[43] The first point is that the social bandit is forced into his outlaw position by an act which, while seen as justifiable or even proper in his own culture, is disapproved of by an outside authority. He is not the enemy of a true king or emperor, one who is just, but only of the local gentry, clergy or other oppressors. He rights wrongs, takes from the rich to give to the poor and never kills but in self-defence or just revenge. He is admired and aided by the people. Through the use of disguises and his ability to blend with the local residents, he is practically invisible to the authorities and appears to be invulnerable. His death can be brought about only through treachery. If he does survive, he returns to his community as an honoured member.

While not all of these points are fully supported by either the legendry or the historical records on Owain Glyndŵr, there are enough for the pattern to be recognizable. Actually, examining Glyndŵr's life and story in relation to the pattern of the social bandit exposes some important differences as well as correlations, showing a certain tension between Glyndŵr's roles as social outlaw and national redeemer.

Glyndŵr was a responsible and respected member of Marcher society. He was baron of lands in North Wales; as a young man he trained at the Inns of Court in London; he was esquire to Richard II and possibly served under Bolingbrooke; he fought in the Scottish campaigns of 1385 and 1387. It was not until he came into conflict over land rights with his neighbour Lord Grey of Rhuthun, and Parliament refused even to hear his case, that Glyndŵr broke with the English. When he could get no redress from the English courts, Glyndŵr attacked Rhuthun, and from then on fought what was essentially a guerilla war against the English. His actions were seen by the Welsh to be perfectly justified. Originally Glyndŵr's argument was not with the Crown, that is with Henry IV, but it soon became so. It is easy to see Grey in the same role of the local antagonist as the Sheriff of Nottingham plays in the Robin Hood materials. One could also argue, along with certain apologists for Glyndŵr, that Glyndŵr's fight with Henry was not a fight with the true and proper king but rather with a usurper, and that he remained faithful to the true king – Richard II – just as Robin fought King John while continuing to support Richard I. The fact is, however, that though Glyndŵr's anger with Grey might not have erupted into war against England had Henry not sided with Grey, it did; Glyndŵr's war was not against a local expression of tyranny, but against the English Crown. This brings out a point of difference between Glyndŵr and most of the other social bandits, for the others are tied to their home areas; their rebellions are narrowly confined to the area surrounding their own villages. Glyndŵr, however, received the support of all of Wales; his was a major rebellion. Some of the nobility, especially in the Marches, stayed loyal to Henry, but the commoners flocked to Glyndŵr. Indeed, as pointed out in Chapter 1, Parliament first began to take it all seriously when it was noted that all the Welsh scholars were leaving Oxford and Cambridge, and Welsh labourers were leaving the English fields in order to return home to fight. In 1401, 119 years after the death of the last Welsh prince, Glyndŵr, who was of the royal lines of both North and South Wales, was proclaimed prince of Wales. Unlike most other social bandits, he had a full court, with diplomatic ties to Scotland and France. For approximately ten years, he had control of all of Wales. Henry and his troops could not even make inroads. They were defeated by Glyndŵr's guerilla tactics, by the mountainous and boggy terrain, and by the weather. In fact, the English thought Glyndŵr was a magician, calling up storms and mists to drive them back. Historically, Glyndŵr's actions were not contained in a small area, and legend would not make them so, because the needs of a national redeemer, which in this case include a wide geographical base, outweigh those of a social bandit.

However, like other social bandits, Glyndŵr did attempt to redress the wrongs of society and to restore the proper, traditional order, a point to which I shall return. And although the English historians report him as being cruel, the Welsh record him as a just, though fierce, warrior. Even when he would burn a whole town, he would leave standing the homes of his supporters. Also like the other bandits, Glyndŵr was supported and aided by the people – not only on the battlefield, but in protecting him. Each legend of his hiding in a cave has the corresponding one of the person who brought him provisions – a matter of pride to the provisioner's descendants down at least into the nineteenth century.[44]

Some of the legendry cited earlier demonstrates Glyndŵr's seeming invisibility, or at least unrecognizability, accomplished through his use of disguise. He could move with ease in and out of his enemy's territory, such as when he stayed the night with Lord Berkrolles. Through various devices, he was able to travel with impunity, as one person explained:

> Glyndŵr was everywhere, and he used even to have people imitate him. This is what confused the English for so long. He used to have people masquerading as him in different parts of the country, so the English never knew where he was, you see.[45]

Reports of his later years tell of his moving about the country in the guise of a shepherd. It is around this point – his seeming ubiquity, invisibility and invulnerability – that many of his trickster's pranks focus.

The social bandit is also characterized by open-handedness, courtesy and humour. It is hard to assess how much Glyndŵr fitted any of these characterizations. Like any proper Welsh lord, Glyndŵr was praised for his generosity. He may have been generous by nature and, since it was one of the duties of his social position, he was undoubtedly generous in fact, but here any perception of his generosity seems to be due more to conceptions of his role as a nobleman, especially as explicated by the poets, than to expectations of him as a social outlaw. There is no particular evidence of his courtesy other than what one would expect from a hospitable lord, and very little for his humour. Slight indications of humour show in the little rhymes he would make about his enemies, but no special point is made of his humour in the legendry. Since we cannot determine whether he actually did compose humorous rhymes, we cannot judge whether the rhymes belong to fact, to his characterization as an outlaw, to a combination of the two, or to other factors.

The social bandits studied by Hobsbawm end their careers in one of two ways. Either their deaths are brought about through treachery or they resume their old positions in society. However, none ever betrayed Glyndŵr. There is even a tale of a man who opposed Glyndŵr but who accepted death rather than betray the man for whom his sons fought.[46] Nor did Glyndŵr resume his position in Anglo-Welsh society. He could have. After the war had turned and England had regained control of Wales, King Henry did offer Glyndŵr pardon, but that is something recorded in the modern histories and not in the legendry.[47] As was discussed in the previous chapter, according to the legendry, Glyndŵr simply never gave in nor died. He faded from sight around 1415, but even as early as 1422 it was recorded that the seers were claiming Owain Glyndŵr had not died. This, of course, is essential for his role as a redeemer. Again the tension between the roles of social bandit and national redeemer is exposed. As strong as the pattern of the social bandit may be for Glyndŵr, it gives way before the demands of the national redeemer. Social bandits may die, but national redeemers must not.

Nevertheless, the connection between Glyndŵr and social banditry exists and is further strengthened by one of the terms used for banditry after Glyndŵr's time, that is *gwerin Owain* (Owain's people). The term apparently arose from those who, unwilling to accept Glyndŵr's defeat, took to the woods and hills, waiting for the opportunity to continue the battle. These disaffected then formed the nucleus of outlaw groups, who made the English their favoured prey.[48] Both written and oral evidence may exist for one of these outlaws in the person of the poet Llywelyn ap y Moel (d. 1440), who may have taken part in Glyndŵr's uprising, thereby earning the epithet 'bronfraith Owain' (Owain's song-thrush), and whose life as an outlaw is the subject of his own *cywyddau* and, probably, of current oral tradition under the name Lewsyn ap Moelyn.[49] The nationalist significance of *gwerin Owain* is outlined in the words of one informant:

> After the Owain Glyndŵr war, there's, there was a period of banditry, and much of this banditry became, was because there's lots of soldiers wouldn't give up to the English and became

outlaws, and these went to the hills, after the Owain Glyndŵr war,
and they kept the struggle going, and they became social bandits,
what's called today social bandits . . . There were these bandits
throughout Wales, and they were mainly poets and bards who'd
been outlawed because they wouldn't take – they were the
propagandists of their day, of course, and they'd become outlaws
and it's sad though that they didn't become as popular as Robin
Hood, you see, because they were our Robin Hoods and there was
a great deal of them, but people don't quite . . . only know one or
two of them, but there was quite a few gangs of them and they
were called the *gwerin Owain*. (Our people have never come to
know that name, only a few people know it – Owain's people.)
They were known as Owain's people years after Owain had died
and the war had ended, Owain's children – meaning they were the
soldiers and they were the leftovers and to us nationalists they
were the ones who kept the struggle alive, and but that's, that
never quite became the popular image.[50]

The patterns of the redeemer-hero, the trickster and the social
bandit do not parallel each other simply by coincidence; they are,
in fact, interrelated. It is significant and not merely curious that
Glyndŵr's primary role is that of redeemer-hero and his
secondary roles that of a trickster and a social bandit. His skills as
a trickster reinforce the hopes for his success as a redeemer. He is
full of the cunning and wiliness which will enable him to succeed
against a treacherous enemy. Considering him as a trickster also
permits discussion and remembrance of him on a more down-to-
earth level – not just as a noble-spirited, prophesied hope, but
also as a very human representative of the people and as an
embodiment of what human traits have been and still are prized
as heroic in Wales.

The patterns of the three roles which I have been discussing –
the redeemer-hero, the trickster and the social bandit – keep
overlapping and intersecting. For example, the roles of the social
bandit and the trickster coincide in their cunning and their
cleverness. Through their ruses, they defeat their enemies. They
appear to be invulnerable and invisible. Even when close to
defeat, they slip away prepared to return and fight again. The
redeemer-hero, too, slips away at the moment of defeat and
awaits a more propitious time. The three roles arise out of a
variety of factors – historical, socio-economic and traditional –
but people's needs, for whatever economic or cultural reasons,

express themselves in the same ways, patterned by expectations of what should be. (Apparently, even very ignoble bandits perceive themselves in the image of the noble robber.[51]) Similar conditions do give rise to similar patterns.

According to Hobsbawm's studies, the pattern of banditry arises in rural areas, which while socially dichotomized between rulers and the ruled, remain traditional and pre-capitalist in structure. Banditry arises when the traditional equilibrium is upset, generally during or after periods of unusual hardship or when outside forces threaten change to the traditional system.[52] Such were the conditions when Owain Glyndŵr was forced into his outlaw position. A century earlier, Edward I had conquered Wales and attempted to establish control through foreign outposts, building castles and walled towns peopled by Englishmen. Wales remained a system of small states with virtual independence from the English capital, but the main offices were held by Englishmen and all but two of the lords were Norman. The English maintained by law a monopoly on business and imposed heavy rents, which were additionally burdensome because they were for money in an economy which had been geared to rents paid in services and provisions. It has been estimated that in Wales, the unfree, who composed one tenth of the population, supplied two-thirds of the royal revenue. Economic hardships were further aggravated by the Black Death, which hit Wales in 1349 and 1350.

Of course, similar problems were troubling all of Europe, which was in upheaval with the breakdown of the medieval order and the emergence of new classes and social systems. These conditions contributed to a number of peasant revolts, such as the French Jacquerie, the English Peasants' Revolt of 1381 and the Hussite Wars.

But Owain Glyndŵr's rebellion was more than a peasant revolt, and Glyndŵr was more than a social bandit. For Wales had an additional problem, in that the Welsh were being not only economically but also culturally overwhelmed.[53] The Welsh did not wish to be made over in the English image. The bitterness of the period and of displacement is reflected in lines composed around 1400 to Glyndŵr's supporter Rhys Gethin:

Lle bu'r Brython Saeson sydd,
A'r boen ar Gymry beunydd.[54]

(Where there were Britons [Welshmen], [now] there are
Englishmen, and the Welsh in pain constantly.)

In the absence of the Welsh princes, whose time ended in 1282,
defence of Welsh tradition was left to the *uchelwyr* (gentry), who,
belonging to an essentially military class, knowledgeable about
their history and literature, and owing their positions to
traditional Welsh law, had both the skills and desire to fight for
freedom. While the gentry did not suffer as much under the new
order as did other Welsh people, often being able to take
positions as intermediaries between the foreign lords and their
own countrymen and to benefit from others' economic hardships
by buying property and thus expanding their own estates, they
were still essentially limited by foreign domination. And though
they might work with the English, they served as leaders and as
conservators of the culture for the Welsh. In this they were aided
by the poets, for whom they served as patrons, and who kept
alive the ideals of the past and strengthened a sense of national
purpose. The Welsh yearned for a redeemer-hero and the poets
prophesied his coming. Often frustrated by their own situation
and encouraged by the poets, the *uchelwyr* rose in revolt
repeatedly in the century following Edward I's conquest.

By 1400, the Welsh were driven to one final, desperate attempt
at freedom. One scholar states that 'the rebellion was the final
protest of a proud and conservative peasantry against the
interaction of alien institutions and money economy with their
former tribal way of living'.[55] But beyond the economic factors,
with all the concomitant anger and frustration, the Welsh were
driven by a sense of themselves as a people with a rich heritage,
by a craving for freedom to live according to their own
traditions, and by the hope that a national redeemer would lead
them back to independence. It was at this point that Owain
Glyndŵr attacked his neighbour Lord Grey and became an
outlaw. It was also at this point that Owain Glyndŵr assumed
the role of a redeemer-hero, the role of one whose task is to
restore the golden age of peace and justice. In the creation of a
better world, the roles of the redeemer-hero and the social bandit

appear to coincide, though serving different needs. For, as mentioned earlier, the social bandit is generally viewed as a righter of wrongs, one who will establish a proper order. Glyndŵr worked to accomplish this on two different levels. As a good social bandit, he took property and goods back from the Anglo-Norman lords and redistributed them amongst his supporters and, as a good redeemer-hero, he tried to establish a just and principled society. As already noted, he set up a parliament, worked to establish a Welsh Church and planned a Welsh university. The significance of this tripartite plan is seen in the frequency with which it is cited by Welshmen speaking of what might have been or could yet be.

Economically oppressed society creates social bandits when it feels the need for a champion and protector. Culturally oppressed society creates redeemer-heroes when it needs a champion. And both may be informed by the wiles of a trickster.

Culture Hero

Culture heroes, whether in the form of gods, humans or animals, a Greek Prometheus or Native American Raven, bring the benefits of culture and an ordered world to the people they serve. In a role often connected with that of the trickster, they may make the land habitable (creating or confining mountains and plains, rivers and lakes; setting the sun and the seasons to run their proper courses), provide necessities for survival (fire, food grain, medicinal herbs, agricultural techniques) or teach important elements of culture (song, ritual, alphabet).

Glyndŵr's tripartite plan argues for considering Glyndŵr as a culture hero also. He is not really a geomorphic constructor, changing the shape of the land, except for a few minor imprints where he knelt or where his horse trod, though he certainly has a fair number of places named after him – caves, mounds, springs, fountains, rocks and mountain routes.[56] However, he did bring, or try to bring, to his people certain cultural benefits – not fire or corn, but rather law, education and religion. His establishment of a Welsh parliament and his work towards a national university and an independent Welsh Church appear from my recorded interviews to be just as important to people's sense of Glyndŵr's greatness, especially as a *national* hero, as his brave and almost successful battle for independence.[57]

Welsh Nobleman and Warrior

The traditions surrounding Glyndŵr display him in many heroic roles. Some of these roles arise naturally from his life as, for example, when tradition deals with Glyndŵr as a nobleman and as a warrior. Iolo Goch, the fourteenth-century poet, describes in a *cywydd* the riches of Glyndŵr's court at Sycharth, with its wooden building, its chimneys, its cupboards as full of goods as a London shop, its orchards and its fisheries. As one would expect, he lays stress on Glyndŵr's generosity, hospitality and patronage of the arts. He describes Sycharth as, 'Llys barwn, lle syberwyd/ Lle daw beirdd aml, lle da byd'[58] (The court of a baron, a place of courtesy, where numerous bards come, a place of the good life). He further describes the abundance of wine, meat and white bread, the tents of the bards spread all around the place and, perhaps most important, no porter at the door.

Glyndŵr was not just a lord, but also a warrior, and his feats while fighting in the Scottish campaign in 1385 are described by both Iolo Goch and Gruffudd Llwyd.

> Pan aeth mewn gwroliaeth gwrdd,
> Goreugwr fu, garw agwrdd,
> Ni wnaeth ond marchogaeth meirch,
> Gorau amser, mewn gwrmseirch;
> Dwyn paladr, gwaladr gwiwlew,
> Soced dur a siaced dew;
> Arwain rhest a phenffestin,
> A helm wen,—gŵr hael am win—
> Ac yn ei phen, nen iawnraifft,
> Adain rudd o edn yr Aifft.[59]

(When he went in stout valour, he was the best man, rough and strong, he did but ride steeds, best of times, in blue-grey trappings; bearing a lance, true brave prince, with a steel socket and thick jacket, bearing a rest [for the lance] and helmet, and a white helm—a man generous with his wine—and on top of it, finely plumed roof, red feathers of the bird of Egypt.)

Pan oedd drymaf dy lafur
Draw yn ymwriaw â'r mur,
Torres dy onnen gennyd,
Tirion grair taer yn y gryd,
Dewredd Ffwg, dur oedd ei phen,
Dors garw yn dair ysgyren.
Gwelodd pawb draw i'th law lân,
Gwiw fawldaith, gwayw ufeldan;
Drylliaist, duliaist ar dalwrn,
Dy ddart hyd ymron dy ddwrn.
O nerth ac arial calon,
A braich ac ysgwydd a bron,
Peraist fy naf o'th lafur
Pyst mellt rhwng y dellt a'r dur[60]

(When your labour was at its heaviest yonder battling with the wall, your shaft broke with you, gentle, insistent relic in the battle, valour of Fulk [Fitzwarin], steel was its head, rough torch into three branches. Everyone yonder saw in your fair hand, fair journey of praise, the fire-flaming spear; you shattered, you smote upon the field, your javelin within your grasp/fist. With strength and spirit of heart and arm and shoulder and breast, you caused, my lord, with your labour lightening shafts between the laths and the steel [i.e. armour])

In the poetry, Glyndŵr is described in the same terms as are used for other lords and other warriors. However, the particular significance of these roles for Owain Glyndŵr is indicated in the number of verses which invoke Glyndŵr's name in order to increase the praise or honour of another. In quite a few of these, Glyndŵr is claimed as a relative, with the family connection most frequently being made through one of Glyndŵr's sisters, though occasionally through his brother Tudur. For example, Hywel Cilan at the end of the fifteenth century refers to Edwart ap Madog Pilstwn, in a eulogy, as:

Nai, gwrol yn ei guras,
Owain y Glyn, onwayw glas.[61]

(Nephew, valorous/manly in his cuirass, of Owain y Glyn, of the green ash spear)

and to the sons of Iorwerth ab Ieuan, in a eulogy, as:

> Deunai, pell a adwaenir,
> Owain ŷnt hwy, enw ein tir,
> Dau etifedd i feddu
> Ar wŷr a thir Iorwerth Ddu.[62]

(Two nephews, who are acknowledged far and wide, of Owain are they, name of our land, two heirs to own on the men and land of Iorwerth Ddu.)

Hywel Cilan says in elegy of one man, Siôn ap Madog Pilstwn, 'Mae'n aeaf am nai Owain'[63] (It's winter for the nephew of Owain); while Guto'r Glyn says in elegy to the same man:

> Gŵr ieuanc oedd gâr Owain
> I'w daro 'mysg derw a main.[64]

(A young man was Owain's kinsman, to be struck amidst oak and stones.)

Lewys Môn refers to Owain Tudur Fychan as 'Owain câr Owain'[65] (Owain kinsman of Owain). *Câr* (kinsman) and *nai* (nephew) are the terms most commonly used to express relationship with Glyndŵr. One should, however, keep in mind that *nai* and *ewythr* (uncle) are used fairly loosely in this poetry and do not necessarily reflect the precise relationship involved, or even any real relationship. Islwyn Jones, editor of Hywel Cilan's work, points out that despite the poet's addressing Llywelyn ap Gruffudd Fychan as 'câr Dewdur,/ A glain doeth Owain Glyndŵr' (kinsman of [Glyndŵr's brother] Tudur, and wise jewel of Owain Glyndŵr), he has been able to find no connection between Llywelyn and Glyndŵr's family.[66] An even more general reference to relationship is found in Tudur Aled's lines:

> Gwaed Owain, gwraidd a geidw'n gras,
> Glyn Dwfr, ag o lin Defras[67]

(Blood of Owain, roots which keep warm, Glyn Dwfr, and of the line of Defras);

or Lewys Môn's lines in praise of Owain ap Meurig which refer to him as 'Gwaed Owain Glyn' (Blood of Owain Glyn) as well as 'Owain lawgoch' (with its dual meaning of bloody hand and Llawgoch the redeemer).[68] Occasionally, comparison without any claim of blood relationship may be made. A *cywydd* to Glyndŵr's officer Rhys Gethin describes him as:

> Milwr yw â gwayw melyn
> Megis Owain glain y Glyn.[69]

(He is a warrior with a yellow spear, like Owain, jewel of the Glen.)

Of course, no direct connection is necessary in order to invoke Glyndŵr's name. For example, Tudur Aled, writing at the beginning of the sixteenth century praises various people with such lines as,

> Llowgoch wyd, llaw â gwayw chwyrn,
> Llwyth Owain, llew a thëyrn;
> . . .
>
> Gŵr wyd a ddwg ar dy ddart
> Arfau Owain i'r fowart;[70]

(Llowgoch [bloody hand] are you, hand with a severe spear, tribe of Owain, lion and ruler; . . . A man are you who brings on your spear, arms of Owain to the vanguard)

and

> Barr Owain Glyn, brân y gloch,
> Bw holl Loegr, bwyall liwgoch[71]

(Spear of Owain Glyn, raven of the bell, terror of all England, [reddened] battle axe [of Llawgoch])

It seems significant that in one and possibly both of the above verses, as well as in Lewys Môn's line to Owain ap Meurig, reference is made not only to Glyndŵr but also to the other redeemer-hero – Owain Lawgoch. The poets seem to play intentionally on the different possibilities of interpretation, that Owain refers to Glyndŵr but may also, especially when taken in conjunction with the military adjective *llawgoch* (bloody hand), suggest Owain Lawgoch. The poets also continue to play with the generic Owain of the prophecies, creating lines such as Lewys Môn's to Owain ap Meurig which, after referring to him as 'cyw Owain Glyn' (Owain Glyn's chick/young one), describe him as 'llun Owain' (Owain's image) and compare him to:

> Gŵr o gudd er budd i'r byd,
> braidd gof, o bridd a gyfyd.[72]

(Man from concealment, as benefit for the world, a faint memory, will arise from the grave [lit. soil].)

Nor are such associations made only through verse; the all-important connection with Glyndŵr may be remarked upon at any time, as for example:

> Here [Camhelig Isa] at the beginning of the fourteenth [*sic*] century, lived Llewelyn ab Adda ap Dafydd of the house of Trefor. He married Myfanwy, a natural daughter of Owain Glyndŵr.[73]

Another form of association which gives weight to the view of Glyndŵr as a military leader is that of ally. A variety of characters who figure in legendry appear to derive their importance from their support of Glyndŵr, or are at least placed in history through him. Two of these men are, of course, Ednyfed ab Aron, who is said to have fed Glyndŵr while he hid in a cave, and Rhys Goch, with whom Glyndŵr was visiting before the two men had to flee the encircling enemy.[74] Some of the others are Howel Gwynedd of Llys Edwin:

> This valiant gentleman, who sided with Prince Owain Glyndyfrdwy against Henry IV, was surprised by his enemies from the town of Flint, about the year 1410, and beheaded in the enclosure of the Camp of Caer Alhwch, on the summit of Moel y Gaer, in Llaneurgain, and his lands were forfeited and given to Bryan Saxton;[75]

Gwilym Glyn:

> At the close of the fourteenth century Lleucu Mortimar of Plas Lleucu was courted by Gwilym Glyn, a freeholder of Glynceiriog, and a friend of Owain Glyndŵr. Lleucu, however, was prevailed upon to refuse his addresses, and Gwilym Glyn was distracted. In the rising of Glyndŵr, Gwilym was made a captain. In a battle near Montgomery Castle in the summer of 1401 he was mortally wounded. In his last moments, he begged of his friend and fellow-officer, Ralph Salesbury, to tell Lleucu that her lover forgave her with his dying breath and hoped she would get the pardon of heaven as well;[76]

and Cadwgan y Fwyall:

> One of Owain Glyndyfrdwy's captains was Cadwgan, Lord of
> Glyn Rhondda, generally known by the name of Cadwgan y
> Fwyall, *i.e.,* Cadwgan of the Battle Axe. When Cadwgan was
> preparing for battle, he used to perambulate Glyn Rhonda,
> whetting his battle-axe as he proceeded along; from which
> circumstance Owain would call out to Cadwgan, 'Cadwgan, whet
> thy battle-axe', and the moment that Cadwgan was heard to do so,
> all living persons, both male and female, in Glyn Rhondda,
> collected about him in military order (for the ladies were in those
> times well drilled and obedient), and from that day to this, the
> battle shout of the men of Glyn Rhondda, has been, 'Cadwgan,
> whet thy battle-axe', and, at the word, they all assembled as an
> army.[77]

Unfortunately, this last example is first noted by Iolo Morganwg,
from whom the above late nineteenth-century text is taken
almost verbatim.[78] As always, any material first found in the *Iolo
Manuscripts* must be suspect. However, while we can have no
confidence in either the existence of Cadwgan y Fwyall or the
story about him, we are still given some indication of Glyndŵr's
importance in Iolo's eighteenth-century world.

Many traditions arise naturally and directly from Glyndŵr's
position as an historical-military figure and from the activities of
his wars. Because of this, it would be difficult in some cases to
say whether a frequently mentioned event was merely a
historical fact given prominence or whether it had more
traditional significance in oral history. The poets, who
apparently kept silent about this period of military activity,
provide no clues. The question of traditional significance first
arises over reports of several of Glyndŵr's battles, beginning
with his opening attack of the war on Rhuthun on St Matthew's
Eve. Next noted are the raids carried out from Glyndŵr's
fastness on Pumlumon. Panton MS 53 records that, 'he marched
with about 120 men in arms into the hills of Plinlimmon, where
he kept his rendezvous, from thence he did very much hurt
sending parties to pillage the countrey all about'.[79] The first of the
battles to come to special attention is the one at Mynydd
Hyddgant, where Glyndŵr and his small band broke out
through the encircling Flemings. Then there are two closely
linked battles:

. . . he [Glyndŵr] met with the English at Mynydd Cwm du, who put him to retreat killing many of his men, but gathering his men suddenly together he overtook the English at Craig y dorth near Monmouth gave them a defeat and pursued them to the very gates of the towns, villages, castles, forts and all places of strength.[80]

Another battle which is repeatedly mentioned is that at Mynydd Pwll Melyn, where Glyndŵr's son Griffith was captured and his brother Tudur was killed.

He sent his eldest son Griffith with an army into Brecknockshire A.D. 1405 there at mynydd Pwll melyn after a hot fight Griffith was overcome and taken prisoner by the King's men and about 1500 of his men were killed and taken. Among the dead bodies besides was found one much like unto Owain, whom they supposed and gave out to be Owain, and that he was there slain, but upon further enquiry it was not him but his brother Tudur who very much resembled him, and was often taken for him, being hardly distinguished asunder, only Owen had a little wart above his eyebrows, which Tudur had not.[81]

It is perhaps to these events that the following, possibly fifteenth-century, account refers.

Ar ol marwolaeth Owen Glyndwr a dug un Madyn ben ir Brenin gan ddywedyd mae'r pen hwnnw oedd Ben Owen, ar Brenin a ymofynnodd ar Cymry a adwaenen hwy ben Owain. ac un a ddywawd os cai ef weled ir adwaenai fo achos bod dafaden ar ei jad, a phan welwyd y pen hwnnw a gwybod nad pen Owain oedd i canodd un o lys y Brenin fal hyn:

> celwydda a ddywad Madyn
> gloff am Arglwydd y glyñ
> am na chad y ddafaden
> garllaw tal y gwr llwyd hen.[82]

(After Owain Glyndŵr's death, one Madyn brought a head to the King saying that that head was Owain's head, and the King asked the Welsh whether they would recognize Owain's head, and one said that if he could see he would know because there was a wart on its pate, and when that head was seen and it was known that it was not Owain's head, one of the King's court sang thus:

falsehood said Madyn
the lame about the lord of the Glyn
because there was not found the wart
near the forehead of the old grey man.)

All of these battles are well established in the early histories and antiquarians' reports, as also is the site of Glyndŵr's conspiracies with Mortimer and the Percys, given as Plas Alcock, the home of David Daron, archdeacon of Bangor.[83] Much less agreement exists as to what exactly happened at the decisive 1403 battle between the Percys and King Henry at Shrewsbury. English tradition claims that Glyndŵr watched the battle from a point of safety across the river, waiting to see which way it would go. A nineteenth-century traveller records the legend thus:

> At Shelton . . . is a celebrated oak, entirely hollow, and of large dimensions, which it is said that Owen Glendwr ascended, at the battle of Shrewesbury, to reconnoitre the forces of the king. Finding them to be very effective, and also aware that Hotspur had not been joined by the Earl of Northumberland, Glendwr fell back upon Oswestry and returned into Wales.[84]

The legend is again cited at the end of the nineteenth century in the *Archaeologia Cambrensis*, which reports that the Shelton Oak is also called Glyndŵr's Oak.[85] Both of these nineteenth-century sources also note an alternative tradition, found in the early Welsh records. Most probably influenced by English evaluations of Glyndŵr's character, these early historians claim that Glyndŵr was twelve miles away in Oswestry at the time of the battle and that, though he had sent on four thousand of his men, he did not go himself.

> A.D. 1403 Sr Henry sirnamed Hotspurr son to the Earl of Northumberland advanced with an army towards Shrewsbury expecting E. Mortimer and Owen Glynndwr with their armies to join with him as they had promised upon the agreement made between them three, the king with his army met Hotspurr before the other two had joined with him, gave him battle near Shrewsbury on St. Magdalene's Eve A.D. 1403 after a cruel fight and great valour shewed on both sides Percy and most of his men being slain, the king obtained a complete victory. Owen was then

with his strength about Oswestry 12 miles from the place of the fight. He had sent four thousand of his men to the aid of Percy but went not in person.[86]

Although the fault is not as great as it would be in watching the battle from the tree on the other side of the river, Glyndŵr is still indeed blamed for his inaction. As Robert Vaughan of Hengwrt (c.1650) says of Glyndŵr's policies in general, they 'cannot be commended, in that he did not come in person to Hotspurs and join his whole power'.[87] However, writing only a few decades later, William Wynne indicates that Glyndŵr was not to blame:

> . . . at length they [Percy and Mortimer] marched with all their power towards Shrewsbury to fight the King, depending mainly upon the arrival of Glyndwr and his Welch-men. But the matter was gone so far, that whether he came in or no, they must fight, . . .[88]

In the eighteenth century, however, Pennant reassesses the events and writes:

> *Glyndwr* had the mortification of being obliged to remain all the time inactive, at the head of twelve thousand men, at *Oswestry*. The *Welsh* historians pass an unjust censure on him for his conduct on this occasion, and blame him for what, it seems, he could not effect. His great oversight appears to me to have been the neglect of attacking *Henry* immediately after the battle, when the royal forces had sustained a vast loss, and were overcome with fatigue; when his own followers, and the remains of the northern troops, would have formed an army nearly double to that of the king . . . [89]

A nineteenth-century encyclopaedia, *Y Gwyddoniadur Cymreig*, while using the story of Glyndŵr watching the battle from an oak tree, puts the full blame on nature – Glyndŵr had arrived within a mile of the battlefield but the river, in strong flood, prevented him from joining the battle; the tree was as close as he could go.[90] In even stronger defence of Glyndŵr, more recent historical evaluations show that Glyndŵr was still several days' march away when the battle took place before the planned time, so that he could not possibly have reached Shrewsbury in time.[91]

Some of the traditions dealing with Glyndŵr's military activities are distinctly localized, such as the caves where Glyndŵr and his men hid during their guerilla activities. Two other examples are his prison (*carchardy*) and his mound (*tomen*), both in the Corwen area. Pennant, in the eighteenth century, first notes that 'The prison where *Owen* confined his captives was not far from his house, in the parish of *Llansantfraid Glyndwrdwy*; and the place is to this day called *Carchardy Owen Glyndwrdwy*', and then goes on to give a physical description of the building.[92] Then in 1878, Hywel Cernyw, in writing about the antiquities of Edeyrnion, records, 'Ceir tai ar fin y Dyfrdwy, yn agos i gapel y Bedyddwyr, yn dwyn yr enw "Carchardy Owain Glyndwr;" a dywedir y byddai yr hen wron enwog hwnw yn cadw ei garcharorion rhyfel yn y lle.'[93] (There are houses found on the bank of the Dee, close to the Baptist chapel, bearing the name 'Owain Glyndwr's Prison-house'; and it is said that the famous old hero used to keep his prisoners of war in the place.) The existence of the prison is recorded in nationalist journals, including one aimed at children, which admits that the association of the prison with Glyndŵr is only a matter of oral tradition, but which nevertheless asks for money to help preserve the building (so that one might have tea in the midst of traditions about Glyndŵr).[94] Apparently, the necessary funds were never gathered, for the building no longer stands. Indeed, in 1982, one man told me that his house was built with the last stones of the original prison. Several people told me that the key had been preserved and by whom it was kept. But perhaps the greatest indication of the local traditions extant concerning the military aspects of Glyndŵr's career are the number of people in the Corwen area who when asked about local associations replied, 'Well, you've seen his *tomen*, and, of course, his *carchardy*, haven't you?'[95]

Tomen Glyndŵr, a small but fairly steep-sided mound, was noted by George Borrow in two pieces of conversation which he reported from his travels in Wales:

> 'Do people talk much of Owen Glendower in these parts?' said I.
> 'Plenty,' said the man, 'and no wonder, for when he was alive he was much about here – some way farther on there is a mount, on the bank of the Dee, called the mount of Owen Glendower, where it is said he used to stand and look out after his enemies.'

'Dyma Mont Owain Glyndwr, sir, lle yr oedd yn sefyll i edrych am ei elynion yn dyfod o Gaer Lleon. This is the hill of Owen Glendower, sir, where he was in the habit of standing to look out for his enemies coming from Chester.'[96]

The *tomen* is further mentioned in various nationalist journals,[97] but again the strength of the tradition is indicated by the residents of the Corwen area. Almost everybody mentions it, and one woman, for example, explained that the mound was where Glyndŵr gathered his men.[98]

One of my Corwen contacts suggested that the mound described by Borrow was not the local Tomen Glyndŵr, but rather another one from which one can see Dinas Brân and which, therefore, served as a sentry post.[99] Two other mounds associated with Glyndŵr have also been noted, one at Caio, 'At Cryg Cyski in Kilycwm parish artificial Mounts, where O. Glyndwr lay. There have been old swords found';[100] and the other at the small village of Aber:

Mŵd – tomen a godwyd gan ddyn yw honno, a lle y dywedir y bu Owain Glyndwr yn cyfarch y bobl ymhlaid rhyddid . . . [101]

(Mŵd – this is a mound raised by man, where it is said that Owain Glyndŵr was addressing the people in favour of freedom).

Another place associated in Corwen tradition with Glyndŵr's military activity is Caer Drewyn. Pennant mentions it when he writes that, after attacking Rhuthun, Glyndŵr 'retired to his fastnesses among the mountains. One I imagine to have been of great strength, surrounded by a vast rampart of stones, near *Corwen*, called *Caer Drewyn*.'[102] In 1822 it was recorded that 'The encampment [Caer Drewyn] may still be distinguished from the church-yard of Corwen, in the direction of the village of Cynwyd.'[103] The current inhabitants of the Corwen area still associate Caer Drewyn with Glyndŵr, who is said to have gathered his army there.[104]

Some of the traditional associations seem to be simply a matter of 'Glyndŵr was here', but other examples of the legendry give a fuller picture of a warrior in action. One minor example was printed in a 1927 newspaper account:

Dywed traddodiad mai heibio'r Bwlchdu y daeth llu Glyn Dwr i wrthdarawiad a'r gormeswyr yn Nant y Gyflafan. Beth bynnag am ystyr y Bwlch Du, fe drodd yn Fwlch gwyn yn hanes Cymru Fu.[105]

(Tradition says that it was past Bwlchdu that Glyndŵr's host came into conflict with the oppressors at Nant y Gyflafan. Whatever the meaning of the Bwlch Du [Black Pass], the pass turned white/ blessed in the history of Wales of Yore.)

An onomastic tale, which the recording antiquarian half retracts, says of the small village of Bryn Saith Marchog (Hill of the Seven Knights):

Y mae blas henaint ar yr enw, a thybia yr Archddiacon Newcome iddo gael ei alw felly am i Owen Glyndwr ddal Arglwydd Grey a saith o'i farchogion yn y fan. Gwyddis i Glyndwr ddal Arglwydd Grey, ai garcharu, a'i orfodi, medd rhai, i briodi ei ferch Sian; ond nid oes fawr o sicrwydd mai yn y lle hwn y syrthiodd ef i'r ddalfa, na bod cysylltiad yn y byd rhwng yr enw âg Owen Glyndwr. Y tebygolrwydd yw fod yr enw yn llawer hŷn nag amser y ddau.[106]

(There is an old flavour to the name, and Archdeacon Newcome supposes it was called thus because Owain Glyndŵr captured Lord Grey and seven of his knights in the place. It is known that Glyndŵr captured Lord Grey, and imprisoned him, and forced him, some say, to marry his daughter Siân; but there is not much certainty that it is in this place that he fell to the capture nor that there is any connection in the world between the name and Owain Glyndŵr. The likelihood is that the name is much older than both.)

An alternative onomastic explanation was told to me thus when I asked whether there were places associated with Glyndŵr:

Oes, mae lle o'r enw – pentre bach o'r enw Bryn Saith Marchog, rhwng Corwen a Rhuthun. A'r stori pam y gelwir y lle yn Bryn Saith Marchog ydi bod Glyndŵr yn ystod y gwrthryfel yn erbyn yr arglwydd Grey o Ruthun wedi anfon saith o'i wŷr, saith o'i farchogion i guddio yn ymyl, yn yr ardal yna, i wylio yr arglwydd Grey i gal gweld be o'dd o'n neud, fel ysbïwyr, a dyna pam, Bryn Saith Marchog.[107]

(Yes, there's a place of the name – a small village of the name Bryn Saith Marchog, between Corwen and Rhuthun. And the story why the place is called Bryn Saith Marchog is that Glyndŵr during the rebellion against Lord Grey of Rhuthun had sent seven of his men, seven of his knights, to hide nearby, in the area there, to watch Lord Grey in order to see what he was doing, as spies, and that's why, Bryn Saith Marchog).

Another recently collected onomastic tradition, which was learned in the 1940s in Llangwm (about seven miles from Corwen), makes a direct association with Glyndŵr's battles.

Brwydr mewn cae ar fferm Tŷ Gwyn Llangwm, Sir Ddinbych – milwyr Owen Glyndŵr yno. Gelwir y cae yn Bryn Owain. Aeth y milwyr i lechu mewn cae a elwir heddiw yn Erw Llech. Aeth gwragedd y milwyr i wylo (udo) ger Ffynnon Garreg Udfan ar y llechwedd i gyfeiriad Dinmael.[108]

(A battle in a field on the farm Tŷ Gwyn Llangwm, Denbighshire – Owen Glyndŵr's soldiers there. The field is called Owen's Hill. The soldiers went to hide in a field which today is called the Acre of Hiding [lit: Acre of the Flat Slab]. The soldiers' wives went to weep/wail near the Fountain of the Rock of Wailing on the slopes towards Dinmael.)

Destroyer

The sites perhaps most closely associated with Glyndŵr's military activities are those places said to have been destroyed by Glyndŵr in the fierceness of battle. While the wars of the fourteenth and fifteenth centuries were certainly very destructive, a special emphasis appears to be placed on Glyndŵr's destructiveness. In describing Glyndŵr's part in the Scottish wars, Iolo Goch introduces a theme which, while a commonplace in descriptions of destructive wars, also became particularly associated with Glyndŵr – the theme of total destruction. According to the poet,

Ni thyfodd gwellt na thafol
Hefyd na'r ŷd ar ei ôl
O Ferwig Seisnig ei sail
I Faesbwrch, hydr fu ysbail[109]

(Neither grass nor dock grew or even corn in his track from Berwick, its base is English, to Maesbury, valiant was the spoil.)

The same statement of great destruction, but in opposite terms, is made concerning Glyndŵr's effect on Llanrwst.

Glyndwr's Wars – beginning 1400, lasted 15 years – brought great desolation on Nant Conwy, so that the green grass grew in the Market place of Lhanrwst, and the Deer out of Snowdon fed in the Church yard.[110]

In each case, the natural order is turned upside down – grass does not grow where it should, and does where it should not; the wilds invade the habited places. This reversal of the natural order along with general destructiveness tie in with Glyndŵr's role as a redeemer for, as seen in the early Welsh prophecies and the apocalyptic visions of other cultures, the coming of the redeemer is generally marked by great destruction.

On an historical level, Glanmor Williams suggests that the destructiveness of Glyndŵr's wars was due in part to the deep resentment which had built up in 'the dispossessed and unfree' who followed Glyndŵr.[111] The most common indication of Glyndŵr's destructiveness is the number of towns and houses he is said to have burned, starting with Rhuthun on the eve of St Matthew's Fair in 1400, the opening move of his war. In 1599, the Englishman John Hayward wrote that Glyndŵr 'proceeded further to inuade the Marches of Wales on the West side of Seuerne; where hee burnt many villages and townes, slew much people, and returned with great prey and praises of his adherents'.[112] Approximately fifty years later, a Welsh manuscript reads: 'he invaded the lands burnt and destroyed the houses and estates of all those that favoured and adhered to King Henry'.[113] Glyndŵr's destructiveness may be reflected in a proverb recorded in a 1620 fair copy of an earlier manuscript list of proverbs compiled by the lexicographer Thomas Wiliems (1545/6–1622): 'Ni weled y cyvriw, er pan vu ryvel Owain'[114] (The like has not been seen since the war of Owain). Without contextual information, we cannot be certain about either the Owain referred to or the meaning, but this sounds like Southerners in the United States saying that they have not seen such destruction since Sherman, or Londoners saying they have not seen anything like it since the Blitz.

The fierceness and thoroughness of the destruction wrought by Glyndŵr are traditionally indicated in the nicknames of two towns, Pentre-poeth and Tre-boeth (Hot Village and Hot Town):

> Oswestry was unfortunate in the year 1400, when Owen Glyndwr seized the town. It was said that the title 'Pentrepoeth' or 'hot town' was due to this calamity, for Oswestry 'was nearly totally destroyed by fire during the wars of the Welsh people'.[115]

> Handbridge, now a peaceful suburb of Chester, was then known as Treboeth, 'the burnt town', because it was so frequently devastated by fire and sword.[116]

Pentre-poeth and Tre-boeth are actually fairly common place-names throughout Wales, with *poeth* (hot/burnt) probably referring to charcoal burning. However, here again, as with Erw Llech, Glyndŵr provides a context for onomastic explanations which, in this case, adopt the strong theme of his destructiveness.

Glyndŵr's destructiveness was in no way reserved for the English territories for, as one seventeenth-century historian notes, Bangor Cathedral was 'burnt by the most profligate Rebel Owen Glyn Dowrdwy, who design'd no less than the destruction of all the Cities of Wales'.[117] The situation is overstated, but Glyndŵr is credited with having destroyed Cardiff and Abergavenny[118] and with having severely damaged Llandaf Cathedral.[119] However, even in the midst of this great destruction, tradition indicates that it was not a matter of uncontrolled violence. Glyndŵr could show restraint when he desired, as with Cardiff, which he totally destroyed, except for the one street on which lived Franciscan friars, an order which favoured Glyndŵr.[120] Some examples of estates destroyed by Glyndŵr are the manor of Gogarth:

> Little is known of the later history of the site, but its traditional destruction by Owain Glyndwr ca.1402, was confirmed by the excavation;[121]

Crickhowell, Monmouthshire:

a ddifrodwyd gan Owain Glyn Dŵr[122]

(which was laid waste by Owain Glyndŵr);

Tretower Court (near Crickhowell):

daeth Owain Glyn Dŵr heibio a gwneud difrod mawr ar y castell a'r tŷ[123]

(Owain Glyndŵr came by and made great destruction on the castle and the house);

and Hay:

Fe'i chwalwyd gan y brenin John, gan Llywelyn Fawr, a chan Owain Glyn Dŵr, bob un yn ei dro.[124]

(It was reduced to ruins by King John, by Llywelyn the Great, and by Owain Glyndŵr, each in his turn.)

Cricieth Castle is another place said to have been burned by Glyndŵr and so well known is it that it serves as comparison for other fires, as in the following statement describing the marks of fire on the walls of a house as 'run fath yn union (â) na hoel tân ar furia y Castall Criciath wedi i Owain Glyndŵr fynd – fod yno'[125] (the same exactly as the mark of fire on the walls of Cricieth Castle after Owain Glyndŵr went – was there). The legendry concerning Dafydd Gam and Hywel Sele relates that Glyndŵr burned the houses of each of those men after they revealed their treachery.[126] The most frequently cited of these destroyed estates are Cefn y Fan and Cesail Gyfarch, both of which were owned by Ieuan ap Maredudd. According to Sir John Wynne, writing in the early seventeenth century, Glyndŵr 'burned them both to cold ashes'.[127] From Pennant on, the same basic information is recorded by a series of historians, antiquarians and travellers.[128] Indication that this is a matter of more than literary-historical tradition is found in a 1954 article which reports: 'Local tradition says that the ruins of Cefn y Fan smoked for a year and a day; and the field in which the remains of the site are now to be seen is called Cae Murpoeth, the Field of the Hot Wall.'[129] Further evidence that the burning of Cefn y Fan by Glyndŵr is more a matter of folk tradition than of historical record is provided by archaeological excavations, which show that the place was never even set on fire, and may not even predate Glyndŵr.[130] Nevertheless, archaeological evidence has no bearing on the general traditional sense that a ruin must be the responsibility of Glyndŵr. It is as if Glyndŵr's battle-fury shows itself not on his features, as would happen with heroes such as the Irish Cú Chulainn,[131] but rather on the land around him. Glyndŵr's war was undoubtedly violent and destructive, as wars generally are, but the point is not how many places he actually did or did not burn; rather it is that Glyndŵr is perceived as being especially destructive. The interplay of history and tradition results in a need to ascribe destruction (no matter how wrought) to Glyndŵr.

Fierce Avenger

Glyndŵr's destructiveness connects with another of his characteristics which emerges in the lore – that is, his fierceness, or in some eyes, his cruelty. This aspect of Glyndŵr appears in the legend known as 'Ceubren yr Ellyll' (the hollow tree of the ghost), which concerns the time when Glyndŵr's cousin Hywel Sele tried to kill him while they were hunting together at Hywel's home Nannau. As mentioned earlier, Glyndŵr was saved from his cousin's arrow by the armour which he wore under his clothes. However, the first records of the conflict between the two men have little of this story. Robert Vaughan of Hengwrt's seventeenth-century account records simply:

> Owen burnt the house of Howel Sele of Nannau who stood out for the king and took him along with him. Griffri ap Gwyn of Ardudwy [Ganllwyd] who came to attempt the rescue of his cousin Howel was beaten and most of his men killed [and buried in the field of battle at Cefn Coch, the place still bearing the name of beddau'r gwyr (graves of the men), Griffri's houses at Berthlwyd and cefn coch were then burnt to ashes] Howel was so disposed of that he was never seen or heard of again by his friends.[132]

In another text attributed to Robert Vaughan in the same period around 1650, additional information is provided: 'It is said that Owen Glendwr caused Howel Sele to be lette down into a hollow oak where he ended his life . . .'[133] By the time of Pennant's writing in the eighteenth century, the whole story had expanded.

> *Howel Sele* of *Nanneu* in *Meirioneddshire*, first cousin to *Owen*, had a harder fate. He likewise was an adherent to the house of *Lancaster*. *Owen* and this chieftain had been long at variance. I have been informed, that the abbot of *Cymmer*, near *Dolgelleu*, in hopes of reconciling them, brought them together, and to all appearance effected his charitable design. While they were walking out, *Owen* observed a doe feeding, and told *Howel*, who was reckoned the best archer of his days, that there was a fine mark for him. *Howel* bent his bow, and pretending to aim at the doe, suddenly turned and discharged the arrow full at the breast of *Glyndwr*, who fortunately had armour beneath his cloaths, so received no hurt. Enraged at this treachery, he seized on *Sele*, burnt his house, and hurried him away from the place; nor could any one ever learn how he was disposed of, till forty years after, when the skeleton of a large man, such as *Howel*, was discovered in the hollow of a great oak, in which *Owen* was supposed to have immured him in reward of his perfidy. The ruins of the old house are to be seen in *Nanneu* park, a mere compost of cinders and ashes.[134]

The tale was recorded over and over again in print, in varying degrees of fullness, and is very much alive in the current folklore of the Dolgellau area. Glyndŵr's fierceness is expressed with the use of verbs such as *gwylltio* (to go wild, lose control of oneself), but even more clearly through the most persistent aspect of the legend, the horrifying motif of the man left buried in a tree; indeed, this one element which gives the legend its name, often stands alone as the whole tale, as in:

> Nannau: In the Garden stands the celebrated old Oak, called Ceubren yr Ellyll, in which tradition says that Howel Selef, who took part against Glyndwr, his Cousin, was inshrined after being put to death by him;[135]

or in the recollections of people living near Nannau.[136] In some accounts, the horror is increased by Glyndŵr's leaving Hywel imprisoned alive in the tree, as in the second of Robert Vaughan's notes quoted above, or as indicated in the following passage:

Ffyrnigodd Glyndwr gymmaint o blegid y brad yma fel y
rhwymodd Hywel yn y fan; ac wedi llosgi ei dŷ cludodd yntau
ymaith na wyddai neb i ba le . . . Ymhen deugain mlynedd wedi
hyny cafwyd ysgerbwd dŷn mawr, o fath Hywel, yng ngheudod
hen dderwen, lle y bwriwyd ef gan Glyndwr, fel y tybid, yn wobr
am ei fradwriaeth.[137]

(Glyndŵr was enraged so much by this treachery that he bound
Hywel on the spot; and after burning his house carried him away
to nobody knew where . . . After forty years, a skeleton of a big
man, of Hywel's type, was found in the hollow of an old oak,
where he was thrown by Glyndŵr, as it is supposed, in reward for
his treachery.)

Glyndŵr's fierce retribution for his cousin's treachery is
generally seen by the Welsh as justified and, since in many cases
Hywel is dead before being encased in the tree, not hideously
cruel.

The English, however, viewed him as exceedingly cruel. Adam
of Usk reports hearing of Glyndŵr that, 'velut alter Assur,
furoris Dei virga, inauditam tyrannidem ferro et flamma
miserime vibravit' (like a second Assyrian, the rod of God's
anger, he did deeds of unheard-of cruelty with fire and
sword).[138] However, the case most often cited as evidence of
Glyndŵr's cruelty more precisely describes the actions of the
Welsh women after a particular battle, when they are said to
have mutilated the English corpses. In the 1580s, Holinshed,
taking his information from Walsingham, writes:

The shamefull villanie used by the Welshwomen towards the dead
carcasses, was such, as honest eares would be ashamed to heare,
and continent toongs to speake thereof. The dead bodies might not
be buried, without great summes of monie giuen for libertie to
conueie them awaie.[139]

A few pages later, Holinshed adds more details to the report:

. . . and such shameful villanie executed vpon the carcasses of the
dead men by the Welshwomen; as the like (I doo belieue) hath
neuer or sildome beene practised . . . yet did the women of Wales
cut off their priuities and put one part thereof into the mouthes of
euerie dead man, in such sort that the cullions hoong down to their
chins; and not so contented, they did cut off their noses and thrust

them into their tailes as they laie on the ground mangled and
defaced. This was a verie ignominious deed, and a worsse not
commited among the barbarous . . . [140]

John Hayward, writing in 1599, also provides a graphic depiction
of what befell the Englishmen:

who sould their liues at such a price, that when manhood had
doone the hardest against them, certaine mannish, or rather
deuilish women, whose malice is immortall, exercised a vaine
reuenge vppon their dead bodyes; in cutting off their priuie partes
and their noses, whereof the one they stuffed in their mouthes, and
pressed the other betweene their buttocks; and would not suffer
their mangled carcasses to be comitted to the earth, vntill they were
redeemed with a great summe of money.[141]

Nevertheless, this appears to be an essentially English tradition
as, even though Pennant repeats it from Holinshed, he makes
clear what were his sources.[142] It was probably the English
influence which led Robert Vaughan to write: 'His cruelty made
the people to leave him, and his covetousness made his soldiers
by degrees to forsake him.'[143] In any case, this view of Glyndŵr
appears never to have been adopted by the Welsh. Indeed, the
whole matter is rejected by Welsh people today, as can be seen in
the words of one Welshman:

. . . ma 'na chwedlau wedi'u creu gan y Saeson ynghylch Owen
Glyndŵr a un yw ynghylch ar ôl brwydro Bryn Glas . . . mae nhw'n
sôn am gwragedd y Cymry yn gwneud petha erchyll i gig y Saeson.
Wel ma hynna dw i di ffeindio allan yn chwedl llwyr oherwydd y
cynta i sôn am hynny ydi yn hanesydd Saesneg Holinshed oedd yn
byw dau ganrif wedyn. Felly mae o'n myth wedi'i creu gan y
Saeson i arbed 'u balchder.[144]

(. . . there are tales created by the English concerning Owain
Glyndŵr and one is about after fighting at the battle of Bryn Glas
. . . they talk about the Welsh women doing hideous things to the
flesh of the English. Well, I found out that it was completely a tale
because the first mention of it is in the English historian Holinshed
who lived two centuries later. So it's a myth created by the English
to save their pride.)

Master of Magic Arts

Another role ascribed to Glyndŵr but which belongs essentially to English tradition is that of magician or wizard. Apparently, several times when Henry IV tried to advance into Wales with his army, he was driven back by terrible storms and heavy mists, while his men wandered lost in the woods and bogs.

> About mid of August, the king, to chastise the presumptuous attempts of the Welshmen, went with a great power of men into Wales, to pursue the capteine of the Welsh rebell Owen Glendouer, but in effect lost his labor; for Owen conueied himselfe out of the waie, into his knowen lurking places, and (as was thought) through art magike, he caused such foule weather of winds, tempest, raine, snow, and haile to be raised, for the annoiance of the kings armie, that the like had not beene heard of; in such sort, that the king was constreined to returne home . . . [145]

Shakespeare further advanced this view of Glyndŵr in his portrayal of him in *Henry IV*, Part I, though he made it appear to be Glyndŵr's own view of himself, and ridiculed it through the sceptical Englishman Hotspur. Glyndŵr is made to say:

> I can call spirits from the vasty deep.
>
> . . .
>
> Why I can teach you, cousin, to command the devil.
>
> . . .
>
> Three times hath Henry Bolingbroke made head
> Against my power; thrice from the banks of Wye
> And sandy-bottomed Severn have I sent him
> Booteless home and weather-beaten back.[146]

The Welsh, on the other hand, perhaps knowing the peculiarities of their weather too well to ascribe to it any supernatural explanation, note the same events with, at the most, some disparagement for the outsider unable to cope with Welsh terrain and weather, and some pride in Glyndŵr's skill in the use of guerilla tactics. Panton MS 53 records quite plainly for 1402: 'About the middle of August king Henry advanced with an army towards Wales, but returned without doing any thing',[147] and for 1405:

The king . . . marched towards Wales with an army of thirty Seven thousand men, but this expedition succeeded not well for the king after he had entred the country lost fifty of his waggons, wherein the provisions treasure Etc were carryed and so was necessitated to return without performing any notable exploit.[148]

At the end of the seventeenth century, however, William Wynne does acknowledge that magical powers are ascribed to Glyndŵr:

But about the midst of August, to correct the presumptuous Attempts of the Welch, the king went in Person with a great Army into Wales; but by reason of extraordinary excess of weather, which some attributed to the Magic of Glyndwr, he was glad to return safe.[149]

Then towards the end of the eighteenth century, Pennant, allowing that Glyndŵr might have made political use of ascriptions of wizardry, describes Henry's ventures into Wales thus:

[1401:] He entered Wales with a great army about the beginning of June, destroyed the abby of *Ystrad Fflur* in *Cardiganshire*, and ravaged the country; but was obliged to make a disgraceful retreat, after his forces had suffered greatly by famine, and the great fatigues they continually underwent.

[1402:] The event of his invasion was very unfortunate. *Glyndwr*, who had too much prudence to hazard a battle against so superior an army, retired to the fastnesses of the mountains, drove away the cattle, and destroyed every means the *English* had of subsistence. The season proved uncommonly bad; for the very elements seemed to have warred against them. A continued course of storms and rains, with the continual watching against an enemy ever hovering over them, and ready to take every occasion of falling on them from the heights, wasted the army with sickness and fatigue; and obliged the king once more to make a most inglorious retreat.

The *English*, willing to cover their shame, attributed the cause of their disgrace to the incantations of the *British* chieftain; 'who,' as an old historian expresses, 'through art magike (as was thought) caused such foule weather of winds, tempest, raine, snow, and haile, to be raised for the annoiance of the king's armie, that the like had not beene heard of.' Perhaps *Glyndwr*, as well to infuse terror into his foes, as to give his people a more exalted notion of him, might politically insinuate his skill in spells and charms, that they might suppose him aided by more than mortal power. This species of credulity was not only strong at this time, but even continued to more enlightened days.

[1405]: *Henry* then returned, and marched into *Wales* with an army of 37,000 men. The same ill fortune attended him in this as in former expeditions. The weather proved so bad, that he was obliged to make a hasty retreat to *Worcester*, aggravated with the loss of fifty of his carriages.[150]

The Welsh were apparently aware of (and amused by?) the English view of Glyndŵr. The nineteenth-century nationalist journals published pieces indicating that magical powers were attributed to him – as for example 'credid ei fod yn medru codi ysbrydion i ymladd drosto'[151] (it was believed that he could raise spirits to fight for him) – but with them it seems to have been more a matter of pride that even the heavens were on their side, the side of right.

Yn Awst a Medi [1402], pan oedd Harri yn Nghymru yn ceisio ei orthrechu, dywedir fod y nefoedd ei hunan fel yn cynorthwyo Owain a'i ganlynwyr: arllwysai y cymylau eu cynwysiad, rhuai yr ystorm, a tharanau y dymhestl; ac yn un o'r ystormydd hyn ysgubwyd hyd yn nod pabell y brenin ymaith.[152]

(In August and September, when Henry was in Wales trying to overcome him, it is said that the heavens themselves aided Owain and his followers: the clouds poured out their contents, the storm roared, and the tempest thundered; and in one of these storms even the king's tent was swept away.)

Nevertheless, as far as I have been able to determine, the only magical powers associated by the Welsh with Glyndŵr are those of the two men who interpreted prophecy for him – Crach y Ffinant, his personal prophet, who encouraged Glyndŵr in his attempt to free Wales, and who advised on the timing for certain military actions, and Hopcyn ap Tomas who warned him away from being captured under a black banner.[153]

International Folk Hero

The heroic category which one might expect to be established in the legendry surrounding Glyndŵr is that of the basic Indo-European or international folk hero. The hero's biographical pattern, found in the lives of male heroes from Moses to Hercules to Daniel Boone, has been studied by a series of scholars beginning with J.G. von Hahn and including Otto Rank, Lord Raglan, Alwyn Rees, Joseph Campbell and Vladimir Propp.[154] Although they differ in the exact details of the pattern and in their interpretations of it, the existence of a traditional heroic biographical pattern has been generally accepted. In broad outline, the hero has a wondrous conception and birth, performs special boyhood deeds, ventures out into the world (either under compulsion or voluntarily), acquires magical aids (weapons, knowledge, helpers), fights with kings and/or monsters, wins a maiden and wins a kingdom (or other form of territory) which he rules until death.

This pattern, however, does not appear in fully developed form for Owain Glyndŵr. There are hints of it and possible elements, but not enough to establish it. As is proper for such a hero, his genealogies put him in royal lines on both the maternal and paternal sides,[155] but since this is also a well-established fact of history, as well as being necessary for his claim to be prince of Wales, one cannot assert that traditional patterning was definitely involved. The traditions of Glyndŵr's birth are both slight and unclear. The best known, or at least most often cited, occurrence is first reported by Holinshed:

> Strange wonders happened (as men reported) at the natiuitie of this man, for the same night he was borne, all his fathers horsses in the stable were found to stand in bloud vp to the bellies.[156]

It has been suggested that this story, despite its international analogues (Motif E761.1.9), was not a genuine contemporary tradition even in England, but rather that Holinshed (or one of his sources) created the story from a misreading of an earlier history. Furthermore, it is unclear whether Holinshed means the story to refer to Glyndŵr or to Mortimer.[157] The story is, however, repeated in the English and Welsh histories.[158] The only indication that it ever became a genuine part of folk tradition comes from a man who grew up in the Bridgend area and who heard as a local legend in Cowbridge:

> One of the prophecies when Glyndŵr was born, the horses in the stables was up to their feet in blood. And of course he fought a battle in Cowbridge and it was so bloody that the horses *were* up to their feet in blood.[159]

Shakespeare does not mention the horses standing in blood, but he does have Glyndŵr describe a birth well-marked by wonders of heaven and earth:

> ... At my nativity
> The front of heaven was full of fiery shapes
> Of burning cressets, and at my birth
> The frame and huge foundation of the earth
> Shaked like a coward.
> ...
> I say the earth did shake when I was born.
> ...
> The heavens were all on fire, the earth did tremble.
> ...
> ... Give me leave
> To tell you once again that at my birth
> The front of heaven was full of fiery shapes,
> The goats ran from the mountains, and the herds
> Were strangely clamorous to the frighted fields.
> These signs have marked me extraordinary,
> And all the courses of my life do show
> I am not in the roll of common men.[160]

These portents are common enough for the international folk hero, a pattern which Shakespeare seems to recognize though it is unlikely that Shakespeare himself was viewing Glyndŵr in that way. Since the material is not taken from Holinshed and the immediate source is not known, we may conjecture either that Shakespeare was expressing an English stereotype about the vainglorious and superstitious Welsh, or that he was recording genuine Welsh tradition learned from the many Welsh at court. In regard to the latter possibility, however, there is no other suggestion of heaven or earth giving forth portents of Glyndŵr's wondrous birth until the beginning of the present century, when Marie Trevelyan records that 'The birth of Owain Glyndwr was said to be heralded by a comet and curious meteors, with falling stars.'[161] However, Trevelyan's indiscriminate use of sources and her generally romanticizing tendencies always make her collections suspect. Moreover, she may well have been influenced by Shakespeare's lines. Nevertheless, even if Shakespeare created the portents, they still provide evidence that he was aware of some, at least, viewing Glyndŵr in heroic terms.

The traditions concerning Glyndŵr's birth which do appear in Wales deal with the place rather than the manner of his birth. In the mid-nineteenth century, *A Topographical Dictionary of Wales* recorded under Little Trefgarn in the parish of St Dogwells (Llantydewi) in Pembrokeshire:

> This parish is noted, on traditional authority as the birthplace and place of burial of that distinguished patriot and chieftain, Owain Glyndwr, who is said to have been born at Little Trevgarn, and to have been interred at the small village of Wolf's Castle, both situated within its limits.[162]

This location for Glyndŵr's birth is claimed again in the journals[163] but, as one might expect, an alternative claim is made by Glyndyfrdwy, which was known as his home area and from which he takes his epithet. In 1953, Thomas Firbank wrote:

> It is said that the old warrior was born at Glyndyfrdwy, though no one is able to give chapter and verse. Yet I remember, when a boy, as I was scrambling about the mount, an old farmer had shown me some long humps in the field below. They formed squares and rectangles, as if the crumbled foundations of a building had become grass-grown. The old man claimed that there had been Owain's palace. It must have been a very small palace, but one could hardly describe Owain's dwelling as a mere house.[164]

The other elements of the international biographical pattern appear even less frequently than the extraordinary birth. The historians and antiquarians tell of Glyndŵr studying at the Inns of Court, but there are no childhood feats or signs of prowess, and unless one chooses to view his time in London and in the Scottish wars as the period of travel when the hero gains magic aids, or in Glyndŵr's case the skills of war, those stages of the pattern are also missing. Moreover, while Glyndŵr did marry, there is no narrative significance to the marriage. Finally, although he fought for a kingdom, it would be difficult to say he won it and ruled it in peace until death.

The basic international folk hero, in addition to his biographical pattern, has certain frequently occurring characteristics, but the only standard heroic characteristic brought out by the legendry on Glyndŵr is that particular heroic strength which can impress itself even in rock. Two legends dealing with this power are told in connection with the church at Corwen. One, included in *A Topographical Dictionary of Wales* under the heading Corwen, states:

> Upon the Berwyn mountain, behind the church, is a place called Glyndwr's Seat, which commands a charming prospect; and from this spot it is superstitiously reported that Owain threw a dagger, which falling upon a stone, formed in it an impression of its whole length, half an inch deep; this stone is now in the south wall of the church.[165]

The other legend, this one sent in to a journal by a minister raised in the Corwen area, relates

> fod Owen Glyndwr wedi ymosod arni o Pen-y-pigyn yr ochr arall i'r dyffryn, ac iddo, naill o lawenydd buddogoliaeth, neu fyrbwylldra siomedigaeth, daflu ei gleddyf o'i law gyda grym aruthrol nes iddo daro yn erbyn mur clochdy Eglwys Corwen, a gadael ei ol ar ei hyd ar feini y mur.[166]

> (that Owen Glyndwr had attacked it [Caer Drewyn] from Pen-y-pigyn the other side of the valley, and that he, whether out of joy of victory or out of testiness/rashness of disappointment, threw his sword from his hand with terrible strength so that it struck against the wall of the bell tower of Corwen Church and left its mark on the stones of the wall.)

Another legend, this time about a stone somewhere between Denbigh and Cerrigydrudion but with the same central motif, relates that, after a major victory, Glyndŵr threw his sword against a rock in which it left its mark, thereby giving the rock its name, Maen Cleddyf Glyn Dwr (stone of Glyndŵr's sword).[167] This heroic strength is further demonstrated in Glyndŵr's leaving the impress of his knees where he knelt and his horse's leaving its hoofprints in stone.[168]

Perhaps the most intriguing aspect of the international heroic pattern in relation to Glyndŵr is its *absence*. As already noted, there are a few elements that commonly belong to the pattern, especially a noble and wondrous birth and the weight of heroic power, but the pattern itself is missing. This absence of pattern may result not from chance, but rather may be peculiarly linked to Glyndŵr's role as a redeemer-hero. Most redeemer-heroes appear to lack the biographical pattern. Arthur and Jesus are notable exceptions but, for most of the others, nothing more needs to be known other than that they will return and will restore the nation to its former glories.[169] As seen in Chapter 2, such is certainly the case with Hiriell, Cynan and Cadwaladr, the earliest in the line of Welsh redeemers. And certainly that is the essence of being a redeemer; what does one's early life matter as long as one will return? The patterns of the basic international folk hero and the redeemer-hero may be in some way antipathetic to each other; the role of the redeemer-hero may preclude the development of the international heroic pattern. Possibly Glyndŵr's role as a national redeemer is so strongly developed that it overrides any tendencies there might otherwise be for tradition to pattern his life as a standard hero.

Nevertheless, the absence of the international heroic bio-graphical pattern from Glyndŵr's legendry does not mean that he is a shallow or slight figure in Welsh tradition. Rather, his wide range of heroic qualities (national redeemer, Welsh lord and warrior with all the concomitant traits, trickster, escape artist, culture hero and purported wizard) indicates something of the depth and significance of the function which Glyndŵr serves. He is not merely the focal point, a central figure around whom legends accrue. He fills a certain function, and there is a direct connection between that function and the type of stories told about him. Other important leaders in Welsh history have quite different legendry associated with them.

Glyndŵr's special role is manifested even in the way that Owain Lawgoch has been treated by tradition. Owain Lawgoch is also a redeemer-hero, whose high point came only thirty-five years before Glyndŵr's and who, as a direct descendant of the Llywelyns, had an even greater claim to the title prince of Wales.

Glyndŵr and Owain Lawgoch have so much in common as redeemer-heroes that at times, especially in the poetry, they may not even be differentiated, with Owain referring to either one or both simultaneously. Owain Lawgoch is used interchangeably with Arthur and Glyndŵr in certain cave legends, but the development of other legendry about him has been quite different, with most of it focusing on his epithet, Llawgoch (Red hand), and how he acquired it. Rather than being depicted as a great military leader who could only be stopped by an English-paid assassin, he now often appears in folk tradition as a malicious figure. In the nineteenth century, he was equated with *y Gŵr Blewog* (the Hairy Man) who would emerge from his cave only to rob people's homes. One night as he was breaking in through her window, an old woman chopped off his hand with an axe. The bloody track led to a cave which has since been called Ogof Owain Lawgoch.[170] In this century, the Museum of Welsh Life has recorded several tales of Owain Lawgoch's malicious spirit. In one case, the spirit is captured and sealed in a bottle, which is then thrown into a lake. The closure-breaking coda to the story is that someone has since seen a red finger working the cork out of the bottle.[171] Owain Lawgoch may be treated differently in part because the fact that he was assassinated, which is an important part of his history, conflicts with, and thus undermines, his role as a redeemer-hero who has never died.

One of Glyndŵr's special functions, and one which manifests his great importance in folklore, is the way in which he serves as a focal point in onomastics, providing an explanatory element. This has been seen repeatedly in legends such as those explaining the derivation of Pentre-poeth, Tre-boeth and Cae Murpoeth from Glyndŵr's destructive fires, Erw Llech from men hiding in the field, Bryn Saith Marchog from seven of Glyndŵr's soldiers, Mynydd y Gaer from his caves extending through to Chester, as well as all those places which have Owain's name as part of theirs because of something he did there.

Another indication of Glyndŵr's strong, accretive role in Welsh folklore might be found (any hesitancy arises from uncertainty as to whether Owain Glyndŵr is the Owain referred to) in a certain *lorica*, a prayer or charm for protection, recorded by Humphrey Foulkes both in a letter to Edward Lhuyd and in a separate report at the beginning of the eighteenth century.

Foulkes notes having heard 'this Popish prayer' near Bala from an old man who had learned it from his grandmother, thereby dating the *lorica* possibly at least as far back as the late sixteenth century.

> Pan godwy'r boreu yn gynta,
> Yn nawdh Beino yn benna;
> Yn nawdd Kerrig, nawdd Patrig,
> Yn nawdd gwr gwyn Bendigedig;
> Yn nawdd Owain ben lluman llu,
> Ag yn nessa yn Nawdd Iesu.[172]

(When I rise first in the morning, under the protection of Beuno chiefly; under the protection of Curig, protection of Patrick, under the protection of the holy blessed man; under the protection of Owain, chief banner of a host and then [next] under the protection of Jesus.)

In the middle of a prayer invoking two Welsh saints, one Irish saint and Jesus, we also have Owain, a secular figure, who is, furthermore, described in military terms. Whether this is Owain Glyndŵr or a generic Owain, the *lorica* suggests first that he was a deliverer (combining military leadership and protective powers), and then that he had such a strong presence in folk imagination that his expected services of protection for the nation could be extended to the individual petitioner. If this is Glyndŵr, as it may very well be, the *lorica* provides yet another example of both the multiformity and inherent consistency of his overlapping roles in tradition.

The elements of Glyndŵr's character – redeemer, trickster, outlaw, nobleman, warrior – have been present in some form in every period. Changes appear either in the details of the versions of a legend, as was seen in discussion of Glyndŵr's early morning meeting with the abbot on Y Berwyn, or in particular legends used to illustrate these traits. For example, stories showing Glyndŵr as a trickster appear throughout the centuries, but what demonstrates his trickery changes. In the sixteenth to eighteenth century, a notable legend has Glyndŵr retaking Aberystwyth Castle by verbal trickery but, in the nineteenth and twentieth centuries, that legend loses its prominence of place to legends of Glyndŵr tricking his enemies with stick figures. Assessing the development of Glyndŵr's tradition is complicated by the interplay of the three factors of legend, source and time period, that is, that certain legends have been recorded only in the medium of certain literary genres, which are in turn characteristic of certain periods. Therefore the appearance or disappearance of a legend from written texts may be affected more by literary fashion than by changes in traditional culture; the absence of a legend from written sources proves nothing about the legend's existence in oral tradition in that same period. The differences between legends recorded in one period and those in another are often subtle, sometimes impressionistic, but the written sources do fall into a couple of broad categories. The two sets of materials, despite the subtleties of difference, reveal certain attitudes of their periods. The histories and chronicles which form the major source in the sixteenth to eighteenth centuries present relatively dry records of Glyndŵr's war, relating traditions of major events. In doing so, they reflect a period in which the need for Glyndŵr was not strongly felt, when he was held in abeyance and moreover, during which English influence was strong and English attitudes prevailed even in the Welsh histories, so that while Glyndŵr's war was recognized as important enough for historical record, it was, for the most part, not given approval or invested with either regrets or hope. The antiquarians' reports and nationalist journals of the late eighteenth and nineteenth century, influenced by romantic nationalism and manifesting a renewed interest in Glyndŵr, contain a mixture of materials culled from both older sources and newly-collected local traditions. They relate slightly more detailed and embellished legends which, while still connected with the war, seem less a military record of specific battles and more about uprising, about the spirit of righteousness which through cleverness and cunning can play with and taunt the enemy. As discussed in the final chapter, twentieth-century fieldwork shows legendry reflecting both local tradition and nationalistic concerns.

The variations in recorded legendry are significant, but one must also remember the danger of assuming that certain traditions were limited to certain periods just because our records of them are thus limited. Beyond the variations is the continuity of tradition about Glyndŵr's roles and character. Moreover, while Glyndŵr's great importance has led to the development of traditions belonging to a wide range of heroic categories beyond that of the redeemer-hero, the traditions also remain consistent with that role of redeemer. Each one in its own special way illustrates Glyndŵr's worthiness for the role – the proper Welsh noble, who should lead; the skilled military leader, with the fierceness to carry out his plans; the trickster, with the necessary cunning and guile; the destroyer, who through chaos will engender a new order; and the culture hero, who will ensure that, when the nation is restored to its former glories, it will enjoy a true golden age.

5

Local Hero and Nationalist Symbol

Owain Glyndŵr continues to be a figure of great import in the modern period: he functions both as a local hero, especially significant to the inhabitants of the areas in which he lived and fought, and as a national hero, who once almost won independence for Wales. Many of the same traditions are used on both the local and national levels, but their transmission, the way in which they are used and the types of details included tend to be very different. Nevertheless, as one might expect in view of the importance of Glyndŵr's war, the legendry all relates in some way to the uprising so that, whether a particular legend shows Glyndŵr gathering his troops, escaping to the wilds, destroying towns, fooling the enemy or leaving the mark of his sword, he remains above all a warrior, heroically resisting the English. Thus it is, as will be shown in the following discussion on Glyndŵr's contemporary role as both a local and a national hero, that while the legendry may display more variation at the local level, it still points in the same direction as the major theme at the national level – a leader endeavouring to redeem his nation.

Local Hero

On the local level, in the valleys where Owain Glyndŵr lived and fought, he is still a national hero, but he is also more importantly and most definitely, a local hero. Both the type and amount of knowledge people have about Glyndŵr changes at the local level. Transmission also differs. On the national level, transmission of information about Glyndŵr is primarily through books and other forms of popular media. Gwynfor Evans and Dafydd Iwan, two active nationalists who frequently invoke Glyndŵr's name, learned of him first through reading history, and had no traditionally-founded knowledge of him before they began using his name.[1] At the local level, though there is naturally some influence from outside sources, knowledge of Glyndŵr is orally derived. Moreover, while on the national level the main points about Glyndŵr are that he is *y mab darogan* and that he had great vision, on the local level there is a great wealth and variety of legendry attached to Glyndŵr. The material emerges even in the midst of denials of its existence. The woman who guided me around the Corwen area would introduce me to people and explain that I was interested in traditions connected with Glyndŵr. Then, to my great frustration, and until I explained the problem, she would add 'but there isn't anything left, is there? It's all died out, hasn't it?' I was used to people telling me that all the folk traditions were gone, but it seemed counter-productive to tell the potential informants so. The people, naturally, would answer, 'No, there's nothing left. I can't tell you anything', but then would add, 'All I can tell you is . . . ', and out would come a series of places associated with Glyndŵr, often to be followed by stories about him. It should be noted that the denial of having any traditional lore may be in part actuated by a distinction drawn between tradition and fact. Several times an informant would say to me, 'Mae hynny wrth gwrs yn ffaith nid yn draddodiad' (That, of course, is a fact, not a tradition). The items they told me ranged from simple statements of a traditional association attached to a particular topographical or constructional feature to full narratives.

The strongest and most peculiarly localized traditions are those associated with specific places; the physical presence acts as a constant reminder of the associated tradition, but only within the relatively limited circle of people familiar with the area. Unusual natural features often become the subject of tradition. Just outside Corwen, there is a stone said to bear the impress of Glyndŵr's knees from when he kneeled on it,[2] and another stone showing the imprint of his horse's hoofs.[3]

Similarly, in the Pumlumon area, at Craig y March (Rock of the Horse), there are hoofprints where Glyndŵr's horse Llwyd y Bacsie walked up the face of the rock.[4] A great deal of onomastic material appears in the local legendry. For example, a woman from Aberhosan reported that Cwm Gwarchae (Valley of the Siege), which is on the side of Pumlumon in the Aberhosan area, got its name because Glyndŵr and his army fought there. Other examples are the traditions about Bryn Saith Marchog being named after Glyndŵr's seven men who spied on Lord Grey from that vantage point, and about Bryn Owain, Erw Llech and Ffynnon Garreg Udfan, where Owain's soldiers gathered and hid, and where the women wept.[5] Sometimes, of course, a place simply bears Glyndŵr's name, indicating that he used it or spent time there, but without any greater specificity, such as Ffos Owen Glyndwr (his ditch), Glyndŵr's Way or Cadair Glyndŵr (his seat) on Y Berwyn.[6]

With many of the places commemorated in local tradition, the main point is that Glyndŵr owned the place or simply visited there. For example, Plas Crug, a fortified medieval mansion which stood between Aberystwyth and Llanbadarn Fawr was said to have been one of Glyndŵr's residences[7] and, in Llanarmon Dyffryn Ceiriog in Denbighshire, local people, taking *wèn* as a contraction for Owen/Owain rather than the more likely *dôl-(g)wen* (fair meadow), have claimed that the farmhouse Dolwen was named after Glyndŵr who often stayed there.[8] Such places were generally the first to be mentioned after people told me they knew nothing about Glyndŵr. In the Corwen area, almost everybody told me about Glyndŵr's *carchardy* (prison). Some of the older people remembered the building standing and had kept mementoes of it, such as a piece of wood. A number of people told me where the key was kept.[9] They also told me about the farmhouse at Carrog Uchaf which was one of Glyndŵr's homes. One man who told me that he had always heard this, said he doubted it because the farmhouse is made of stone and he assumed that in Glyndŵr's period it would have been made of wood.[10] Nobody else, however, expressed such doubts; in fact, one woman told me that the stairs in the farmhouse are stained with the blood of one of Glyndŵr's soldiers.[11] The owners of the house, which is a beautiful stone building, told me that they used to have in the house a table belonging to Glyndŵr – a huge,

round table standing on one centre leg. It was so big that they
had to pull out a window to remove it from the house.[12] A
nineteenth-century collection of antiquities in the area contains
the following note:

> Mae traddodiad yn yr ardal fod hen fwrdd cegin mawr a arferid
> gan Owain Glyndwr ar gael eto yn ffermdy Carog. Bu amryw o
> enwogion y Gymdeithas Hynafiaethol Brydeinig yn ei weled ar
> adeg eu cylchwyl yn Llangollen yn Awst, 1877; ond barnent oll, er
> fod y bwrdd yn hen, nad oedd mor hen a hyny.[13]

> (There is a tradition in the area that a big, old, kitchen table which
> was used by Owain Glyndŵr is still in Carrog farmhouse. Various
> notables of the British Antiquarian Society saw it on the occasion of
> their meeting in Llangollen in August 1877; but they all judged,
> although the table was old, that it was not as old as that.)

Another frequently mentioned place is Llidiart y Parc (The Park
Gate), said to mark a park belonging to Glyndŵr. One woman
explained that it was his deer park (*parc ceirw*).[14] Several people
in the Corwen area also told me about the ruins of an old house
belonging to Glyndŵr, but the following example is worth
quoting for what it shows of the life and transmission of these
local traditions. First, the traditional site is given precise location,
complete with directions. Next, despite not having looked
closely for himself, this person accepts what he was told by his
parents and grandparents. Furthermore, despite doubts, he
cannot help but think of the legend every time he passes the
place.

> Dach chi'n dod lawr 'rŵan o Garrog Ucha i'r ffordd fawr. Dŵad i
> gyfeiriad Carrog dipyn bach. Yn y cae ar draws y ffordd ma 'na
> bwll o ddŵr. Ne' mi o'dd 'na bwll o ddŵr, pwy bynnag. Wn i ddim
> ydi o'n dal yno. Ma 'na yma eto, do's gynna i ddim ffaith
> hanesyddol am y peth. Ond mi glywes 'y mam a nhad, a nhaid a
> nain yn sôn bod yn fanno. Ma 'na gerrig yno, glampie o gerrig
> ynde, bod yna rei o adeiladau Owain Glyndŵr yn y fan honno ond
> bod nw wedi suddo i mewn i'r tir glyb 'te ond unwaith eto ma
> cerrig ynde, a faswn i'n dychmygu na fasa Owain Glyndŵr yn y
> pymthegfed ganrif ddim yn adeiladu â cherrig, er nad ydw i ddim
> yn awdurdod ar bethe felly chwaith ynde. Ond dyna fo. Dyna be
> glwes i. Bod 'i adeilade fo wedi suddo i'r lle glyb 'ma. Mae o i weld
> ranny bob tro fydda i'n pasio fydda i'n meddwl am 'ny 'de.[15]

(You come down now from Carrog Uchaf to the main road. Come in the direction of Carrog a little bit. In the field across this road there's a pool of water. Or, there was a pool of water anyway. I don't know if it's still there. Here again I don't have any historical fact about the thing. But I heard my mother and father, and grandfather and grandmother mention that it's there. There are stones there, massive stones, that there's some of Owain Glyndŵr's buildings in that place but they've sunk in the wet earth, but once again there are stones, aren't there, and I would imagine that Owain Glyndŵr in the fifteenth century wouldn't build with stones, though I'm not an authority on such things either. But there it is. That's what I heard. That his buildings have sunk in this wet place. It can be seen for that matter; every time I pass, I think about that.)

Later in the conversation, this man remembered that the place where the buildings sank was called Pwllinein (Pool . . .) and wondered about the meaning of the second element of the name.[16]

This same man went on to describe the next place of interest down the road. In speaking with people living in one of Glyndŵr's areas, one becomes aware of how the whole landscape is alive with associations for them. It is not simply a matter of casual statement, 'Oh, yes, Glyndŵr was here', but rather that he was *here*, on this road, on this field and on this hillside. Without the accompanying scene and gestures, the following words of a man looking out of his window in Carrog, can only give a partial impression of the situation but, even so, they give some indication of how intimately Glyndŵr and his traditions are tied to the local landscape:

Carrog Ucha de, wedyn ma Carrog Isa wedyn yn is i lawr. Wel rŵan ta ma nw'n deud bod Glyndŵr yn dod dros y mynydd 'ma i lawr i Glyndyfrdwy de, draws yr afon yma 'nde yn Glyndyfrdwy ac ymlaen wedyn dros y mynydd i Rhuthun. A dyna'r ffordd o'dd o'n i chymryd yn de. A ma'n debyg 'na dyna'r ffordd o'dd o'n gerdded pan o'dd o'n llosgi Castell Rhuthun ynde. Ac wedyn ddaru 'na ferch iddo fo ddod i fyw i ffarm o'r enw Blaen Cwm ynde, reit yn top fanna. Dyna'r traddodiad, yndê.[17]

(Carrog Uchaf [Upper], then there's Carrog Isa [Lower] then lower down. Well now, they say that Glyndŵr came over this mountain

down to Glyndyfrdwy, across this river in Glyndyfrdwy and on
then over the mountain to Rhuthun. And that's the route he took.
And it's likely that that's the route he walked when he burned
Rhuthun Castle. And then a daughter of his came to live on a farm
by the name of Blaen Cwm, right on top there. That's the tradition,
isn't it.)

A number of places are remembered, or even named, for
events that took place at them, rather than because they are
simply marks of the hero's presence. The most important of these
in Corwen is Tomen Glyndŵr (his mound) which, as noted in the
last chapter, is thought of as a look-out post and as the place
where Glyndŵr gathered his men. One woman in Carrog
suggested that Glyndŵr's soldiers are sleeping in the mound, but
the ensuing group discussion determined that they were buried
and that they might even be in another, nearby mound at
Hendom.[18] Another of my contacts in the area also had trouble
determining whether the two mounds were the subject of the
same or different traditions, and he, too, decided that they were
separate.[19] Bwrdd y Tri Arglwydd (Table of the three lords) is
another frequently mentioned place in the Corwen area,
described by one person as:

> lle roedd Owain Glyndŵr yn cyfarfod â'r Iarll Grey ac un uchelwr
> arall. Dw i ddim yn cofio 'i enw fo ond allwn i edrych i fyny. A mi
> fydden nw'n cyfarfod o gwmpas y bwrdd yma, a ma hwnnw i'w
> weld heddiw, bwrdd carreg mawr, a thair carreg fel coese yn dal y
> garreg i fyny . . . Dw i wedi'i weld o. Mae o'n ymyl y ffordd ond ar
> y ffordd gefn rwle tua Chapel Cefn Wern.[20]

> (where Owain met with Lord Grey and one other nobleman. I don't
> remember his name, but I could look it up. And they would meet
> around this table, and that's to be seen today, a big stone table, and
> three stones like legs holding the stone up . . . I've seen it. It's near
> the road but on the back road somewhere towards Capel Cefn
> Wern.)

When a companion and I located the place, we found only a
stone marker with a plaque which read, 'Bwrdd y Tri Arglwydd.
This Ancient Boundary stone marks the meeting point of four
Parishes and of the Lordships of Ruthun, Glyndyfrdwy, and
Yale.' Another tradition of a stone table in the area, or possibly
even of the same table, is of Bwrdd y Brenin:

If we go over the bridge and pass the mill, we come to the extensive farm of Plas Tregeiriog. On a field at the top of the road, called Sarn, and within the angle formed by that road and the mountain road to Llanarmon, is a large stone, called Bwrdd y Brenin ('the King's table'). In the summer of 1403, Prince Henry, afterwards Henry V, left Shrewsbury with a large force, and marched to Sychart, Llansilin, with the intention of meeting Owain Glyndŵr in battle. Not finding Owain at his mansion, the Prince burnt Sychart, and hastened with his troops by the shortest cross-country route over the Berwyns to Glyndyfrdwy, hoping to meet Owain there. While on this journey, Prince Henry took refreshments on this stone, which, ever since, according to tradition, has been called Bwrdd y Brenin.[21]

In the Pumlumon area, another meeting-place is also marked by stones, Cerrig Cyfamod Owain Glyndŵr (Stone of Owain Glyndŵr's Treaty), where local tradition claims that Glyndŵr and Hugh Mortimer made their pact to end the war.[22] Again in the Pumlumon area, are Y Stablau (the Stables), crags or a cave where Glyndŵr is said to have stabled his war-horses.[23] Another tradition provides explanation for the name of a farm, Esgair Gadwyth, in the parish of Darowen near Machynlleth. It is explained that an older name, Esgair Cadw Wyth (Ridge of Keeping Eight), came from the fact that the family living there was responsible for providing lodging for eight of Glyndŵr's men when the army was in the area.[24] All of the caves, in whatever part of Wales, to which the people in the area point as a place from which Glyndŵr waged his guerilla war, to which he retreated or in which he hid or now sleeps, also exemplify this aspect of local tradition.

Other places, noted not just with an explanatory phrase but rather with a full narrative, also figure in the local legendry. The most prominent of these in the Corwen area is the church, or rather a stone built into the wall over one of the church doors. Into the stone is cut the shape of a cross-hilted knife or sword, more than twenty inches long and approximately one inch deep. An early reference to the stone, associating it with Glyndŵr but without a narrative explanation, appears in a late eighteenth-century manuscript:

> Cleddyf Owen Glynn-dyfr, the Sword of Owen Glyndwr, which is engraved in a stone over a door on the South side of Corwen

Church, in Merionethshire, which is said to be the door where he used to go to Church at: The above sword is about 23 Inches long.[25]

There then follows a sketch. Some of the early nineteenth-century works describe it as a very rude cross shown to strangers as the sword of Owain Glyndŵr.[26] Eventually, the antiquarians began to record the story, one example of which is given in Chapter 4, in which Glyndŵr threw his knife from the top of the mountain behind the church, and the knife landed on a rock leaving its impress.[27] These nineteenth-century accounts report Glyndŵr as sitting in *Cadair Glyndŵr* on Y Berwyn. The people in Corwen and the neighbouring Cynwyd and Carrog who told me about the sword in the church generally described Glyndŵr as throwing the knife from Pen y Pigyn, the hill rising steeply behind the church on the other side of the churchyard. With the placement of the hill, the churchyard and the church, and the existence of the incised sword acting as safeguards, the stories told were essentially the same, but they differed in length, detail and emphasis. The first version told to me, by a man cleaning the churchyard, was very short and without much detail:

> And the story of him throwing the sword from that mountain, that's Pen y Pigyn, that is, that's what that's called. And he's supposed to have thrown the sword from there and hit – well, I don't think he hit there [the stone above the door], but he must have hit a stone somewhere, and they carved it out.[28]

An equally short version from a woman in Carrog, however, stresses Glyndŵr's fine aim, rather than allowing that the stone might have been moved. In answer to a question about throwing a knife in the churchyard, she said:

> O Pen Pigyn reit at y trawst ynde uwchben y giat yr eglwys. O'dd Owain Glyndŵr yn gallu anelu o Pen Pigyn Corwen i fanno de.[29]

> (From Pen Pigyn right at the lintel above the gate of the church. Owain Glyndŵr was able to aim from Pen Pigyn, Corwen, to that place.)

Others told much fuller stories with more colour, as for example this version from a man in Corwen, in which Glyndŵr is shown as a normally flawed human.

Mae 'na ym mynwent eglwys Corwen, garreg. Ag ar y garreg 'ma,
mae 'na siap 'run fath a fasa rywun wedi torri mewn llun dagr, yn
y garreg. A'r chwedl ydi bod Owain Glyndŵr ryw ddiwrnod yn
sefyll i fyny yn y coed acw ar Ben y Pigyn, a mae Pen y Pigyn yn lle
mae'r television mast yn fan acw – fanna ma Pen Pigyn – bod
Owain Glyndŵr yn sefyll yna, a bod rywun wedi'i wylltio fo. Oedd
o, o doedd o ddim yn sant, Owain Glyndŵr, wchi, o nag oedd. Ma
hynny'n ffaith 'de. O'dd o ddim yn sant o lawar iawn, o bell ffordd.
Ond ro'dd o 'di gwylltio'n ofnadwy wrth rywun a bod o 'di tynnu
'i ddagr allan ag wedi'i daflu o, a bod y dagr wedi fflio heibio pen
pwy bynnag o'dd wedi 'i wylltio fo 'te ac wedi disgyn ar y garreg
'ma i lawr ym mynwent eglwys Corwen, ag wedi gneud 'i farc, 'i
hôl yna. A ma hwnnw i weld yna ar y garreg o hyd te. Ond ma
hwnna'n hen chwedl yn dydi.[30]

(There is in the churchyard at Corwen church, a stone. And on this
stone, there's a shape the same type as someone would have cut as
an image of a knife, in the stone. And the story is that Owain
Glyndŵr one day was standing up in that wood on Pen y Pigyn,
and Pen y Pigyn is where the television mast is up there – up there
on Pen y Pigyn – that Owain Glyndŵr was standing there, and that
someone had angered him. He was, he wasn't a saint, Owain
Glyndŵr, you know, oh, he wasn't. That's a fact. He wasn't a saint
by a lot, by a long way. But he was terribly enraged by someone
and had pulled out his knife and had thrown it, and that the knife
had flown past the head of whoever had angered him and had
fallen on this stone down in the graveyard of Corwen church, and
had made its mark, its impression there. And this is to be seen there
on the stone still. Oh, that's an old tale, isn't it.)

In the following variant, told by a man in Cynwyd, Glyndŵr's
anger is directed not just at an individual, but at the people of the
area:

Ma Pen y Pigyn reit o du ucha eglwys y plwy – cewch 'ma. Cerwch
i tu nôl i'r eglwys ma 'na ddrws yn 'r ochor ac uwchben carreg y
drws ma 'na slab o garreg, carreg sy'n dal y wal i fyny 'n de, a ma
'na siap cleddyf ar hwnnw, a be glywes i bod Owain Glyndŵr wedi
melltithio pobol Edeirnion am droi yn dipyn o gachgwns, yndê
ddim yn fodlon i'w helpu o, ac yn 'i wylltineb bod o 'di lluchio'r
cleddyf i lawr a bod o 'di landio ar ryw glwt go feddal a bod
hwnnw mewn amser wedi c'ledu a throi'n garreg, yndê. Ond y, yr
unig beth, ydi hynny'n wir dw i'm 'n gwbod, dê, ond yr unig beth
wn i ydi bod y garreg uwchben y drws ochr Corwen, ochr yr

eglwys yng Nghorwen a ma 'na siap cleddyf cyntefig yno, 'ntê. Jest fel 'na, dydi o ddim yn gleddyf ffansi o gwbwl.[31]

(Pen y Pigyn is right above the parish church – you have here. Walk behind the church, there's a door in the side and above the lintel there's a slab of stone, a stone which is holding up the wall, and there's a shape of a sword on that, and what I heard is that Owain Glyndŵr had cursed the people of Edeirnion for turning a bit into cowards, not willing to help him, and in his fury that he had thrown his sword down and that it had landed on some fairly soft piece and that that in time had hardened and turned into rock. But the, the only thing, whether that's true I don't know, but the only thing I know is that the stone is above the door on the Corwen side, the side of the church in Corwen, and there's a primitive sword shape there. Just like that, it's not a fancy sword at all.)

This man, a retired schoolmaster, who is suggesting that the sword's imprint was fossilized after being made in soft matter, is the same one who doubted that Glyndŵr's house would have been made of stone. He knows all the local legendry, but keeps questioning and rationalizing it, though never letting that interfere with transmission of the basic information. Only one person in the Corwen area told the story with a change in a fundamental detail. Instead of reporting that the knife had fallen lengthwise on a stone, a man in Carrog related that Owain Glyndŵr was on Pen y Pigyn and that when he threw his knife the point went between the stone and the wall.[32]

As already mentioned, despite variation in the narration, the stories of the sword's or dagger's imprint in the stone are all bound to the church and Pen y Pigyn. However, local legend, even when presumably attached to a specific place, may actually be ascribed to a number of places in the area. A good example from Corwen is the story, discussed in the previous chapter, of Glyndŵr dressing up stick figures to create the illusion of an army. The events are most often, in printed accounts anyway, reported as having taken place in the field known as Dôl Pennau, but there is some disagreement as to where Dôl Pennau is, with accounts placing it east, west and north of Corwen, and at various distances. In the accounts which I heard in Corwen, Dôl Pennau does not figure particularly strongly. One of these accounts, which has already been cited in Chapter 4, places events at the field with the sewage works, and another makes the connection with Dôl Pennau only indirectly, by telling the story immediately after describing the field's location.[33] In another variant collected in Corwen, the narrator associates the ruse with yet another geographical feature, Rhiw y Saeson (Hill of the English):

> . . . ma 'na draddodiad – ym – ma Rhiw Saeson, dw i ddim yn sicir lle ma Rhiw y Saeson. Y – ma 'na ryw ffordd i'w gweld ar ochr Y Berwyn wrth ben Carrog yn fan hyn. Fydda i'n meddwl bob amsar ma hwnnw 'di Rhiw y Saeson ond hwrach mod i ddim yn iawn de. I ddod i 'mosod ar Glyndŵr a'i fyddin yng Nghaer Drewyn mi fydda'n rhaid i'r Saeson ddod i lawr y ffordd honno 'dach chi'n gweld ac wrth iddyn nhw ddod i lawr y ffordd honno, oeddan nhw'n gweld beth oedd yma ar Gaer Drewyn. Wel yr unig beth wn i ydi bod Glyndŵr wedi gwisgo'r polion 'ma hefo dillad a wedyn bod y Saeson o fanno wedi gweld nw'n de ag wedi meddwl bod ganddo fo anferth o – o fyddin fawr, mwy o lawer nag oedd ginno fo.[34]

> (. . . there's a tradition in Rhiw Saeson, I'm not sure where Rhiw y Saeson is. Uh – there's some road to be seen on the side of Y Berwyn above Carrog here. I think every time that that's Rhiw y Saeson but perhaps I'm not correct. To come to attack Glyndŵr and his army in Caer Drewyn the English would have to come down that route, you see, and in coming down that route, they saw what was here in Caer Drewyn. Well, the only thing I know is that Glyndŵr had dressed these poles with clothes and then that the English from that place had seen them and had thought that he had a huge – a big army, far bigger than he had.)

This example indicates how a local tradition may become assigned to a variety of sites. A person hears the story, but unsure of the location, may associate the legend with any place he thinks likely. This type of movement is much more possible with this legend than it would be of the sword in Corwen's church, because while the latter depends and centres on the physical element of the incised stone, the former focuses on Glyndŵr's cleverness, which can be transported to any of the numerous fields with accompanying high places in the area.

Despite the mobility of the legend of the stick figures within the Corwen area, the legend is not told elsewhere. The legend itself may be a migratory legend, readily adapted for any hero and any place, but within Wales, it is a local legend. This and the other Corwen traditions discussed thus far in this chapter are definitely local legends, told in the immediate area of Corwen, but not generally beyond that particular cluster of villages. For example, a man who listened to an account of the sword being thrown into the churchyard had never heard it before, but he came from a village on the other side of the mountain.[35] Each area in which Glyndŵr was particularly active has its own set of legendry. Just as Corwen's traditions are confined to Corwen, Pumlumon's traditions are peculiar to its immediate circle. In Dolgellau, only a short distance (*c.*40 miles) by modern transportation from Corwen, but a very long distance for transmission of local legends, the Corwen stories are not told. Instead, Dolgellau has its own Glyndŵr legend – the story of 'Ceubren yr Ellyll', in which Glyndŵr encases his cousin Hywel Sele in a hollow tree. The story takes place at Nannau, an estate just outside Dolgellau. Almost everybody with whom I spoke in Dolgellau associated Glyndŵr with Nannau and some variation of the name Hywel Sele, such as Huw Selef, and many told at least some part of the story of Hywel Sele's treachery and resulting punishment. Many people emphasized the ghost which haunts the tree, or what is now left of the tree. Sometimes, people were confused about the story, as was one woman who thought Glyndŵr was 'the one who hid in a tree, to escape someone'.[36] The legend of Glyndŵr's staying overnight, unrecognized in the home of his enemy Berkrolles, which was also discussed in the previous chapter, is particular to the Bridgend area in South Wales, where people learn it orally. People in other parts of Wales who knew the story knew it only from the nineteenth-century ballad, which had been taught in the schools. A northern variant of the legend, in which Glyndŵr is travelling in the North and in which no particular host is named, does exist in the Dolgellau area, where I heard it.[37] The importance of localism in the transmission of the Glyndŵr legends emerged with the realization that, no matter where I interviewed people, if they were able to tell me something specific about Glyndŵr (other than a few chance items and information learned from nationalist sources), the tradition would turn out to be localized in the person's home area. For example, a person from Bridgend told me the Lord Berkrolles story, that a battle at Cowbridge fulfilled the omen at Glyndŵr's birth because the horses were up to their feet in blood, and that a certain house in Cowbridge was, according to Iolo Morganwg, said to have been used by Owain Glyndŵr.[38] A woman from Pembrokeshire told me that Glyndŵr was born there:

> . . . ma nhw'n *dweud* bod e 'di cal i eni yn Sir Benfro . . . mewn lle bach o'r enw Trefgarnowen . . . tua milltir a hanner o Freudeth.[39]
>
> (. . . they *say* that he was born in Pembrokeshire . . . in a little place by the name of Trefgarnowen . . . about a mile and a half from Breudeth.)

Another person, who had moved into the Aberhosan area of Pumlumon, could point to a specific farm said to be associated with Glyndŵr.[40]

Some of the legends told about Glyndŵr are migratory, even in Wales. Such is obviously the case with almost any legend involving a cave. These legends are localized with appropriate details for any given area. Some of the legends have become localized in more than one specific place, but others have become generalized to the point that they may be told anywhere in the country without naming any particular location. The localization of a migratory legend is seen in the transfer from London Bridge to Bala Fair of the story about the herdsman who meets a wise man who shows him the warrior asleep in a cave.

One interesting aspect of localization of legendry is the way in which the legends are placed within contemporary local geography. This process, which seems to result naturally from trying to describe a locale, encourages a more personal interest in the legend by linking it intimately with people's everyday world. One example, already noted several times, is the field in which Glyndŵr set up stick figures, described as the field with the sewage works. One contact who explained that Glyndŵr was standing on Pen y Pigyn when he threw the knife into the churchyard located the site by reference to the television mast, which serves also to indicate that Glyndŵr was on the highest point in the area, where one might expect a hero to perform a special feat. One person located Caer Drewyn in relation to a swimming pool, and another explained the location of one of Glyndŵr's caves with reference to an acquaintance's house.[41]

Another way in which the intimate relationship between

Glyndŵr and the Welsh is maintained is through artifacts, both their preservation and awareness of them. Even people who did not have any would tell me about others who did. For example, in Corwen more than one person told me about Glyndŵr's table at Carrog Uchaf, about the key to the old prison and about pieces of wood from that prison. One person even claimed to have Glyndŵr's hunting-knife.[42]

None of this is to suggest that everybody in an area which is special to Glyndŵr is replete with traditional knowledge or even interest. Awareness of a legend can even exist side by side with great ignorance about Glyndŵr. For example, a man in Corwen told me that Glyndŵr threw a sword from the hill into the churchyard and that the stone left its mark in a stone, but that he had not seen it and did not know whether or not it was true. However, the only other thing he knew about Glyndŵr was that 'he just happened to be a prince around here sometime or other'.[43] So while individuals may not be imbued with extensive knowledge about Glyndŵr, they may still acquire some of the local legendry. Moreover, the feeling of special connection with Glyndŵr may become part of the atmosphere of a community. As one Corwen man explained, after noting that the name Bro Glyndŵr had been adopted for the area of local government and that the local competitive choir called itself Côr Meibion Glyndŵr:

> O ydi ma'r enw ac mae 'na ymdeimlad a rhyw wybodaeth dipyn yn niwlog ynde yn dal yn fyw yma o hyd. A mae o'n dal yn arwr.[44]

> (Oh yes, there's the name and there's the feeling and some pretty hazy knowledge continuing to live here still. And he's still a hero.)

Nor is any of this meant to suggest that people living in areas with less specific links to Glyndŵr or those who could offer no traditional knowledge of him are devoid of all legendry. They are often able to tell narratives concerned with their own local heroes, as did the woman in Llanrwst who told me about the prankster Dafydd ap Siencyn[45] and the couple on the Llŷn peninsula who told me about their local hero, Dic Aberdaron.[46]

One more way in which traditional associations with Glyndŵr are localized is in family lore, whether claiming descent from the man who protected him while he hid in a cave (see Chapter 3) or descent from Glyndŵr himself. John Rhŷs noted a letter from a G.B. Gattie in 1882 in which the writer stated, 'I believe my esteemed grandfather went so far as to trace his descent from the great patriot, Owen Glendower himself!'[47] In January 1995, the *Western Mail* carried a reference to four people who claimed not only descent from Glyndŵr but also to know the family secret of where he was buried.[48]

National Hero

Glyndŵr's role has expanded from that of traditional hero, appearing in various forms of folklore, to that of nationalist hero, appearing in various forms of propaganda. The nationalists have recognized in Glyndŵr a natural symbol of nationalist aspirations. Since the traditions about him already depicted him as the embodiment of national hopes, *y mab darogan* who one day would return, it was logical for the nationalists to begin to use him consciously as a readily available emblem of the struggle to achieve those hopes, as well as a means to teach people about their history and why they should strive for independence. In turning a relatively passive, legendary figure into an active, charged symbol, the nationalists, in effect, have accentuated a role which Glyndŵr was already playing.

In order to understand how Glyndŵr has come to function as a nationalist symbol, one must first know something of Wales's history since Glyndŵr and of the development of the Welsh nationalist movement. The joy of prophecy fulfilled and the hope of a shining future with which the Welsh welcomed Henry VII's ascension to the throne proved unwarranted. Rather than Wales achieving freedom through regaining control, it almost lost itself through absorption into England. Henry VII's London became a new centre of activity for the Welsh, drawing to itself Welshmen with talent and aspirations. Setting a social and cultural pattern which still plagues Wales, England – and particularly London – became the place in which to achieve and measure success. Though potentially harmful to Welsh culture, this was an innocent and natural effect associated with centres of power, but a certain perniciousness (even if the unintentional result of political necessity) entered the relationship between England and

Wales with the Act of Union of 1536. The Acts of 1536 and then of 1542, taking 'union' to mean uniformity, had the purpose not so much of uniting the two nations as of subsuming one within the other. They specifically and openly determined to obliterate all cultural differences in Wales, that is, customs, practices and language, so that the Welsh might more readily become like the English and thus be joined as one people. With laws against offices being given to any but English speakers, the Welsh felt the effects of anglicization not only through the legislature but also in the judiciary and the Church.

In fact, however, in the next couple of centuries, the greatest damage appears to have been done to individual Welsh men and women who, deprived of their own leaders, suffered the hardships of laws and economic forces imposed on them from without, rather than to Welsh culture itself, which could not be driven from the Welsh hearth as easily as the English might have wished. Protestant religion became one of the protective forces helping in the survival of the Welsh language and, despite changes in denomination and sect, remained strongly so into the nineteenth century and even into the twentieth century, although with diminished power. In the sixteenth century, the anglicizing efforts of the Church itself, with its English churchmen who could not even speak the language of their Welsh parishioners, were counteracted by the publication of the Bible and the Prayer Book in Welsh. The decision to give priority to the making of good Christians over the making of good Englishmen gave added strength to the language. Later, Sunday schools purposely taught Welsh and, with the increasing influence and development of Nonconformity from the mid-eighteenth and throughout the nineteenth centuries, a major concern was the establishment of chapels worshipping in Welsh and congregations literate and fluent in the language.

Nevertheless, even those who loved and honoured their language and who used it with joy did not necessarily see any problem with being ruled by an English Crown and Parliament. Since almost everybody within the country still spoke Welsh and the culture apparently continued without any abrupt changes, an individual was unlikely to notice the dangers threatening the Welsh world. Present-day historians write with a mixture of pity and contempt for the generations of Welsh who, whether wilfully or not, failed to see that they were not free, that though they might have rulers in London, they had no guardians there. Even in the eighteenth century, despite deep interest in the American and French Revolutions, no one rose to claim the same rights for Wales. Interest in Welsh culture was relegated to antiquarian concerns. In the nineteenth century, however, the Welsh began to react against laws and actions which took no account of Welsh life and needs. The Nonconformist chapels grew in number and strength. When rural Wales found the toll-roads introduced by the 1835 General Highways Act too burdensome, people responded with the Rebecca Riots, in which bands of men destroyed toll-gates. Industrial Wales was in turmoil as the working class began to form unions and to claim their rights, with many confrontations, of which the 1831 insurrection of Merthyr Tudful is the most noted. In 1865, the Welsh colony of Patagonia (Y Wladfa) in Argentina was founded under the guidance of Michael D. Jones, who came to believe that the only chance for the Welsh to live as a free people in their own land was for them to start anew, that they would never be granted freedom in the land of their ancestors or, if they were, it would be too late, when their culture had already been destroyed.

But while the nineteenth century saw these brave actions of a people reawakening, it also saw acts to make a nation despair. Probably the most serious of these began in 1847 with what has come to be known as 'Brad y Llyfrau Gleision' (the Treason of the Blue Books).[49] This was the Report of the Commission of Inquiry into the State of Education in Wales, in which three monoglot Englishmen, who had obtained their information primarily from Anglican clergy and anglicized Welsh gentry, reported that the people in Wales were suffering under the burden of the Welsh language, that their failure to use English was resulting not only in economic hardship but in immorality as well. This report led to the Education Act of 1870, which declared education compulsory, but with the critical rider that it must be in English. Welsh was not only driven from the schools but also made to appear to be some dirty habit better wiped out of the land. The Education Act and the attitudes it fostered among Welsh speakers are held to be largely responsible for the near death of the language. The percentage of the inhabitants of Wales who could speak Welsh dropped from 90 per cent before the Act to just over 50 per cent by 1891 and to 40 per cent by 1911.

In the second half of the nineteenth century, Welsh nationalism began to grow and leaders began to emerge. For one thing, Wales finally insisted on having its own university. The University College of Wales in Aberystwyth was founded in 1872 and was followed by the University College of South Wales and Monmouthshire in Cardiff in 1883 and the University College of North Wales in Bangor in 1884; the three colleges together became the University of Wales in 1893. But before that, Thomas Gee, the publisher, used his newspaper *Baner ac Amserau Cymru* along with other publications to promulgate his radical and liberal (and effectively nationalist) views. In 1886, the political movement Cymru Fydd (Wales of the future) was formed with the purpose of establishing a national legislature for Wales. Amongst the new activists were Thomas Edward Ellis, David Alfred Thomas and David Lloyd George, all of whom took seats in Parliament; John Viriamu Jones, the first principal of the University College of South Wales in Cardiff and proponent of a system of secondary education; and Owen Morgan Edwards, a historian who worked to improve Welsh education and who, through his journals, restored to the Welsh knowledge of much of their history and literature. These men and others working at the same time were, however, hampered to varying degrees by confusion as to their identity. While they were very conscious of being Welsh, they also accepted that they were British, in the sense of being part of a United Kingdom. This caused them sometimes to compromise their nationalist aspirations and to give priority to British concerns. For some, the needs of the Liberal Party took precedence over Cymru Fydd's nationalist needs. By the twentieth century, there were many people who, although able to accept dual identities by differentiating between British economics, politics and government, and Welsh religion and culture, were never aware of the influence of the former on the latter; however, the activist leaders were clear that their political commitment, like their social and cultural concerns, should be first and foremost to Wales and her well-being. The consequences of a predominantly English-constituted Parliament and other bodies, regarded at times as thoughtlessly ignoring and at others as wilfully disregarding Welsh needs and aspirations, have been seen as threatening the survival of Welsh language and culture, not just the attainment of basic national rights.

Twentieth-century Wales has, however, seen more and more movements working specifically to counteract and reverse those effects. Urdd Gobaith Cymru, an organization for the youth of Wales, was founded in 1922 by Sir Ifan ab Owen Edwards. Plaid Cymru (Welsh Nationalist Party) was established in 1925, and in 1966 Gwynfor Evans became its first Member of Parliament. In Aberystwyth in 1939, the first Welsh-language primary school was established. A period of more direct action began in 1937 when Saunders Lewis, Lewis Valentine and D.J. Williams – a university lecturer, a minister and a schoolmaster – burned down an RAF bombing school and gave themselves up to the police. Twenty-five years later, inspired by Saunders Lewis's 1962 lecture 'Tynged yr Iaith' (Fate of the Language), Cymdeithas yr Iaith Gymraeg (Welsh Language Society) was founded with the aim of gaining wider public use of and official status for the language, using the courts to mobilize the community. Some people chose more violent techniques. The first clandestine violence was a small, symbolic explosion in 1963 at the construction site for a dam in the valley of Tryweryn, whose Welsh community was dispersed and the valley drowned to provide a reservoir for the English city of Liverpool. This action was linked to the self-styled 'Free Wales Army', which again achieved considerable publicity, though having little impact and drawing little public support, near the time of the investiture of the prince of Wales in 1969. A series of more serious explosions at water pipelines and government offices in the same period was eventually traced to one man, John Jenkins, at the time an army sergeant, operating under the name of MAC (Mudiad Amddiffyn Cymru – Movement for the Defence of Wales). Such actions, however, were repudiated by the more established nationalist organizations, including Cymdeithas yr Iaith, who – quoting Gandhi and Martin Luther King – adopted strategies of open non-violent direct action.[50] The successful impact of this sort of approach is seen in the following comments about Cymdeithas yr Iaith:

> . . . quite a few people I know, including one highly respectable lady who wouldn't have anything to do with it to begin with and

now is one of their biggest supporters because they've converted her. I mean this habit of being in prison and singing hymns, I mean seriously singing hymns, and not destroying anything on a Sunday.[51]

As happened in many other countries, the nationalist movement in Wales was given much of its impetus by the Romantic movement in thought and literature. Throughout the centuries Welsh literature has reflected national interests, and not only in the early and medieval poetry, discussed in Chapter 2, with its relatively direct comments on political and other social matters. The literature of the later antiquarians also indicates the degree and direction of nationalist concerns, and then goes further by nourishing nationalist sentiments, as happened in the Romantic movement. Antiquarian studies in Wales began in the sixteenth century, when, inspired by English antiquaries and supported by a sense of national unity under the Tudor reign, Welshmen such as George Owen of Henllys and Rhys ap Meurig began collecting and recording traditional information. In the seventeenth century, Edward Lhuyd, using new standards of scientific observation, through a combination of questionnaires and fieldwork, studied numerous and wide-ranging aspects of Wales and the other Celtic countries. He gave new attention to old manuscripts, collecting and preserving them and, by redis-covering ancient prose and verse, awakened the interest of others in them. Lhuyd's efforts played an essential role in the eighteenth-century rebirth of Welsh scholarship. Foremost in the eighteenth century were the Morris brothers of Anglesey and others of like mind (including Richard, one of the brothers) in London, who in 1751 founded the Society of Cymmrodorion to encourage arts, science and literature in Wales. Their work, and the antiquarian collections which they inspired, preserved many manuscripts along with a great deal of information about Welsh culture. In 1771 another society, the Society of the Gwyneddigion, based in London and devoted to the study of Welsh literature, was formed; it provides the first clear example of the influences of the Romantic movement. As one historian explains:

An interest in all that was strange and remote led to pride in the legendary and historical past of the nation. This was particularly

strong in a group of London Welshmen, for in them it combined
with the attachment of exiles for the land of their birth.[52]

The society formed by these London Welshmen gathered
together as much medieval prose and poetry as it could and
published it in the *Myvyrian Archaiology of Wales* between 1801
and 1807. The editors, Owen Jones and William Owen Pughe,
called on the services of Iolo Morganwg, who, as was his
practice, contributed his own creations along with his genuine
discoveries. Like other Romantics, Iolo was fascinated by the old
customs, ceremonies and beliefs, but he was also driven by fear
that the traditional literature and ways would disappear under
the incoming wave of Methodism.[53] Although his love for his
native Glamorgan was overwhelming and he was always trying
to claim honours for it by crediting it with the greatest of poets
and other heroes, he was also intent on recording the history of
Wales, to which he felt folk culture and the development of that
culture were basic.[54] In his attempts to establish an ancient
literary tradition for Glamorgan, Iolo became interested in the
druids and invented ceremonies for them, which he worked to
're-institute'. Through his efforts, the ritual of the *gorsedd* (bardic
congress) was integrated into the eisteddfod, which had been
reborn in its modern form in 1789.

It was at this point – the end of the eighteenth and beginning of
the nineteenth century – that revived interest in Owain Glyndŵr
began to emerge. The histories compiled in the previous
centuries had taken note of him but had mostly depended on
earlier works, not only for detail but also for attitude, which
means that Welsh historians often echoed English views. At the
end of the eighteenth century, Thomas Pennant wrote his history
of Glyndŵr, making use of all the previous histories but re-
evaluating them. Then Iolo Morganwg included tales of Owain
Glyndŵr in his collections. As was discussed in previous
chapters, we cannot be certain to what extent these tales record
genuine tradition rather than Iolo's creativity, but they begin to
show Glyndŵr as a Welsh hero.

Nevertheless, though dusted off and brought to the fore along
with a few other figures from Wales's past, Glyndŵr is not yet a
nationalist symbol or a call to freedom. In this period before
nationalist interest, Glyndŵr is recognized as important but,

because he represents behaviour and attitudes inimical to the current state, some way must be found to come to terms with his existence. We can see the ambivalent attitude towards him in the antiquarian publications appearing in the early nineteenth century. For example, in *The Cambro-Briton* (vol. 3), published in the 1820s, the tone for a biography of Glyndŵr is set by the verses which head the article:

> And he was once the glory of his age,
> Disinterested, just, with every virtue
> Of civil life adorned – in arms excelling:
> His only blot was this, that, much provoked,
> He raised his vengeful arm against his sovereign.[55]

The article, which mainly gives a basic history of Glyndŵr's wars, also comments on Glyndŵr's character, describing what a good and admirable man he was. Moreover, in a burst of consciousness of national self-worth, he is described as embodying all that is best of the Welsh character:

> The most prominent features in the character of Owain Glyndwr were boldness and activity, ambition, bravery, and no small portion of military skill. Hospitable to profuseness the patron and liberal encourager of bards, – eager and faithful in his friendship – unforgiving and revengeful in his enmities – patriotic, enthusiastic, and irascible – in him were combined all the characteristics of the warm-hearted Cambro-Briton; and his gallant spirit, undaunted and unsubdued to the last, achieved those exploits, which are familiar at this day to the mountain peasant of Merionethshire.[56]

However, the article also views Glyndŵr's military actions as improper and illegal; no matter how provoked, he should not have risen against his king. The concluding paragraph expresses all the ambivalence of one who considers the present state right and proper but who, while content that no traces of revolution remain, recognizes that Glyndŵr was a true Welsh hero.

> . . . although, in this enlightened age, we cannot but regard with detestation the cruelties he often committed on those who fell into his hands, yet we must admire his heroism, and admit that his incitement to arms, in the first instance, was a just and powerful extenuation of the illegality of his conduct. But it is of little

importance now, whether he was justified or not in the course he pursued. Years have rolled on, and repaired the ravages which he committed; – the bones of his brave warriors have mouldered into dust, – and no traces of his valiant exploits remain, save such as tradition will supply in the minds of his admiring countrymen.[57]

We see the same attitudes expressed in a lengthy (286-line) poem, entitled 'Owain Glyndwr: An Historical Poem' and printed in the *Transactions of the Cymmrodorion* in 1826. The poem, following previous histories, gives a detailed account of Glyndŵr's conflict with Lord Grey, a summary account of the subsequent battles, a brief note of the parliament at Machynlleth and the encounters with Dafydd Gam and Howel Sele, concluding with the battle at Shrewsbury. After commenting on the setting of Glyndŵr's sun, the poem ends:

> Byth gwedi er lloni'r llys
> Un Brenin biau'r Ynys.
> Tano'n awr a'i rwysgfawr rym
> Dedwydd yn ein gwlad ydym.[58]

(Ever after, for joy of the court, one King holds the Island. Under him now and his majestic strength, happy/content are we in our land.)

Nevertheless, as nationalist sentiment grew, the attitude towards Glyndŵr changed. No longer did the Welsh scholars feel the need to be apologists for him, explaining how despite all the awful things he did, he really was a good man. Part of the change of attitude reveals itself in the shift of emphasis in interpreting Glyndŵr's uprising. At the beginning of the nineteenth century, the emphasis was on the conflict over land claimed by Lord Grey; at the end of the century, the emphasis was on revolt against unjust treatment and the struggle for freedom. In an early debate about Glyndŵr's motivation, an article in an 1829 journal demonstrates both the difficulty and importance of changing the frame of reference. The author, whose attitude is made clear by an opening declaration of the importance to those who love their country and nation of remembering Glyndŵr's efforts to free his country from the yoke of slavery, concludes by responding to those who claim that Glyndŵr engaged in battle merely for personal revenge rather than for the sake of national honour and freedom. He does not rebut the argument; he simply suggests that one motivation can grow out of the other.[59] Half a century later, the debate over motivation was clearly resolved. For example, in an 1882 article on Glyndŵr, the author comments on the tendency of English authors to attribute every type of cruelty to the Welsh in their wars by pointing out that considering the laws of the time, it is no wonder that the people were full of revenge. He then goes on to list all the laws treating the Welsh as inferiors and non-citizens and denying them basic rights, and concludes with the simple statement, 'Dyna y gyfraith pan oedd Owain yn ymdrechu rhyddhau ei wlad o afaelion yr estron'[60] (That was the law when Owain tried to free his country from the foreigner's grasp).

The nationalists were quite conscious of their role in rehabilitating Glyndŵr's image. They saw the need to re-educate the Welsh, not just to teach them about their past, but also to show them the fallacies of English-inculcated views. This shows clearly in the introduction to an article on Glyndŵr published in *Y Llenor*, one of the journals under the editorship of Owen M. Edwards. The writer begins the article by discussing how heroes become obscured by half-truths presented by differing factions, and points to Glyndŵr as one who is rising from that obscurity. He notes that the people who were then (1897) middle-aged had been taught that Glyndŵr was a half-barbarous revolutionary fighting against king and law but, he goes on to assert, they will live to see the tarnish removed from his glory and him recognized 'fel un o'r gwladweinwyr goreu fu'n ceisio codi a gwella'r ynysoedd hyn'[61] (as one of the best statesmen who tried to raise and improve these islands). He then notes that even the English writers are being forced to admit, though with some surprise, what a great man Glyndŵr was. This same article also shows clearly how in this period Glyndŵr begins to shine forth not just as a national hero, but more importantly as a representative of nationalism. At one point in recording Glyndŵr's history, the author notes, 'Ac yr oedd y werin ymhob man, yng Ngwent fel yng Ngwynedd, ar y gororau fel ar y mynyddoedd, yn edrych arno fel y gŵr a'u gwaredai o'u caethiwed'[62] (The people in every part, in Gwent as in Gwynedd, on the borders as on the mountains, were looking to him as the man who would save them from their enslavement). The author's summation of Glyndŵr's history in four words is even more expressive: 'amdiffynnydd gwerin, ymgorfforiad cenedl-garwch'[63] (defender of the people, embodiment of patriotism). Although O.M. Edwards, Owen Rhoscomyl and others are no longer being apologists for Glyndŵr, they are still responding to English views of him. Their re-evaluations of his character and of history tend to address points, or rather criticisms, made by the English.

The same views are expressed again and again in this period. A paper presented to the Society of Cymmrodorion by Owen Rhoscomyl criticizes the historians who repeat the same material over and over:

> with pages of mild disquisitions, born of the holy horror of the holy orders at Owen's deplorable habit of breaking eggs merely because he had an omelette to make; and also with timid deprecations of distress that Owen should have so far forgotten the elegancies as to use fire and sword in making war. Such rehashes of Pennant are scattered from one end to the other of Welsh-English literature; all elegant, deprecating, apologistic, and unspeakable![64]

Rhoscomyl goes on to re-examine history and shows that the disastrous battle at Shrewsbury was not in any way the fault of Glyndŵr, who was working according to the agreed plan, but was rather the fault of Hotspur, who changed the plans and tried to claim victory on his own. Furthermore, we see in this paper not only that Glyndŵr is becoming identified with nationalism, but also that he is recognized as becoming so identified.

> The air being now so full of the dash and movement of the 're-awakening of Wales,' the writing of this paper is only one of the things to be expected. For amongst the many names and catchwords which in a sort are shibboleth of the present unrest, that of Owen ab Gruffydd, lord of Glyndwrdy and Coron'd Prince of Wales, is one of the most frequent and potent.[65]

The turn of the century was a period of great education for Wales in a way that had nothing to do with, and in fact was in opposition to, the Education Act of 1870. Welsh scholars were re-examining every aspect of their history and culture, but were not merely studying it; they were disseminating it through every means possible. John Edward Lloyd, historian and supporter of Cymru Fydd, wrote an important history of Wales up to the Edwardian conquest,[66] providing both a much-needed, well-researched, scholarly examination of Welsh history and a new way for the Welsh to regard their past. John Rhŷs, philologist, principal of Jesus College and professor of Celtic at Oxford, undertook a scholarly examination of Welsh folklore.[67] Perhaps the most important of the educational media used by the nationalists were the periodicals. *Y Geninen* (The Leek), which was founded in 1881 by John Thomas as a literary journal with a Nonconformist outlook, declares its nationalist sentiments in its motto 'Fy iaith, fy ngwlad, fy nghenedl' (My language, my land, my nation) and in the words enscrolled on its seal, 'Y ddraig coch a ddyry cychwyn' (The red dragon will give a beginning). *Y Llenor Cymreig* (The Welsh Litterateur), founded in 1882 by John Goronwy Mathias, carries the slogan, 'Goreu Arf – Arf Dysg' (The best weapon – the weapon of learning). Owen M. Edwards was particularly active in publishing; he founded a series of periodicals serving various parts of the community, but all with the purpose of promulgating cultural information through a popular and easily accepted form. Again, the information on the title-pages alone indicates the purpose of these periodicals. *Cymru* (Wales), founded in 1891, describes itself as, 'Cylchgrawn misol i ymdrin â hanes, llenyddiaeth, cân, celf, ac addysg Cymru' (A monthly periodical to treat history, literature, song, art, and education of Wales), and bears the motto, 'I godi'r hen wlad yn ei hôl' (To raise the old land again). *Cymru'r Plant* (Wales of the Children), founded a year later, bears the same motto. The material in this journal, obviously aimed at children, includes, along with items of natural history, songs and literature, short accounts of historical figures and interesting descriptions of places, such as Glyndŵr's prison-house and the cave in which he is said to have been provisioned by Ednyfed ab Aron.[68] *Wales*, founded in 1894, was 'A national magazine for the English speaking parts of Wales'. *Y Llenor* (The Litterateur), founded in 1895, took a more academic approach than did the earlier journals. A fifth journal, *Heddyw* (Today), was founded in 1897. All of these journals served to arouse national awareness and raise nationalist sensibility.

In these periodicals, the importance given to Glyndŵr is demonstrated not only by the articles about him but also because he is the subject of much poetry. For example, *Cymru* published at least five poems to Glyndŵr just between the years 1892 and 1898. Many of the poems printed in the journals are simply historical accounts in verse, sometimes covering Glyndŵr's whole life and sometimes selected incidents as, for example, in one lengthy account of 'Ceubren yr Ellyll', the story of Glyndŵr killing his cousin Hywel Sele.[69] Nor are such poems confined to the turn of the century. A 1974 edition of the weekly paper *Y Cymro*, for example, carried a poem about the battle at Hyddgen.[70] The same nationalist sentiment that is present in the articles runs through these poems, as can be demonstrated with even just a few examples. One poem on Glyndŵr's death, printed next to a short article on his life and under a picture of his parliament house in Machynlleth, contains the following lines:

> Pan suddodd haul Llywelyn
>   Dan gymyl duon Brad,
> Daeth gwawr i wenu wedyn,—
>   Glyn Dŵr yn blaid i'n gwlad;
> Gwladgarwch sydd yn galw
>   Dros frig canrifau pell,
> Gan herio Cymru heddyw
>   I ddangos Cymro gwell.[71]

(When Llywelyn's sun set under black clouds of treachery, a dawn came to smile afterwards,—Glyn Dŵr to the support of our land; it is patriotism which is calling over the top of distant centuries, challenging/daring Wales today to show a better Welshman.)

The poem goes on to explain that despite the loss of Glyndŵr,

> Cawn ganu mewn llawenydd
>   Wrth gofio hyn bob gŵr,—
> Fod gobaith Cymru Newydd
>   Yn fyw ar fedd Glyn Dŵr.[72]

(We shall sing in joyousness at each man's remembering this—that the hope of a New Wales lives on Glyn Dwr's grave.)

The *awdl* which won the chair at the Llangollen Eisteddfod of 1895 gives an interpretive history of Glyndŵr's wars and then ends with the verse,

> Bu Cymru'n dysgu o dan—ei faner,
>   Drwy fynych gyflafan
> Fyw yn rhydd, fynnu ei rhan,—yn unol
>   Wlad anibynnol. Adnabu'i hunan.[73]

(Wales learned under his banner, through frequent battles, to live in freedom, to demand its share,—a united, independent land. She knew herself.)

Glyndŵr is the subject of these verses, but he is also serving as the means for expressing the ideals and hopes of the political movement Cymru Fydd. Another poem, which has sections labelled with such titles as 'Ei febyd a'i freuddwyd' (His youth and his dream) and 'Ei wladgarwch' (His patriotism), ends the last section, 'Ei neges i ni' (His message for us), with this little anthem:

> 'I fyny', fy ngwlad, fo'th arwyddair,
> I fyny mewn urddas ac undeb,
> I fyny mewn bywyd di-anair,
> I fyny mewn cenedlaetholdeb,
> I fyny mewn meddwl a moesau,
> I fyny mewn crefydd ac awen,
> I fyny, wlad anwyl fy nhadau,
> I fyny gan gofio dy Owen.[74]

('Up', my land, may your motto be, Up in dignity and unity, Up in an irreproachable life, Up in nationalism, Up in thought and morals, Up in religion and muse [i.e., culture], Up, dear land of my fathers, Up, remembering your Owen.)

The distinguished position accorded Glyndŵr shows clearly in a 1920 article in which the historian J.E. Lloyd quotes a verse by Mynyddog, one of the most popular nineteenth-century poets:

> Glyndwr annwyl! mae dy enw
> Fel y byw oleuni pur;
> Nid oes berygl iddo farw
> Tra bo Cymro yn y tir.

(Beloved Glyndŵr! your name is like the pure, living light; There's
no danger of it dying while a Welshman be in the land.)

and then declares, 'Every line of Mynyddog's song finds a ready
response from a popular audience, for whom Glyn Dŵr is the
immortal embodiment of the spirit of the Welsh nation.'[75]

In addition to the periodicals, there were, of course, a number
of monographs trying to accomplish the same purpose. One such
work, *Flame-Bearers of Welsh History*, written for children by
Owen Rhoscomyl, shows the further development of Glyndŵr as
a hero of the people. The section on Glyndŵr begins with the
statement:

> No other of all our heroes ever seated himself so firmly in the
> hearts of our race as this Owen. And if it be asked why, the answer
> is, that it was because he was the champion of poor folk, of folk that
> live ever too near to misery, of the man who must earn house and
> fire, bread and clothing, for his wife and his children by the labour
> of his hands. Working folk live close enough to sorrow. When they
> find a prince who fights for them, toils for them, plans for them,
> and dreams for them, then they are not likely soon to forget.[76]

It ends with the statement:

> But other and learned men have vexed themselves looking for his
> real grave. They say they cannot be sure where it is. But that is
> because their eyes have wandered from the right way – looking to
> Kentchurch or to Monnington, in the green shire of Hereford,
> where his loving daughters lived.
>   They are all wrong. His grave is known – well known. It is beside
> no church, neither under the shadow of any ancient yew. It is in a
> spot safer and more sacred still . . . Time shall not touch it; decay
> shall not dishonour it; for that grave is in the heart of every true
> Cymro. There, for ever, from generation unto generation, grey
> Owen's heart lies dreaming on, dreaming on, safe for ever and for
> ever.[77]

The historical romance, whether in serialized or monograph
form, also provided a forum for disseminating both historical
information and nationalist inspiration. In his study of the
historical romance, E.G. Millward reports that in a genre notable
for its emphasis on heroes, Owain Glyndŵr was a favourite

subject.[78] He appeared sometimes as the main character, as in the serializations 'Owain Glyndwr' and 'Bronwen', which were published in the radical, working-class newspaper *Tarian y Gweithiwr* (The Worker's Shield) in 1877–8 and 1880–1 respectively. At other times, he simply played a significant role in the protagonist's life, as in 'Madog Llwyd', serialized in *Y Gwladgarwr* (The Patriot) in 1868–9, in which the title character is one of Glyndŵr's ardent supporters; or as in *Owain Tudur*, published first in 1874 after winning the Porthaethwy Eisteddfod of 1873 and then in 1913 being serialized in *Cymru*. Owain Tudur's story begins in December 1414 with Glyndŵr appearing as an old, essentially-defeated man who disappears from the narrative (into a cave) after only fifty-five pages. Nevertheless, he is an important contact for the title character, who was to become the grandfather of the next redeemer, Henry Tudor. The narratives make use of the traditions concerning Glyndŵr, as for example in *Owain Tudur* where Glyndŵr's going about in disguise and living in caves play an important part. Given their attention to traditional details and given that they were written in a time when other genres were emphasizing Glyndŵr's continuing life, whether in body or spirit, it is curious that both 'Owain Glyndwr' and *Owain Tudur* report Glyndŵr's death.[79] The clear statement of his death may have been part of the need, described by Millward, for authors to keep their patriotism and anti-English sentiments within safe bounds, as something appropriate for the past but of no danger in nineteenth-century Britain. However, these historical romances did provide their history lessons. The importance of that aspect of the narrative is underlined in a note placed by O.M. Edwards in the Table of Contents of *Cymru* under the entry for the serialization of *Owen Tudur*:

> Rhamant hanesyddol y Parch. W. Prichard [*sic*] yw hon, nid hanes. Eto nid yw'n gwneud cam a hanes. Gweir iddi hanes Owen Glyndwr, Iolo Goch, ac Owen Tudur; ac nid oes dim yn ei phenodau raid anghofio wrth ddarllen hanes y cyfnod.[80]

> (This is the Revd W. Pritchard's historical romance, not a history. Yet it does not do an injustice to history. It weaves into it the history of Owain Glyndŵr, Iolo Goch and Owen Tudur; and there is nothing in its chapters that need be forgotten in reading history of the period.)

For a time, these historical romances and other popular works such as the Englishman Arthur Granville Bradley's *Owen Glyndwr and the Last Struggle for Welsh Independence* (1901) – and similarly, though much later, John Cowper Powys's *Owen Glendower* (1940) – were major sources of information on Glyndŵr. Though safely set in the distant past, the historical romances did present a nationalist message. Take, for example, the opening and concluding passages of one of Glyndŵr's speeches to his troops:

> Gwyddoch fod ein gwlad wedi mynd yn sathrfa – estroniaid wedi ei meddianu bob cwys, a ninau wedi myned yn gaethion bob copa. A ydym i barhau fel hyn yn dragwydd? . . . Safwch yn wrol, a mynwch rhyddhau eich gwlad. Gadewch i ni eu gyru yn ol dros y clawdd, a dileu olion eu traed oddiar wyneb y tir.[81]

> (You know our country has become a trampling place – foreigners have occupied every furrow, and we have become slaves of every summit. Are we to continue this way forever? . . . Stand bravely and insist on freeing your country. Let us drive them back across the ditch, and erase the tracks of their feet from the face of the land.)

In 1931, J.E. Lloyd, an established academic historian, published a history of Glyndŵr, which was both sympathetic and well-balanced, and he closed it with the line, 'He may with propriety be called the father of modern Welsh nationalism.'[82] This statement was taken up and repeated by numerous nationalists, who both took a lesson from it and used it to teach others. Thus Glyndŵr's name is invoked by politicians, by protest singers and by other activists.

The invocation may take a variety of forms, some more obvious than others. It may be as indirect as Gwynfor Evans including in his book *Rhagom i Ryddid* a photograph, not immediately connected with the text, of a statue of Owain Glyndŵr. Furthermore, under the photograph he prints a line taken from a Glyndŵr's Day lecture: 'Goleuir y meddwl Cymreig o hyd gan luchedyn y weledigaeth o bobl a fu'n rhydd'[83] (The Welsh mind is still lighted by the lightening vision of a people that was free). Perhaps the simplest, most straightforward invocation appears in the name of a group calling themselves Meibion Glyndŵr (Sons of Glyndŵr). This group is most noted for its campaign, begun in 1979, of burning English-owned holiday-homes in Wales, with the purpose of driving out the English – or even England – who destroy pocket after pocket of Welsh culture by necessitating the use of English, by driving up property values so that the local people can no longer afford them and by turning the economy into one viable only in the summer. The impression is that Meibion Glyndŵr, in burning intrusive English homes, are simply following their hero's example in both this particular act and in the more general fight to free Wales. They echo Glyndŵr's guerilla tactics with their own – moving easily in and out of the community, unidentified and striking unexpectedly. The group further heightens its connection with Glyndŵr by signing its letters to the public and to the authorities with the name of his officer, Rhys Gethin. Meibion Glyndŵr's political threat, which appears to be far greater than their practical one despite their having burned more than 200 homes, is underlined by various police and social authorities trying to undermine their image by labelling them as 'sick' and 'fanatics' and by attempting to link them to the Irish Republican Army and the fascist National Front, allegations which have not stuck.[84] Glyndŵr's name lends the group a symbolic authority, which makes it easy for some to believe that the only people so far tried for Meibion Glyndŵr activities, in 1993, were framed and that the real Meibion, just like their namesake, have continued to escape.

Other political action groups have also invoked Glyndŵr fairly directly. In 1911, Cynghrair Cenedlaethol Cymreig (The Welsh Nationalist League), as part of its campaign for a Welsh nationalist party, issued a booklet entitled *Yspryd Glyndŵr: neu y clêdd lle metho hêdd* (The Spirit of Glyndŵr: or the sword where peace fails).[85] More recently, Cymdeithas Cyfamod y Cymry Rhydd (Society of the Covenant of the Free Welsh) which was founded in 1987 and demands independence by 2000 for a Welsh-speaking, totally Welsh Wales, has claimed Glyndŵr as their authority by purportedly quoting him in a scroll on their pamphlets and fliers:

> Rydym yn eich hysbysu ein bod gyda chymorth Duw a chwithau, yn gobeithio y gallwn ryddhau pobl Cymru o gaethiwed ein gelynion Seisnig, sydd am hir amser a aeth heibio, wedi ein gorthrymu ni a'n cyndeidiau.[86]

(We inform you that with God's help and yours, we hope to be able to free the people of Wales from the captivity of our English enemies, who for a long time past, have oppressed us and our ancestors.)

Glyndŵr has also been invoked in a call to arms on the world stage. In a November 1914 editorial in which he praised Britain (which he saw as an almost perfect combination of unity and freedom) for being the defender of small nations and called on the small nations to stand up for each other, O.M. Edwards concluded with the following call to action:

> Rhyfedda ambell un, ond odid, fod Cymru heddychlon yn troi'n filwriaethus. Mewn heddwch y gobeithiem fedru dathlu pum canmlwyddiant Owen Glyndwr. Ond am ymdrech debyg i'w ymdrech ef, ac un anrhaethol ehangach y dywedir heddyw,–
>
> 'Mae Owen Glyndwr a'i fyddinoedd
> I'r frwydr yn ymbaratoi.'[87]

(One or two wonder, probably, that peaceful Wales is turning militant. We had hoped to celebrate Owain Glyndŵr's five-hundred-year anniversary in peace. But of a struggle like his struggle, and one infinitely broader, it is said today, – 'Owain Glyndŵr and his armies/are preparing themselves for battle.')

Sometimes Glyndŵr is invoked by comparison with current activists, who are presented as his direct, worthy heirs. Gwynfor Evans writes of the 'young nationalist leaders of this decade [1970s] who have shown a heroic commitment not seen in Wales since the days of Owain Glyndwr'.[88] 'Not since . . . ' almost becomes a formula in political exhortations. In comparisons of the present with the past, the attitude that 'if he could do it, we can too' often appears. This approach can be seen, for example, in another passage by Gwynfor Evans:

> In the year 1400, when Owain Glyndwr rose, Wales was under the control of the English and their Welsh collaborators. They were the all-powerful establishment throughout the land. Yet Owain built a powerful movement, and established a Welsh state which would have taken Wales into Europe centuries ago had its success being [sic] longer-lived. Behind him he united, as we are trying to do, all

sections of Welsh life; and he evoked a heroism which still awakens a response in Wales. Our task is no harder than his.[89]

Running throughout the political declarations is the theme that present-day activists are simply carrying on Glyndŵr's work. A 1964 letter to the police from the Free Wales Army explaining their actions, includes the statement, 'Glyndwr had from an early period of his insurrection the aim of independence for his country; dream though it might be, we also have this in mind.'[90] Since the work must be carried on, evocation of Glyndŵr becomes an exhortation to action. This technique of holding him up as a moral model is demonstrated in the following passage, taken from a speech promoting the work of Cymdeithas yr Iaith Gymreig:

> Cychwyn chwyldro a wnaeth Glyn Dŵr, ac fe wnaeth hynny am ei fod e'n gwybod mai dim ond chwyldro a allai achub ei genedl. Mae'r rhai ohonon ni nad ydym yn estrysiaid â'n pennau yn nhywod Prydeindod, yn gwybod mai dim ond chwyldro a all achub yr iaith.[91]

> (Glyndŵr started a revolution, and he did that because he knew that nothing but a revolution could save his nation. Those of us who aren't ostriches with our heads in the sand of Britishness know that nothing but a revolution can save the language.)

Nevertheless, Glyndŵr is invoked not just as a reminder of what work must be done; since he is a redeemer-hero, he himself may return. His return, even if only in spirit, is a hope for the future. At a rally held in 1969 at Cilmeri, the site of Llywelyn's death, Emyr Llewelyn stressed in his speech the theme embodied in the words of a *cywydd*, 'Myn Duw, mi a wn y daw' (By God, I know he will come). The *cywydd*, variously ascribed to the antiquary Meredith Lloyd (1620–95) and with greater likelihood to the poet Gruffudd Llwyd ap Dafydd (*c*.1380–*c*.1420), promises that Owain will come when hope is at its lowest (i.e., the need is greatest). In his speech, Emyr Llewelyn insisted that, despite doubts, Glyndŵr would return, but that it was up to people now to make it possible. Courage and effort were required to make the dream come true.[92] This idea that Glyndŵr's return is dependent on the people's efforts is consonant with the traditional views about his return which were discussed in Chapter 3. Glyndŵr as a redeemer-hero is not a magic solution to be imposed from outside; the people must be ready for him. Also at the Cilmeri rally, Dafydd Iwan, a singer and protest-song writer in the nationalist cause, introduced a song inspired by the same *cywydd*'s theme of Glyndŵr's return:

Mae gwaed y rhai fu'n brwydro
Ac a lifodd ar y gwellt
Ers talwm wedi'i olchi gan y glaw;
Ni chlywaf gan y daran,
Ni welaf gan y mellt,
Nid oes ond cri anobaith ar bob llaw.
Ymhle mae Owain yn awr?
Ymhle mae Owain yn awr?

Mae Owain, gyda'i filwyr,
Wedi cilio draw o'n gwlad,
Ac nid oes mwy ond atgof ar ei ôl.
Nid oes ond oer gelannedd
Lle gynt bu maes y gad,
Ac nid yw rhyddid mwy ond breuddwyd ffôl.

Owain, ni ddaw yn ôl.
Owain, ni ddaw yn ôl.
Daw llanw wedi'r trai,
Daw enfys wedi'r glaw,
Ac wedi'r nos mi wn y wawr a ddaw.
O! mi wn y daw Owain yn ôl –
O! mi wn y daw Owain yn ôl,
Fel llanw wedi'r trai,
Fel enfys wedi'r glaw,
Fel gwawrio wedi'r nos,
Myn Duw, mi a wn y daw,
Myn Duw, mi a wn y daw.

Nid yn ofer y bu'r brwydro,
Nid yn ofer tywallt gwaed,
Mae eto fuddugoliaeth yn y gwynt.
Mi glywaf leisiau'r milwyr,
Mi glywaf sŵn eu traed
Yn cerdded o Eryri ar eu hynt.
Rhowch heibio bob anobaith,
A'r holl amheuon lu,

Mae Owain eto'n barod am y dydd.
O'i loches yn Eryri,
Fe ddaw â'i ffyddlon lu,
I'n harwain gyda'r wawr i Gymru rydd.
Fel llanw wedi trai,
Fel enfys wedi'r glaw,
Fel gwawrio wedi'r nos,
Myn Duw, mi a wn y daw,
Myn Duw, mi a wn y daw.

Ymrestrwn yn ei rengoedd,
A'r iaith Gymraeg yn arf;
Dioddefwn warth caethiwed awr yn hwy.
Gorseddwn iaith ein tadau,
Dilewn olion brad,
Dangoswn nad taeogion monom mwy!

Rhown heibio bob anobaith
A'r holl amheuon lu,
Mae Owain eto'n barod am y dydd.
O'i loches yn Eryri,
Fe ddaw â'i ffyddlon lu
I'n harwain gyda'r wawr i Gymru rydd.
Myn Duw, mi a wn y daw.
Myn Duw, mi a wn y daw.
Myn Duw, mi a wn y daw.[93]

(The blood of those who were fighting and which poured on the grass has for a long time been washed by the rain; I do not hear because of the thunder; I do not see because of the lightning; there is nothing but the cry of despair on every hand. / Where is Owain now? (×2)//Owain with his soldiers, has retreated from our land, and there is nothing more but memory of him. There is nothing but cold corpses where formerly was the field of battle, and freedom is nothing more than a foolish dream. //Owain will not come back. (×2)/ High tide comes after ebb, a rainbow comes after the rain, and after the night I know the dawn will come. / Oh! I know Owain will come back. (×2)/ Like high tide after ebb, like a rainbow after the rain, like dawn after the night, / By God, I know he will come. (×2)//Not in vain was the fighting, not in vain the pouring of blood, victory is again in the wind. I hear the voices of warriors, I hear the sound of their feet, walking from Snowdonia on their way. Put aside every despair and the whole host of doubts, Owain is again ready for the day. From his refuge in Snowdonia, he will come with his faithful host to lead us with the dawn to a free Wales. Like high tide after ebb, like a rainbow after the rain, like dawn after the night, /By God, I know he will come. (×2)// Let us enlist in their ranks, with the Welsh language as a weapon; let us not suffer the shame of slavery an hour longer. Let us enthrone the language of our fathers, let us erase the traces of treachery, let us show we are not serfs any more! // Let us put aside every despair and the whole host of doubts, Owain is again ready for the day. From his refuge in Snowdonia, he will come with his faithful host to lead us with the dawn to a free Wales. /By God, I know he will come. (×3))

We see here historical continuity not just in the hope for a redeemer but also in the poetic expression of that hope. Dafydd Iwan's verses pick up and present anew the declaration of hope which concludes the *cywydd brud* – 'Myn Duw, mi a wn y daw.' (This line has, furthermore, become a catchphrase, independent of the *cywydd* which originally contained it.) Dafydd Iwan's verses echo, moreover, the refrain (and title) of Siôn Cent's *cywydd* 'Gobeithiaw a ddaw yddwyf' (My hope lies in what is to come), which was discussed in Chapter 2.

Not only does Glyndŵr serve as a rallying cry; the celebration of him serves as a rallying point. Some political activist groups treat Glyndŵr's Day (Dydd Gŵyl Owain Glyndŵr), 16 September, as a national holiday, a time for flag-waving and speech-making. There are both local celebrations and a national one, held in Glyndŵr's home area, Corwen, though neither of these can be said to be folk, or even popular, celebrations. They are engineered by the group Cofiwn, in their attempt to awaken Welsh historical awareness. A similar linking of Glyndŵr with historical awareness appears in *Cof Cenedl* (Memory of a Nation), an annual volume of essays on Welsh history by established scholars, which has the express purpose of deepening and strengthening the consciousness of the Welsh-speaking Welsh about their lineage and inheritance; since the second volume in 1987, the editor has dated the foreword, Gŵyl Owain Glyndŵr.[94]

Because of what is known of his wars and because of associated traditions, Glyndŵr is a natural symbol of nationalist aspirations, but that does not mean that the public figures who employ him thus are not fully conscious of what they are doing. Indeed, as in the case of Dafydd Iwan, they may think of him more as a useful symbol than as an actual hero. This point came out when I asked Dafydd Iwan who, apart from Glyndŵr, were Wales's heroes, and he responded:

Wel, dw i ddim yn gwbod faswn i'n galw Owain Glyndŵr yn arwr oherwydd mae o tu allan ch' gwbod; mae o'n fwy o symbol nag yn arwr yndê.[95]

(Well, I don't know that I'd call Owain Glyndŵr a hero because he's outside you know; he's more of a symbol than a hero, isn't he.)

He then went on to explain what he meant by a hero:

Faswn i'n deud mai arwyr ydi pobol dw i'n nabod yndê . . . Pobol dw i 'di cyfarfod. Ne faswn i ddim yn galw ffigur mewn hanes fel 'na yn arwr. Sut dw i'n edrych ar bethe ydi hwnna, yn arwyr i mi ydi pobol dw i wedi gyfarfod ac sydd wedi'n ysbrydoli fi fel cenedlaetholwr, pobol oedd yn credu beth bynnag oedd yr 'odds' yn byw y peth i'r pen draw, fel D.J. Williams a Waldo Williams a Gwynfor Evans.[96]

(I'd say that heroes are people I know . . . People I've met. I wouldn't call a character in history like that a hero. How I look on these things is this, heroes to me are people I've met and who have inspired me as a nationalist, people who believed whatever were the odds in living the thing to the end, like D.J. Williams and Waldo Williams and Gwynfor Evans.)

Dafydd Iwan also explained how he saw Glyndŵr as a symbol:

. . . roedd Owain Glyndŵr yn symbol o'r frwydr genedlaethol ac yn fwy felly na Llywelyn, yndê . . . Mae Glyndŵr yn symbol o arweinydd, wel yr arweinydd dwetha ddaru ymladd gyda byddin dros Gymru. Faswn i'n deud fod o'n fwy tebyg i arwr na Llywelyn. Mae Llywelyn yn rhy bell, neu dw i'n meddwl yn yr ystyr yna fod Glyndŵr yn fwy potent fel symbol o arweinydd cenedlaethol yn ymladd er ein bod ni nawr wrth gwrs yn pwysleisio mwy ar Llywelyn gan bod hi'n saith gan mlwyddiant, yndê. O na, mae Glyndŵr yn wastad wedi bod yn symbol o'r frwydr genedlaethol ac yn naturiol felly yn ymddangos mewn caneuon yndê.[97]

(. . . Owain Glyndŵr was a symbol of the national battle and more so than Llywelyn . . . Glyndŵr is a symbol of a leader, well, the last leader who fought with an army on behalf of Wales. I'd say that he was more like a hero than Llywelyn. Llywelyn is too far away, or I think in that sense that Glyndŵr is more potent as a symbol of a national leader fighting, although we now, of course, are emphasizing Llywelyn more since it's the seven hundredth anniversary [of his death]. Oh no, Glyndŵr has always been a symbol of the national battle and so, naturally, he appears in songs.)

Gwynfor Evans, too, considers Glyndŵr a better symbol than is Llywelyn. When I asked him whether, when he used Glyndŵr and Llywelyn in speeches, they both had the same significance and were the same type of symbol, he explained:

> O ydyn, ydyn, yr un fath, ond Glyndŵr yw'r un cryfaf dw i'n credu . . . Mae'n gliriach. Achos etifeddodd e ddim [grym yn y wlad]. Doedd ganddo ddim byd ond ei ystad ei hun. Wel mae'n wir am Llywelyn ein Llyw Olaf. Roedd yn rhaid iddo ef frwydro wrth gwrs i gael Gwynedd, hyd yn oed, dan 'i reolaeth, ond roedd ganddo safle fel un o'r teulu o'dd wedi bod yn rheoli yng Gwynedd trwy'r canrifoedd ond ro'dd Glyndŵr yn dechre 'from scratch' heb ddim byd fel 'na, wrth 'i gefn e, ac ro'dd e wedi diffinio 'i weledigaeth yn llawnach nag y gwnaeth Llywelyn . . . Fel mae e'n fwy cyflawn ac mae'n nes atom ni mewn amser hefyd. Mae hynny yn ffactor – yn y bymthegfed ganrif.[98]

> (Oh yes, yes, the same type, but Glyndŵr is the stronger one, I believe . . . He's clearer. Because he inherited no power in the land. He didn't have anything but his own estate. Well, that's true about Llywelyn our Last Leader. It was necessary for him to fight, of course, to get Gwynedd, even, under his rule, but he had standing as one of the family that had been ruling in Wales through the centuries, but Glyndŵr was starting from scratch without anything like that, at his back, and he had defined his vision more fully than did Llywelyn . . . Thus he's more complete and he's closer to us in time also. That's a factor – in the fifteenth century.)

Just as they are very conscious of their use of Glyndŵr as a symbol, these leaders are also very aware of the need for the people to have the necessary background information to be able to appreciate the symbol. They must be properly educated. When I asked Gwynfor Evans how effective he thought Glyndŵr was as a symbol, considering how many people seemed to know almost nothing about him, it touched off this response:

> Wel, rydw i'n gweld rhan o'r hyn ydych chi'n ddweud – 'dyw pobl ddim yn gwybod llawer amdano . . . yn gyffredinol achos dydyn nhw ddim yn gwybod llawer am hanes Cymru o gwbwl, ac mae'r

myth [am hanes Cymru] oedd yn bod hyd at ddiwedd y ganrif dd'wetha 'falle ymhlith y werin, 'ma hwnna wedi diflannu . . . mae addysg wedi 'i ladd e, ac wedyn y cyfan sydd gan bobl yn gyffredinol nawr yw'r hyn maen nhw wedi 'i gâl drwy'r ysgolion, a dyw'r ysgolion ddim wedi bod yn cyflwyno hyn o gwbl. Dydyn nhw ddim wedi bod yn sôn am hanes Cymru at 'i gilydd, neu os oeddwn nhw, o'dd e fel atodiad bach dibwys i hanes Lloegr, neu hanes Prydain, a gan hynny dydi Glyndŵr ddim wedi bod yn ffigur mor bwerus, mor nerthol yn ein bywyd ni fel symbol, ac fel myth, ag y dyle fe fod ond mae'n câl ei adfer. Ac ŷn ni'n ceisio adeiladu Llywelyn nawr [hefyd] trwy'r hyn sy'n digwydd eleni [1982, saith gan mlwyddiant]. Neud pobl yn ymwybodol ohonyn nhw, ac o'u pwysigrwydd nhw a cheisio sefydlu yn 'u meddwl nhw rhyw batrwm – myth mewn gwirionedd . . . o hanes Cymru – fel rhywbeth ar wahân i Loegr.[99]

(Well, I see part of what you're saying – people don't know much about him . . . generally because they don't know much about the history of Wales at all, and the myth [of Welsh history] which was in existence up to the end of the last century perhaps amongst the ordinary people, that has disappeared . . . education has killed it, and afterwards all that people generally have now is what they had got through the schools, and the schools haven't been presenting that at all. They haven't been mentioning the history of Wales on the whole, or if they have, it was as a small, unimportant appendix to the history of England, or the history of Britain, and because of that Glyndŵr hasn't been a figure as powerful, as strong in our life as a symbol, and as a myth, as he should be, but he is being restored. And we are [also] trying to build up Llywelyn now through what is happening this year [1982, seven hundredth anniversary]. Making people conscious of them, and their importance and trying to establish in their minds some pattern – myth, really . . . about the history of Wales – as something separate from England.)

Dafydd Iwan, too, recognized the importance of education in understanding the symbol, but he seemed to be a little more satisfied with the size of the audience being reached:

Faswn i'n deud fod arwyddocâd Glyndŵr yn eitha eang, oherwydd mae o'n gymeriad sydd yn câl 'i gydnabod mewn cylchoedd eitha eang, ond wrth gwrs ma'r hyn yden ni'n dysgu mewn ysgolion, neu oedden ni'n dysgu mewn ysgolion amdano fo yn baragraff neu ddau am 'this Welsh rebel', yndê. Ond 'da chi'n gwbod ma – erbyn hyn ma plant yn cael dysgu hanes Glyndŵr yn llawer mwy llawn ac mae o – yr arwyddocâd felly yn gryfach, yndê. O na, faswn i'n deud yn sicr, ma llawer mwy o bobol yn gwybod am Owain Glyndŵr a'i arwyddocâd nag am Llywelyn er enghraifft.[100]

(I'd say that Glyndŵr's significance is quite extensive, because he's a character who's recognized in quite wide circles, but, of course, what we learn in schools, or were learning in schools, about him is a paragraph or two about 'this Welsh rebel'. But you know it's – by now children are taught Glyndŵr's history a lot more fully and he is – so the significance is stronger. Oh no, I would certainly say, that a lot more people know about Owain Glyndŵr and his significance than about Llywelyn for example.)

A point that emerges in these interviews is that, while some people must be educated to understand what Glyndŵr represents when his name is invoked, there is the reciprocal effect that, in emphasizing Glyndŵr, the nationalists are teaching the people about their own history. They teach them pride in their heritage. A further point is that Glyndŵr is always present as a popular name with a vague nationalistic connotation upon which education and greater understanding can be built.

Glyndŵr is understood as having a special role in teaching the Welsh about the need for freedom. Unlike the preceding Welsh princes, who were fighting in an independent Wales to maintain that independence, Glyndŵr was fighting for freedom in a land where no one then alive had ever known it. He fought for his vision of a free and independent nation. Owen Rhoscomyl makes this same point in contrasting Glyndŵr with earlier princes:

> In Glyndŵr's day every freeman in Wales was still a warrior, but instead of being accustomed to national independence, they were accustomed rather to the idea of national fetters, though they were also accustomed to the dream of one day winning back their freedom . . . It is his abiding claim on us that he . . . gave Welsh nationalism a fresh lease of life . . .[101]

Gwyn A. Williams explains Glyndŵr's particular significance thus:

> And if there is doubt about Welsh national consciousness, even Welsh nationalism, before the revolt, there can be none after it, for

the Welsh mind is still haunted by its lightning-flash vision of a
people that was free.[102]

That Glyndŵr really does symbolize the struggle for freedom,
and not just in the minds of historians and political activists, is
seen in the response of a man who indicated that he was not
well-versed about Glyndŵr. When I asked what came to mind
when he heard the name Glyndŵr, he immediately replied, 'Wel
un yn brwydro dros ryddid'[103] (Well, one fighting for freedom).
Glyndŵr is recognized as a worthy exponent of nationalist aims
because of his fight against oppression and because of his vision.
One young woman explained his significance by reporting what
she had been taught in school:

> . . . bod o wedi penderfynu 'i bod hi'n hen bryd i gael gwared o'r
> gyfundrefn oedd yno bryd hynny ac i gael – wel, i gyfuno Cymru
> fel un cenedl, ac i sefydlu senedd i Gymru . . . o'dd yr athrawon
> falla yn pwysleisio'r ffaith bod o nid yn unig yn filwr o'r Canol
> Oesoedd ond fod ganddo fo weledigaeth ar y dyfodol, a bod rhai
> o'r syniada o'dd gyno fo hyd yn oed yn y bymthegfed ganrif, o'dd
> rheini'n addas i'n hamser ni.[104]

> (. . . that he had decided that it was high time to get rid of the order
> that was there at that time to get – well, to unite Wales as one
> nation, and to establish a parliament for Wales . . . the teachers
> perhaps stressed the fact that he was not only a warrior of the
> Middle Ages but that he had a vision of the future, and that some of
> the ideas that he had even in the fifteenth century, those were
> suitable to our time.)

Another contact, a retired man, gave his view of Glyndŵr in this
way:

> Faswn i'n deud, wel y fo o'dd yr ola o'r gwrthryfelwyr, yndê. Os
> leiciwch chi alw fo yn rebel heddiw, 'ndê. Dyna be'di o. Dyna'r
> enw fasa nw'n roi arno fo heddiw fydda rebel, 'ndê. Yn erbyn y
> system ddieflig sydd yn bod heddiw ac yn bod, yr un, un, yndê . . .
> Ond yr un, un ydi'n problemau ni ddoe, a'r un, un ydi'n
> problemau ni heddiw. Glyndŵr yn cwffio yn erbyn yr un petha ag
> ydan ni'n cwffio yn 'u herbyn nw. Dan ni 'chydig bach gwell rŵan,
> ma'n wir, 'ndê, ond – ym – ond dyna fo yr un, yr un, un, ydi
> sylfaen y cwbwl i gyd. Owain Glyndŵr yn ymladd yn erbyn y
> system Seisnigaidd dramoraidd, Lloeger a'i frenin. A dyna 'da
> ninnau'n neud heddiw.[105]

(I would say, well, that he was the last of the rebels. If you like to
call him a rebel today. That's what he is. That's the name they
would give him today, would be rebel. Against the devilish system,
which exists today and exists, the same one, isn't it . . . But our
problems yesterday are the same ones, and our problems today are
the same ones. Glyndŵr fighting against the same things as we are
fighting against. We have it a little better now, it's true, isn't it, but
– um – but there it is, the same, the basis of the whole lot is the
same. Owain Glyndŵr fighting against the foreign, anglicized
system, England and its king. And that's what we ourselves are
doing today.)

Another important characteristic which emerges in Glyndŵr's
use as a symbol is his leadership. The first thing that Gwynfor
Evans told me about him was that:

> Ro'dd e'n arweinydd. Ro'dd e'n gallu arwain. Ro'dd yn amlwg yn
> gallu deffro brwdfrydedd mewn pobol ac ennyn teyrngarwch
> pobol. Ro'dd pobl yn ffyddlon iawn iddo fe ac yn barod i'w ddilyn
> e. Ac roedd ganddo weledigaeth.[106]

> (He was a leader. He was able to lead. He was obviously able to
> awaken enthusiasm in people and to kindle people's loyalty.
> People were very faithful to him and ready to follow him. And he
> had vision.)

He then went on to describe the plans for a parliament and an
independent Welsh Church. A member of Cofiwn, a group
devoted to inspiring nationalism through educating the Welsh
about their history, explained to me why Glyndŵr is so
important to his group:

> Well, Glyndŵr is, is, to modern Welsh nationalism, he represents
> the father of Welsh nationalism, you see, and um, certainly
> amongst political Welsh nationalists he's looked upon as the chief
> medieval figure, not just because he was more or less the last
> struggle for independence, but, um, the fact that it was quite a
> modern revolution, the war that he led was quite modern in many
> ways, like he had a concept of a Welsh state, and, uh, they still
> believed in the crown of Britain prophecy, where the Welsh would
> take over the crown of London and take over England again. But
> Glyndŵr wanted to create a state, so he's very –, not only, – he
> wanted to create a Welsh church, a Welsh parliament, he wanted

to, um, reclaim certain lands back from England, and made a
tripartite indenture with some English allies, and so to the modern
Welsh nationalist he's constitutionally and politically the leading
figure. And, uh, also important to modern nationalists is the fact
that in our historiography Llywelyn is very much, has been written
up by the British historians as an ending point for Welsh nationalism, you see. And certainly to the Tudors in the sixteenth century,
Llywelyn was a logical end for them, for the Tudors. And the
Tudors were anti-Glyndŵr. They give him a very bad press in
those days, the Tudors, because he didn't fit into the policy, you
see, of going to London. And see in the last century the Liberals
were saying, they would cut off at Llywelyn, you see. And it was
British history, Welsh-British history. So to the modern Welsh
nationalist, you've got to focus, focus on Glyndŵr because he rose
up after the conquest of Wales. So he is the most popular cult figure
in our history.[107]

The clearest expression of what Glyndŵr represents, of the
force behind his use as a symbol, often appears in comparison
with Llywelyn y Llyw Olaf. At the first listening to the speeches
and the protest songs, it appears as if Llywelyn and Glyndŵr are
used interchangeably as political symbols. Both can, with reason,
be called the last prince of Wales – Llywelyn was the last
Welshman recognized as such by the English, and Glyndŵr was
the last Welshman to bear the title. In the months preceding Prince
Charles's investiture as prince of Wales in 1969, both men were
frequently presented as evidence that Charles had no right to the
title. Nevertheless, differences do emerge and, as has been seen in
some of the preceding quotations, Glyndŵr emerges as the
stronger symbol of the two. Even a speech given at Cilmeri, the
site of Llywelyn's memorial stone, and beginning with discussion
of why memory of Llywelyn is so alive, makes more use of
Glyndŵr than of Llywelyn. It is this speech which ends in the
assertion, 'Mi a wn y daw'[108] (I know that he will come). To see
how Glyndŵr actually functions and what he signifies, it is worth
looking at some of the statements comparing the two princes. A
late nineteenth-century article on Glyndŵr includes the assertion,

Ac ni charwyd neb erioed fel y carwyd Owen Glyn Dŵr gan werin
Cymru. Mewn hanes y mae Llywelyn, ond y mae Owen Glyn Dŵr
fel pe'n byw gyda'r genedl; ac nid rhyfedd ei fod, – fel Moses ac
Arthur a Chalfin, – heb fedd a adwaenir.[109]

(And no one was ever loved as Owain Glyndŵr was loved by the people of Wales. Llywelyn exists in history, but Owain Glyndŵr is as if he's living with the nation; and it's no wonder that he is, – like Moses and Arthur and Calvin, – without a known grave.)

Repeatedly, people expressed this sense of greater feeling for Glyndŵr. One man, who admittedly may be slightly biased by living in Corwen, in response to my question whether or not he considered Glyndŵr a hero on a national level, answered:

Cenedlaethol, o ydi, cenedlaethol, o ydi, am wn i mae o'n fwy o hynny na unrhyw un o'n tywysogion ni. Mae eleni wrth gwrs yn ddathlu saith gan mlwyddiant lladd Llywelyn ein Llyw Olaf, yndê, a maen nw'n ceisio'n galad, pobol sy'n perthyn i rai pleidia a phetha felly codi brwdfrydedd a ma 'i'n anodd 'dydi, ond ma 'i'n haws efo Glyndŵr 'dydi. Ma Glyndŵr yn ffigwr a ma ganddon ni fwy o edmygiad ohono fo rwsut. Achos un gododd o wrthryfel yn erbyn Saeson mewn gwirionedd ag o blaid y petha gwir Gymreig ac ro'dd ganddo fo weledigaeth yn doedd o sefydlu nid yn unig wladwriaeth ond hefyd cael cyfundrefn addysg a phetha felly.[110]

(National, oh yes, national, oh yes, for all that I know he's more of that than any of our princes. This year, of course, is commemorating the seven hundredth anniversary of the slaying of Llywelyn ein Llyw Olaf, isn't it, and they're trying hard, people who belong to some parties and such things to raise enthusiasm and it's hard, isn't it, but it's easier with Glyndŵr, isn't it. Glyndŵr is a figure for whom we have more admiration somehow. Because he was one who rose from rebellion against the Englishman really and in favour of the truly Welsh things, and he had vision, didn't he, of establishing not only a state but also having a system of education and such things.)

Both public figures and private individuals kept making the same point to me, that Glyndŵr was closer, that people had more feeling for him and more admiration for what he tried to accomplish. His tripartite plan and his image as a rebel serve as anchors for people's impressions of Glyndŵr in a way unparalleled by any such associations for Llywelyn, helping to make Glyndŵr a more potent symbol and more easily comprehended. Also, again and again, they made reference to his never having died – that he still lived, whether in a cave or in people's hearts – which is important both as a contrast to

Llywelyn, who so definitely died when he was ambushed, and as a reminder that Glyndŵr, unlike Llywelyn, is a redeemer-hero. Glyndŵr appears to be more satisfying than Llywelyn, more able to fill the needs of nationalists, whether activists or not, and in this, romanticism plays a large part. One member of Cofiwn, after explaining that Glyndŵr was the more important of the two because he was more modern and was trying to establish an independent state with its own parliament, university, Church and diplomatic relations, paused because he could not think what else to say, and then added:

> Ma rwbeth romantic am Owain Glyndŵr dw i'n meddwl, i fi, ac er mod i'n aelod o'r gymdeithas sy'n atgoffa Llywelyn.[111]

> (There's something romantic about Owain Glyndŵr I think, for me, and despite my being a member of the society which commemorates Llywelyn.)

Another member of Cofiwn elaborated on this a little:

> [There's] something about Glyndŵr that does raise emotions in people . . . Strange you don't find that so much about Llywelyn. Llywelyn hasn't got that romantic image so much. But there again a lot of the stuff written about Llywelyn is very much in the terms of English constitutional struggles. It's very much seen as a constitutional thing, but Glyndŵr is seen as a people's man, because he was a guerilla leader, of course, and he wasn't quite, he was of princely descent, but at the same time he was a minor chief in the fifteenth century. So he's got this more popular image you see.[112]

In an article published in 1969, entitled 'Pam Llywelyn?' (Why Llywelyn?), the author claims that Llywelyn was not really so great. Glyndŵr, on the other hand, really did unite Wales, and not just through force. He wanted a free Wales and never gave in to the English, even at the end, when he could have received a pardon. He taught the Welsh national self-respect, which is reflected in the fact that, unlike Llywelyn, he was never betrayed. The article ends with the following two expressive paragraphs:

> Ac ni bu farw chwaith, fel nad oes angen galarnadu amdano. Arhosodd Owain Glyn Dŵr yn fyw ac yn annwyl yng nghof ei

werin, ac er i haneswyr ac eraill geisio ei nodi'n rebel ac yn bopeth, yr oedd enw Owain yn golygu rhywbeth i'r Cymro am ganrifoedd. Pobl a fagwyd ar fersiynau llyfr o'n hanes sydd wedi llyncu'r sôn am fawredd ac arwyddocâd 'Llywelyn y Llyw Olaf'. Pobl y 'Celtic twilight' ydynt hwy. Owain Glyn Dŵr, y gŵr a fore-godai yn ôl y chwedl olaf amdano'n cyfarfod ag abad Glyn y Groes, yw'r arwr i bobl sydd â'u hwyneb tua'r wawr.[113]

(And he did not die either, so there is no need to lament him. Owain Glyndŵr stayed alive and dear in the memory of his people, and despite the historians and others trying to mark him a rebel and everything, the name Owain meant something to the Welshman for centuries.

People who were raised on book versions of our history have swallowed the claim of 'Llywelyn y Llyw Olaf's' greatness and significance. They are people of the 'Celtic twilight'. Owain Glyndŵr, the man who rose early according to the last tale about him meeting the abbot of Glyn y Groes, is the hero for people who have their face to the dawn.)

A question that comes up in comparing Glyndŵr's status as a nationalist symbol with that of other Welsh heroes, especially when considering the importance of romanticism, is whether Arthur, another well-known redeemer-hero, can serve the same function. It appears that he cannot. He is not invoked in political rhetoric, and the reason seems to be that Arthur, even more than Llywelyn, belongs to a distant past, in contrast to Glyndŵr with his war for a modern state. In fact, Arthur belongs so much to the past that even his existence is in doubt. Furthermore, though it is good for the symbol to be a romantic figure, he seems to be too romantic. He is so much a figure of romance that he has lost the edge needed in a political symbol. He makes a good literary subject, as shown by poetry written for eisteddfodau and various periodicals, but his stories rarely reverberate with the same intensity of real struggle as Glyndŵr's. Moreover, Arthur has been pre-empted by the English. Television and the movies depict him as an Englishman so that, though there are still many legends about him in Wales, he has become useless to the nationalists. A member of Cofiwn explained to me the problem with using Arthur as a nationalist symbol thus:

Arthur's been usurped by the English, you see, and so to many nationalists he's gone down, like he's been so dominated. But they've used him, the English have usurped him from a long time back . . . And we have such a surfeit of Hollywood films where Arthur's an Englishman fighting Saxons . . . Arthur was always English and it confused people in their minds, and so you know many people have got so confused about Arthur . . . and now English television series, where Arthur is an Englishman, and they're in England which didn't exist in Arthur's time of course, so to modern nationalists, yes Arthur's not so important any more. To me he is, you know, knowing the story, I've read history. I'm still waiting for Arthur's return, but – . However, in terms of folk stories, yes Arthur is around, like, it's just the meaning's gone. With Glyndŵr, I can identify with the nationalists [a few] centuries back. With Arthur, while there's a mass of folk stories about Arthur around Wales . . . to a nationalist he wouldn't stand out any more because he's been usurped by the English.[114]

Glyndŵr is seen as more real, more pertinent to modern needs than Arthur, Llywelyn or even Owain Lawgoch. Arthur, and to a great extent, Owain Lawgoch, belong to misty pasts but Glyndŵr is very real and therefore potentially dangerous. Arthur has so little political significance that he poses no threat, but Glyndŵr carries with him an aura of rebellion and of danger. These points arise in some observations made by a retired clergyman about Glyndŵr:

> If I was using, as you know I sometimes do in a sermon, local associations and things in Wales, if I wanted to play safe I would tell a story about Owain Lawgoch, or King Arthur. I would hesitate to tell one about Glyndŵr . . . unless I would transfer the name to –, unless I was very sure of myself, because Glyndŵr is – I'm quite sure of this – he's not regarded by the older school in Wales as quite nice.
>
> There was this feeling that Glyndŵr is too real. He's very real, Glyndŵr, you see. Owain Lawgoch isn't real. King Arthur isn't real. But this is what I meant when I said he's almost too recent for folklore.
>
> He [Owain Glyndŵr] represents rebellion . . . Owain Lawgoch is a harmless enough figure; you can put him in all sorts of things. But Glyndŵr – I can understand people in Machynlleth . . . they associate him with such things as vandalizing telephones, and other things that make life less comfortable.[115]

Glyndŵr has strength as a nationalist symbol because of his

realness and his modernness. However, the use of him as a symbol by a host of political activists has given him an added layer of dangerousness. While the activists invoke him, Glyndŵr's name has come to evoke the activists. One woman, in response to my question of what came to mind at mention of Glyndŵr, responded immediately, 'trwbwl, dim ond iwso fo fel esgus i wneud trwbwl'[116] (trouble, just using him as an excuse to make trouble).

The danger associated with Glyndŵr goes even deeper than acts of vandalism done in his name, and his significance lies deeper than that he is a symbol used by politicians. Perhaps there is real truth about his living in the hearts of his countrymen, because many Welsh are certainly protective of him. He is a subject not always safely talked about with an outsider. One woman whom I approached was perfectly friendly and willing to talk to me until I mentioned the topic; then she literally ran away from me.[117] In my fieldwork, I found that many people would not talk to me about Glyndŵr until they saw that I was somehow vouched for by another Welsh person. Even that was not always enough, however. One woman simply would not talk to me about Glyndŵr. On my broaching the subject, she immediately looked terrified and kept saying things like, 'I can't talk to you about this, I have to get on with the English; I can't talk with you, my boss is English; I can't talk with you.'[118] This was in Machynlleth, and I would have been pleased even with some story about the parliament held there, but apparently, even that seemed too dangerous to her. Glyndŵr, though he may embody the people's hopes and dreams, is a threat to the establishment and to the *status quo*, and sometimes one must be brave not only to chance but to admit such risk. A farmer, with whom I talked one market-day in Machynlleth, expressed this unwillingness to risk the present status:

> . . . there's such a palaver here in Wales now about Plaid Cymru wanting to have a prince of Wales, that the present prince is not the one that should be qualified for the job, but Owain Glyndŵr was our last prince, wasn't he. He was the prince of Wales. But all that thing is in the past, you see. We don't want to bring something from the past which can do any um, any um friction. You can bring friction in there, you see . . . we don't want that, do we. Yes, we don't want that . . . The present is more essential [than history] to

me, and we're living very peacefully at the moment in, in this town.[119]

I do not believe that the vehement refusals by some people to discuss Glyndŵr were due simply to fear that admitting knowledge of Glyndŵr might somehow associate one with political activism, but rather to a very deep, traditional cognizance of him. This view is supported by a retired priest, whose last parish was Machynlleth; he said that while the people there take great public pride in the Parliament House, they will not discuss the man but instead treat him as a dark, personal secret.

Apart from these people who are not politically active and who are uncomfortable talking about Glyndŵr, there are others who are critical of the political use made of him, and their criticisms take a variety of forms. Some do not like the goal he represents: one man, who feels 'that Glyndŵr is still very much the symbol of a very definite resistance', reported of his father:

> Now he, when I was at University and first sort of began to think about things in connection with Wales, and with devolution, and things like that, and some measure of self determination, which was very lacking then, ah, he would say a very interesting thing, he would say that the Welsh cannot rule themselves, and he was saying this to me, he wasn't saying this to please someone. Because he said when we try to rule ourselves . . . we fall out.[120]

This is an attitude which the nationalists have been trying very hard to change and which may well die out with the last generation into which it was inculcated as part of the anglicized education system. Some do not like the romanticism and what they see as its illusions: one man views the current emphasis on Glyndŵr as

> Romantic mythology. In that they quote him as a sort of – . Let's put it this way – so many of the youngsters of today, they want to go back. Their concept of Wales as such is somewhere in the mid-nineteenth century, and they go back further to Owain Glyndŵr – is this great leader of the Welsh. But of course, those days, Wales was broken up into various parts with no unity about them at all . . . You need somebody like Ifan ab Owen Edwards, who would have a natural concept of Welshness, without having to embellish it with romantic heroes of the past.[121]

Some do not like the effects of romanticism blurring the issues.
One young man explained:

> . . . what I don't like about it, they sort of bring in these sort of
> characters like Glyndŵr and what have you, on a sort of political
> level and, you know 'I have the heart of Glyndŵr burning under
> my breast' sort of thing – well, when the situation today is
> completely different. It's not a matter of just straightforward
> political oppression, it's sort of much more indirect *social*
> oppression . . . It's not a matter of just sort of Welsh heroes in battle
> falling against the English and vice versa and what have you – it's
> much more *vast* than that now and Dafydd Iwan seems to a certain
> extent much more sort of – so much of a sort of romantic and sort of
> wanting to go back to the good old days and this sort of thing –
> rather than looking at the situation – well to a certain extent it
> doesn't matter that we are still politically British if we can have
> everything that's required to keep the Welsh language alive. You
> know, I mean, that sort of thing about talking about Glyndŵr just
> means sort of Wales and England and then 'ne'er the twain shall
> meet' sort of thing – it just doesn't sort of bring into account
> anything which is relevant today, I don't think . . .[122]

And some simply do not like Glyndŵr: one shopkeeper
explained that Glyndŵr had no import for him because

> . . . dwy i erioed wedi edmygu yr uchelwyr . . . achos y ffordd rwy
> i'n edrych ar y bobl fel Owain Glyndŵr a Llywelyn a rhain, fydda
> i'n meddwl amdanynt hwy, mae'n siwr, eu bod nhw wedi rhoid
> amser anodd iawn i bobl fel fi yn y cyfnod hwnnw, y gweithwyr . . .
> dwy i ddim yn edmygu milwyr . . . a dydwy i'n dychmygu bod na
> hen hen hen daid imi wedi cael amser anodd a chaled iawn o dan
> Owain Glyndŵr a llawer ohonyn nhw wedi cael eu lladd, doedd
> dim ots, gan Owain Glyndŵr . . . [123]

> (I've never admired the noblemen . . . because the way I look at
> people like Owain Glyndŵr and Llywelyn and those, I would think
> about them, it's sure, that they had given a very hard time to people
> like me in that period, the workers . . . I don't admire soldiers . . . I
> imagine that a great great great grandfather of mine had a very
> difficult and hard time under Owain Glyndŵr and many of them
> were killed, it was no matter, by Owain Glyndŵr . . .)

In the discussion of the political treatment of Glyndŵr, there
are a few other non-traditional presentations of Glyndŵr to

consider. Like the political materials, while they may reflect traditional as well as popular attitudes and may draw on traditional
narratives, they do not themselves come directly from tradition.
For example, Glyndŵr has been the subject of a number of
dramas and pageants. An examination of three of these, none of
which was composed specifically for propaganda purposes,
shows a change in attitude and historical perception. The first,
Owen Glendower, a Dramatic Biography which was published in
1870, is a cross between apologia and reconstruction, with the
idea that Glyndŵr becomes much more respectable if one looks
at him in the right way. Some of the points, as explicated in the
book's preface, are that Glyndŵr was not at fault in not showing
up for the battle at Shrewsbury, because not only had he never
contracted with Hotspur to be there, but he had never even met
Hotspur; he cannot be condemned as a rebel for rising against
King Henry because he was actually remaining true to the only
king to whom he ever swore allegiance, that is, Richard; and that
'national feelings gave the Welsh resistance a nobler character
than that of rebellion'.[124] The second drama was a local pageant,
in English with Welsh verses, written and performed by people
in the Corwen area in the late 1960s. It was written by a local
woman from Cynwyd, and the part of Glyndŵr was played by
the man who lent me the script. The pageant includes scenes of,
or reference to, almost all of the most famous traditions
associated with Glyndŵr. The author even created scenes which
illustrate traditional characteristics, such as the opening scene in
which Glyndŵr infiltrates the king's camp in the guise of a wild
man, a good illustration of his wily trickery. Some of the other
references are to the English belief that Glyndŵr was a wizard,
horses standing in blood at his birth, the man who would rather
die than betray his sons' leader, Cadwgan whetting his battle-axe,
ceubren yr ellyll and, finally, the early morning meeting with the
abbot. The drama shows the English as both foolish and
treacherous and shows the Welsh as clear-thinking and devoted
to a worthy cause. The bloodshed and ravaging of the
countryside resulted only from necessity, not uncontrolled blood-
lust. However, the suggestion at the end is that once the battle
was lost, though it was noble of the proud Owain to go off alone
and refuse the king's pardon, it was wiser for the people to turn
back to Henry. The Narrator speaks these bitter lines:

Wales had become so impoverished that even the means of
sustaining life could not be obtained, except by rewards from the
king. Thousands cursed Glyndwr, as they looked upon the havoc
of the last decade . . . They returned to what remained of their
homes, or to hide from the wrath of Glyndwr – who was still an
unsurmountable obstacle to the good government of Wales.[125]

The final phrase was later crossed out. In contrast to this drama
which, while not condemning Glyndŵr, seems to accept his
defeat and leave him very much a figure in the past, the third
drama ends with a message to the present with the hope of
Glyndŵr's dream. *Y Mab Darogan* is a rock opera prepared for
and first performed at the 1981 National Eisteddfod at
Machynlleth and then taken on tour. The drama shows Glyndŵr
being accepted in leadership as *y mab darogan* and carefully
weighing the potential consequences of his actions. Owain sings
of his dream, which includes:

> Senedd i Gymru, a thegwch i bawb;
> A gwir democratiaeth,
> Yw'r unig athrawiaeth,
> Fe gewch chi eich cyfle, cyfoethog a thlawd.[126]

(A parliament for Wales, and fairness for everyone; and true
democracy is the only doctrine, you will get your chance, rich and
poor.)

However, the society, which he had struggled to create, withered
because individuals began looking for material rewards. In a
song in which Owain looks on the ruins, there are two lines
which echo the theme, discussed earlier in Chapters 3 and 4, that
the hero is as dependent on the people as the people are on the
hero.

> Pobol – roeddwn i yn nwylo'r bobol,
> A'r bobol yn fy nwylo i.[127]

(People – I was in the hands of the people, and the people in my
hands.)

The end of the show is one of hope, a call for the future. As the
programme notes explain,

Er i Owain Glyndŵr ddiflannu, mae ei freuddwyd yn fyw, a'r arwr ei hun yn ddiogel yng nghalonnau'r Cymry am byth (Y GWANWYN GWYRDD).
> 'Welsoch chi'r haul yn hwylio'r nen,
> Welsoch chi'r byd yn codi ben?'[128]

(Although Owain Glyndŵr disappeared, his dream is alive, and the hero himself safe in the hearts of the Welsh forever (THE GREEN SPRING).
> 'Did you see the sun sailing the heavens,
> Did you see the world raising its head?')

Many people with whom I spoke during the course of my fieldwork told me what a wonderful spirit there was in the audience at each performance and how the show inspired people with new hope. One of the performers explained to me what she tried to do with the final song, which she directed to the audience rather than to the other characters.

> . . . ar y diwedd ro'n i'n siarad â'r gynulleidfa a dweud 'Chwi yw y gwanwyn gwyrdd', hynny yw mae o i fyny i chi, ag i ninne wrth gwrs, ond mae i fyny i chi i wneud beth ellwch chi i – wel i godi Cymru'n ôl 'te.[129]

> (. . . at the end I was speaking to the audience and saying 'You are the green spring', that is that it is up to you, and us, of course, but it is up to you to do what you can to – well, to raise Wales again.)

Another way in which Glyndŵr appears in popular culture is in the names of inns and pubs. This, too, though it is a matter of commercial, popular culture, indicates something of the depth of Glyndŵr's importance in traditional culture, because while Welsh pubs are not generally named after Welsh heroes, many of them are named after Owain Glyndŵr. As one person pointed out, even a working-class pub in the industrial town of Merthyr Tudful is named after him. Even in New York City, a pub called the Owain Glyndŵr Tavern attracted Welsh exiles in the 1850s.[130] Glyndŵr's name appears in other odd places, as for example in the Vale of Rheidol Light Railway operating from Aberystwyth where, since 1956, locomotive No. 7 has been named Owain Glyndŵr, while No. 8 and No. 9 have been named Llywelyn and

Prince of Wales.[131] Spring water, bottled at its source in the village of Bow Street near Aberystwyth, is marketed under the name *Glyndŵr*. The bottlers may have been playing with the name's meaning 'glen of water', but the juxtaposition of 'Glyndŵr' with a red dragon on the label leaves little doubt about allusion to a cultural hero. The Countryside Commission, in a presumably non-political move but recognizing the popularity of the character, has named one of Wales's long-distance footpaths Glyndŵr's Way.

There is, as well, a small amount of iconography associated with Glyndŵr. These items, too, reflect both nationalist and traditional attitudes. A statue of Glyndŵr, made in 1916, stands in a hall of Welsh heroes at the City Hall in Cardiff. The contemporary catalogue citation for it indicates the need, still felt at that time, to assert that Glyndŵr was better than a rebel, that he actually had a cause and ideas:

> The statue represents the great Welsh patriot as the soldier statesman – the enthusiast with lofty ideals and noble aims – not a mere ambitious rebel as wrongfully depicted in English histories, but a man who fought with splendid courage for the independence of Wales and the advancement of the people. Spiritual aspirations rather than desire for material success is depicted in the figure.[132]

Wax figures now illustrate the display at the Parliament House in Machynlleth, which, after several less glorious incarnations, opened in 1982 as a historical interpretive centre, a development which reflects both the growing demand for educational resources in Welsh history and Glyndŵr's own importance. A further piece of iconography is a Glyndŵr postage stamp (part of a Post Office series on United Kingdom heroes), which decorated the first-day cover for Plaid Cymru's fiftieth anniversary in 1975. One more item, found on sale at Welsh gatherings, is a stained-glass colouring-sheet of Glyndŵr, a black outline on plastic which one can colour in with felt-tip pens and then hang in the window. Sometimes the iconography can go astray; the statue which Corwen had planned to honour their native son has been met upon its unveiling in 1995 with disappointment and dismay that Glyndŵr looks more like a 'hill-farmer', 'troll' or 'dalek' than a princely hero.

Glyndŵr's usage in popular culture may tie in also with his

having become to some extent a symbol of Wales, on a par with dragons, leeks and daffodils, for outsiders' recognition. The New York tavern, the locomotive, the bottled water and the ramblers' footpath may in part reflect that function, as may certain postcards printed in the early part of this century (the available examples are postmarked between 1905 and 1926). The postcards depict a young woman in identifiably Welsh dress being accosted (on several cards, apparently while she is working) by a man dressed as an Englishman on holiday. Accompanying this picture is the following doggerel:

> 'Where are you going, my pretty maid?'
> 'To Llyncochdywarchen, sir,' she said.
> 'Shall I go with you, my pretty maid?'
> 'If you climb Tecwynuchelochrau, sir', she said.
> 'Is it as rough as its name, my pretty maid?'
> 'Rough as Bwlchardudwy, sir,' she said.
> 'I like not your Welsh, my pretty maid.'
> 'Glyndwr Fawrglod did, sir,' she said.
> 'I'll never learn Welsh, my pretty maid.'
> 'Nobody asked you, sir,' she said.[133]

These postcards (some of which are printed with bilingual instructions) convey an ambiguous message. They present an English stereotype about Welsh place-names and language (their unpronouncability), a stereotype recognized by the Welsh, so that the message can be satisfactorily read by an English person as mocking the Welsh language, and by a Welsh person as mocking English linguistic (and cultural) limitations (as well as their unwelcome intrusions). The reference to Glyndŵr displays the same semiotic duality – on the one hand a recognizable (but also dismissable) Welsh figure or on the other hand, a hero whose honouring of the language and culture far outweighs any outsider's disparagement and whose stand against the English can be emulated by the maid. Another postcard design devotes half of its space to established icons of north-west Wales (the longest place-name, the Menai Straits and the Menai Suspension Bridge) and half to a seemingly unrelated coat of arms labelled 'Arms of Owen Glyndwr'. Given some of the other evidence of Glyndŵr as a symbol, perhaps this image is simply another way of declaring 'Wales'.

So far in this discussion, I have quoted only those who have definite knowledge or opinions about Glyndŵr and the use of him, but this does not cover the views of all those interviewed, let alone all Welsh people. I did fieldwork in various parts of Wales, speaking with a wide range of people of all age-groups and many occupations, and I found that when Glyndŵr is looked at on a national level, those people actively involved in nationalist concerns are full of information and consistently speak of Glyndŵr's vision in his plans for a Welsh parliament, church and university. Those not actively involved, however, were much more vague in their knowledge. They all knew his name and that he was supposed to be important, and some even provided the information that his parliament house was in Machynlleth, though others said that he had lived there. Some simply said they knew nothing about him, explaining either that they had no interest in history or that they were not taught Welsh history in school. Schoolchildren were also very vague. The three points that they did bring out, however, were the Parliament House in Machynlleth, Glyndŵr's attacks on castles, including the one in Aberystwyth, and his unknown grave.[134] Generally, the better-informed children knew things because, according to them, their parents had mentioned them or had taken them to the sites involved – in Machynlleth or on Pumlumon. Other people did try to provide information but, when questioned further, were not sure of Glyndŵr's rank – one person guessed at a prince? a king? a soldier?; of his time period – one person suggested, 'Arthur's time, no, eighteenth century, or was it somewhere around 1200?', and another was undecided between the sixteenth and eighteenth centuries; or what he did – one person could suggest only that he had fought somebody and, when asked whom, could only guess that it was the English. People also tended to confuse Glyndŵr with Llywelyn y Llyw Olaf, which is not surprising in view of the way the two names are used by speech-makers and, further, that the year of my most intensive fieldwork was the year commemorating the seven hundredth anniversary of Llywelyn's death, with all the attendant publicity. People would also confuse Glyndŵr with other Llywelyns, including the Llywelyn of the Beddgelert story – the story of the dog slain by his master, who mistakes the blood on the animal's jaws for that of his infant son, when it is really the blood of a wolf killed by the dog defending the child. This particular confusion may have arisen because one of Glyndŵr's caves is located near the village of Beddgelert. In some cases, people did know something about Glyndŵr, but only through a chance association, as for example the shop assistant in Betws-y-coed who knew that Glyndŵr had lived in a particular cave because she had gone there with a college walking-group.[135] Two women in Llanrwst were able to tell me that Glyndŵr came from the Corwen area because they knew that there was a Hotel Glyndŵr in Corwen, although, by that reasoning, they might have placed him in any number of towns.[136] One young woman associated him with Snowdon only because she had heard a song about his having been there.[137] Nevertheless, no matter what the degree of ignorance, when asked whether they personally considered Glyndŵr to be a national hero, most of these people said yes.

It is not that Glyndŵr has no real significance for those who are not politically active; as was seen in the cases of those too frightened to discuss him, he may have too much significance. Rather, this material indicates that it is possible for people to respond to Glyndŵr as a symbol without necessarily knowing what lies behind the symbol.

Although I have treated local tradition and national use of Glyndŵr separately in this chapter, none of the discussion is intended to suggest that the nationalist propagandists acquire their knowledge solely through non-traditional means, while those enjoying a rich tradition about Glyndŵr are somehow pure of outside influences. Even ardent nationalists come from the people and may have traditional lore, and local bearers of tradition may be ardent nationalists and/or students of history. As with any aspect of human culture, the boundaries are not clear. The old inhabitant imbued with local lore offers political analysis, and the young political activist provides a traditional tale. Nevertheless, the forces which keep traditions about Owain Glyndŵr alive and viable in a local setting – the physical reminders, the natural interest in a local boy – do not function at any great distance from that local source, and cannot sustain him as a hero on a national scale. For that, the nationalists must create anew the awareness of him as a leader and a visionary and must consciously revive him as a symbol of the fight for a better world.

Notes

1 Introduction

[1] While his name has been spelled in a variety of ways, including *Owen Glendower*, the form familiar to readers of Shakespeare's *Henry IV*, Part I, I use the standardized Welsh form *Owain Glyndŵr*.

[2] Jan Morris, *The Matter of Wales*, p.4.

[3] Glanmor Williams, *Owen Glendower*, p.25.

[4] Since at the time of writing there is a local government reorganization, I have considered it safest to revert to the old nomenclature of the thirteen counties.

[5] Gwynfor Evans, *Land of My Fathers*, pp.252–71; J.E. Lloyd, *Owen Glendower / Owen Glyn Dŵr*; Roderick, ed., *Wales through the Ages*, vol.1; Williams, *Owen Glendower*; John Davies, *Hanes Cymru*, pp.186ff.

[6] Jarman and Hughes, eds., *A Guide to Welsh Literature*, I, 118.

[7] See for example, Jarman and Hughes, *A Guide to Welsh Literature*, chs.1, 2.

[8] David Powel, *The Historie of Cambria*, Preface.

[9] Ibid., p.387.

[10] Ibid., Preface.

[11] Aberystwyth, NLW MS 13074D, p.14a. This was brought to my attention by Mary Burdett-Jones.

[12] BL MS Harleian 2261; printed in Higden, *Polychronicon Ranulphi Higden*, VIII, 513–18. See also John Taylor, *The Universal Chronicle of Ranulf Higden*, esp. pp.1–3, 139–40.

[13] Aberystwyth, NLW MS 7006D; published in Thomas Jones, ed., *Brenhinedd y Saesson*, p.274.

[14] Aberystwyth, NLW Peniarth MS 44, p.93 (fol.48r). See also Brynley F. Roberts, 'Astudiaeth Destunol'. I am grateful to Mary Burdett-Jones for helping me decipher the text.

15 Burdett-Jones, 'A Note on a Welsh Legal Manuscript'.
16 Ibid.
17 Aberystwyth, NLW Peniarth MS 135, pp.59–60; translated in 'Welsh Sources for the History of the Glyn Dŵr Movement', in J.E. Lloyd, *Owen Glendower*, p.150.
18 Adam of Usk, *Chronicon Adae de Usk*, p.78.
19 BL MS Harleian 2261; Higden, VIII, 514.
20 Aberystwyth, NLW MS 13074D, p.14a.
21 Personal communication from Mary Burdett-Jones, who helped clarify for me the relationship of Gutun Owain's manuscripts (extant and lost) to Robert Vaughan's.
22 Harleian 2261; Higden, VIII, 513.
23 *Holinshed's Chronicles of England, Scotland, and Ireland* (1808 edition), III, 17.
24 Ibid.
25 Powel, op. cit., p.386.
26 Ibid., p.387.
27 Aberystwyth, NLW MS 39B, p.68.
28 Hartland, *The Science of Fairy Tales*, chs.7, 8.
29 Friedman, 'The Usable Myth', p.41.
30 Schneider, *A Madman of Ch'u*.
31 Davidson, 'Folklore and History'; Lanczkowski, *Verborgene Heilbringer*; Oinas, 'Kalevipoeg and His South Slavic Relations', p.378 esp. and n.53. This last article shows the shift of interest as Oinas discusses both the origins of the pertinent legends and their particular significance in Estonian culture.
32 Eliade, *Myth and Reality*, pp.64f.; Cohn, *The Pursuit of the Millennium*.
33 Keen, *The Outlaws of Medieval Legend*; Nagy, *The Wisdom of the Outlaw*; John W. Roberts, *From Trickster to Badman*.
34 R. Rees Davies's *The Revolt of Owain Glyndŵr* (Oxford: Oxford University Press, 1995) was not published until my own work was in press but, if taking the same approach as in his 1995 National Eisteddfod lecture, 'Owain Glyn Dŵr: Hanes a Chof Gwlad', Davies acknowledges the interplay of oral tradition and history more extensively than previous historians have.
35 Lanczkowski, op. cit., p.28; translated from the German by Mary Beth Stein in personal communication.
36 Rosenberg, *Custer and the Epic of Defeat*, p.177.

2   The Pattern of the Redeemer-Hero

1 Cohn, *The Pursuit of the Millenium*, esp. p.72.
2 Ibid., pp.90–3, where Cohn quotes a contemporary observer as saying of Baldwin that, 'at Valenciennes people await him as the Bretons await King Arthur'.

3   Ibid., pp.113–18.
4   R.R. Davies, 'Law and National Identity in Thirteenth-Century Wales', p.52.
5   The number of redeemer-heroes is a striking difference between Wales and the European countries, for whom the printed sources report only one or two per country. However, since I do not know the individual cultures well enough to know whether there were other heroes who have fallen from memory or discussion, I hesitate to make too much of this point.
6   Gildas, *The Ruin of Britain*, esp. chs.2, 4, 21 (pp.89, 90, 95–6).
7   Nennius, *British History and the Welsh Annals*, §45. The attitudes expressed by Gildas and 'Nennius' are examined in Brynley F. Roberts, 'Testunau Hanes Cymraeg Canol', pp.274–7 esp.; idem, 'Geoffrey of Monmouth and Welsh Historical Tradition', pp.29–40.
8   Nennius, *British History*, §42, pp.71(original)/31(translation). (The slash alone [e.g. 71/31] will be used to indicate original/translation in a single publication in future notes.)
9   For discussion of this, see Brynley F. Roberts, ed., *Brut y Brenhinedd*, Appendix, pp.55–74; Roberts, 'Testunau Hanes Cymraeg Canol', pp.280–8.
10   Roberts, 'Testunau Hanes Cymraeg Canol', p.288; Roberts, *Brut y Brenhinedd*, p.xxiv.
11   Bullock-Davies, 'Exspectare Arturum', pp.433–5. Another translation might be 'Oh you who are awaited, come'. In either case, Carausius is seen as a redeemer. That Carausius presented himself as a redeemer of Britain is supported by contrast with the commander who reconquered Britain for Rome and who was greeted as *Reddito Lucis Aeternae* (Restorer of the Eternal Light), placing him as a *Restitutor* of the Roman Empire (Ashe, *The Discovery of King Arthur*, p.28). Ashe presents an overview of the importance of the *Restitutor* throughout the Roman Empire (pp.19ff.) and that importance in the third, fourth and fifth centuries raises the question of how much Roman concepts influenced Welsh concepts of a redeemer. However, although the British were probably aware of Roman hopes, there is no evidence that the British redeemer was dependent on the Romanist one. Indeed, the redeemer-hero is just as, if not more, likely to be an independent creation or to date back to an older, shared heroic stock. Nor is there any indication that the admiration for Rome shown by writers from Gildas to Geoffrey of Monmouth gave rise to redeemers who were more *Restitutors* of the Roman Empire than deliverers of Wales. As will be shown in subsequent discussion, and no matter how much the Britons may have assimilated aspects of Roman culture, the Welsh redeemers were quite clearly called on to fight for an independent and united Wales, freed of all aliens.
12   R. Wallis Evans, 'Trem ar y Cywydd Brud'; idem, 'Prophetic Poetry'.
13   J. Gwenogvryn Evans, ed., *The Book of Taliesin* (BT), 78; Marged

Haycock, 'Llyfr Taliesin' (BT–Haycock), 485.64. Marged Haycock's dissertation has been extremely valuable in guiding my translations of verse from *Llyfr Taliesin*. With this and the following excerpts of verse, it is not always possible to give anything but tentative translations because the poetry is mostly unedited and often textually corrupt. Nevertheless, it is possible to understand the general sense of the verses.

14 Ifor Williams, BBCS, 3 (1927), 50–2; Ifor Williams, ed. and Rachel Bromwich, trans., *Armes Prydein* (AP[2]), p.xi.

15 Geoffrey of Monmouth, *History of the Kings of Britain*, xii:15–18, pp.280–4.

16 Bromwich, ed. and trans., *Trioedd Ynys Prydein* (TYP), p.292–6; *The Dictionary of Welsh Biography Down to 1940* (DWB), q.v. Cadwaladr, Cadwallon; Geoffrey of Monmouth, *Life of Merlin*, pp.169–70.

17 Geoffrey of Monmouth, *History*, v:12–14, pp.139–41

18 J. Gwenogvryn Evans, ed., *Llyfr Gwyn Rhydderch*, cols.189–91; Gwyn Jones and Thomas Jones, trans., *The Mabinogion*, pp.86–8.

19 TYP, pp.318–19; Geoffrey of Monmouth, *Life of Merlin*, pp.175–6.

20 J. Gwenogvryn Evans, ed., *Poetry from the Red Book of Hergest* (RBP), 1051.18.

21 Jarman, ed., *Llyfr Du Caerfyrddin* (LlDC), 17.89–92. J. Gwenogvryn Evans, ed., *The Black Book of Carmarthen* (BBC), 57.3–6.

22 LlDC 16.33–4; BBC 49.13–14.

23 BT 76; BT–Haycock 484.9–12.

24 Geoffrey of Monmouth, *Life of Merlin*, ll.965–8, pp.104/105.

25 RBP 1052.8–10.

26 RBP 579.19–21.

27 BT 71.56; BT–Haycock 449.16–17.

28 LlDC 16.12; BBC 48.12–13.

29 AP[2] 1.1, pp.2/3.

30 AP[2] ll.12–14, pp.2/3.

31 BT 77; BT–Haycock 484.34–5.

32 BT 80; BT–Haycock 499.5.

33 LlDC 16.77, 16.84; BBC 51.16, 52.3.

34 RBP 581.32–3, 37–8.

35 BT 77; BT–Haycock 484.23.

36 AP[2], ll.163–70; pp.12/13.

37 BT 30; BT–Haycock 443.18–22.

38 BT 76; BT–Haycock 484.1–8.

39 LlDC 17.148–9; BBC 60.2–4.

40 AP[2] ll.73–6, pp.6/7.

41 AP[2] ll.89–94, pp.8/9.

42 AP[2] ll.113–22, pp.10/11.

43 LlDC 16.7–10; BBC 48.8–11.

44 LlDC 17.150–3; BBC 60.4–6.

45 AP[2] ll.7–8, pp.2/3.

46 AP[2] ll.28–9, pp.4/5.

47   BT 77; BT–Haycock 484.32–3.
48   RBP 1051.20–2.
49   LlDC 17.51–2; BBC 55.1–2.
50   BT 31; BT–Haycock 443.23–4.
51   BT 80; BT–Haycock 499.11.
52   LlDC 17.183–4; BBC 61.7–8
53   LlDC 17.186; BBC 61.9.
54   LlDC 17.189–90; BBC 61.11–13.
55   RBP 581.32–4, 37–8.
56   LlDC 16.77–8; BBC 51.16–17.
57   LlDC 16.84–5; BBC 52.3–5.
58   LlDC 17.122–3; BBC 58.12–13.
59   Geoffrey of Monmouth, *Historia Regum Britanniae*, vii:3, p.388; translated in *History*, vii: 3, p.175.
60   RBP 1053.23–6.
61   LlDC 17.124–7; BBC 58.13–16, where the lines read 'allv alledrad a divahaur./ An bi ni inaeth guared guydi guaeth.'
62   AP^2 ll.2–4, pp.2–3.
63   LlDC 15.20–3; BBC 47.16–48.3.
64   LlDC 16.86–8; BBC 52.5–8.
65   Geoffrey of Monmouth, *Life of Merlin*, ll.972–3, pp.104/105.
66   Ibid, ll.930–68, pp.102–5.
67   See for example, BBC 72, 79, 94–5.
68   *Gododdin* in *Canu Aneirin*, ed. Ifor Williams, l.1242.
69   Nennius §56, pp.35/76.
70   LlDC 18.133–5; BBC 67.12–13.
71   William of Malmesbury, *De Gestis Regum Anglorum*, vol.II, §287, p.342; quoted in TYP, pp.369–70. William F. Hansen and James Halporn, in personal communication, suggest that 'fabulatur' be emended to 'fabulantur'.
72   Henry of Huntingdon, *Epistola ad Warinum*, p.74.
73   Gerald of Wales, *De Principis Instructione*, I:20, p.127; translated in Gerald of Wales, *The Journey through Wales*, p.281.
74   Gerald of Wales, *Speculum Ecclesiae*, II:8–9, p.48; translated in *Journey through Wales*, p.285.
75   Gerald of Wales, *Speculum Ecclesiae*, II:9, p.49; translated in *Journey through Wales*, p.286. Translation of *adhuc venturum* (come back/ come to this place) is problematic because, while Jews would assert that the Messiah has not yet come once so that his awaited coming would not be a matter of 'return', we cannot be certain of how Giraldus understood the situation. Nevertheless, the parallel he tried to draw between the hopes of the Jews and of the Britons for an expected deliverer is clear.
76   TYP 51, pp.132/133.
77   For examples of these, such as Hermann of Tournai's report in 1113 of the violence which erupted in Bodmin when some visiting monks suggested Arthur was dead, see Chambers, *Arthur of Britain*; Roger

Sherman Loomis, 'The Oral Diffusion of the Arthurian Legend', and 'The Legend of Arthur's Survival' in *Arthurian Literature in the Middle Ages*; Bullock-Davies, 'Exspectare Arturum', pp.438–9.

78 Aberystwyth, NLW Peniarth MS 50, p.43; in EVW, p.145.
79 Aberystwyth, NLW Llanstephan MS 119, p.83; in EVW, p.147.
80 Aberystwyth, NLW Peniarth MS 26, p.42; in EVW, p.157.
81 NLW Llanstephan MS 119, p.77; in EVW, p.146.
82 Aberystwyth, NLW Peniarth MS 53, p.22, in EVW, p.153.
83 NLW Llanstephan MS 119, p.83, in EVW, p.147.
84 EVW, pp.139–41.
85 Glanmor Williams, 'Prophecy, Poetry, and Politics', pp.71–86.
86 Rowlands, 'Iolo Goch', p.130.
87 For discussion of the role of the Welsh poet, see Ceri W. Lewis, 'The Court Poets', pp.123–56; J.E. Caerwyn Williams, *The Poets of the Welsh Princes*; Glanmor Williams, 'Prophecy, Poetry, and Politics', pp.71–86; Thomas Parry, *A History of Welsh Literature*, chs.3, 6.
88 See Edward Owen, 'Owain Lawgoch – Yeuain de Galles'; DWB; and A.D. Carr, 'Who was Owen of Wales?' (as well as for other aspects of his life).
89 Aberystwyth, NLW Mostyn MS 133, p.174b, found in THSC (1901), 96–7.
90 IGE², xxx, p.92, ll.1–18. This poem was once thought to have been composed by Iolo Goch for Owain Glyndŵr, but further examination has revealed it to be for Owain Lawgoch by an unidentified poet. See THSC (1901), 90–2; EVW, pp.159–61.
91 IGE², xxx, p.91, ll.5–12.
92 BL Additional MS 31057, p.115b; found in THSC (1901), 95–6, ll.34–46, 56–64, 77–84.
93 DWB; J.E. Lloyd, *Owen Glendower*, pp.8–17.
94 The socio-economic situation is discussed further in Chapter 4, where references are also cited.
95 Brynley F. Roberts, 'Un o Lawysgrifau Hopcyn ap Tomas o Ynys Dawy', p.227.
96 IGE², LXXXVIII, p.267, ll.30–4.
97 Glanmor Williams, 'Prophecy, Poetry, and Politics', p.32; Rowlands, 'Dilid y Broffwydoliaeth;' p.43; idem, 'Iolo Goch', p.134; *Brut y Brenhinoedd*, pp.56–9; also Ceinwen Thomas, 'From the Fall of Llywelyn to the Tudor Period', pp.68–78.
98 See lists in R. Wallis Evans, 'Prophetic Poetry', pp.288–91.
99 For discussion of *cywyddau brud* of these times, see also Henry Lewis, 'Rhai Cywyddau Brud'; W. Leslie Richards, 'Cywyddau Brud'; W. Garmon Jones, 'Welsh Nationalism and Henry Tudor', esp. pp.29, 32; T. Gwynn Jones, 'Cultural Bases: A Study of the Tudor Period in Wales', esp. pp.166–8.
100 Henry Lewis, 'Cywyddau Brud', pp.305–7 (IG xiv), ll.35–6, 45–6, 53–8, 67–70. This *cywydd* was once thought to have been written by Iolo Goch to Owain Glyndŵr, but further examination has shown it

[100]   to be written later in the fifteenth century to Henry Tudor. See W.J. Gruffydd, 'Iolo Goch's 'I Owain Glyndwr ar ddifancoll'; Lloyd, *Owen Glendower*, p.155; Henry Lewis, 'Rhai Cywyddau Brud', pp.251–4.

[101]   W. Leslie Richards, ed., *Gwaith Dafydd Llwyd o Fathafarn*, no.33, p.82, ll.29–30, 35–6, 39–48.

[102]   Jarman, 'Wales a Part of England 1485–1800', p.79; DWB.

[103]   T. Gwynn Jones, 'Cultural Bases', p.167.

[104]   The power of a narrative paradigm which can shape people's perception of events and inspire imitation is explored by Bruce A. Rosenberg for the pattern the 'epic of defeat' in *Custer and the Epic of Defeat*, where he also discusses the sometimes related pattern of the returning hero (pp. 273–8).

3   Legends of Glyndŵr the Redeemer

[1]   IGE², XI, XII, XIII.

[2]   IGE², XLI.

[3]   IGE², XII, p.34, l.13.

[4]   IGE², pp.xiv–xv.

[5]   IGE², XLII, p.126, l.33–p.127, l.4.

[6]   J.E. Lloyd, *Owen Glendower*, pp.155–7; IGE², p.xx; Ifor Williams, 'Llyma Fyd Rhag Sythfryd Sais'.

[7]   David Johnston, 'Iolo Goch and the English'.

[8]   IGE², pp.li–lii.

[9]   IGE², LXXVIII, p.235, l.16 and note on p.235.

[10]   Adam of Usk, *Chronicon Adae de Usk*, pp.72/240; also in Matthews, ed., *Welsh Records in Paris*, p.111.

[11]   Adam of Usk, pp.73/241; *Welsh Records*, p.112.

[12]   David Powel, *The Historie of Cambria*, p.386.

[13]   William Wynne, *The History of Wales*, p.317.

[14]   Pennant, *Tours in Wales*, p.322.

[15]   *Henry IV*, Part I, Act 3, sc.1, ll.147–54. Holinshed (1587), p.149. It is also possible that Pennant was drawing his information from either Holinshed or Shakespeare.

[16]   J.E. Lloyd, *Owen Glendower*, pp.31, 35, 68–9; Gwilym Arthur Jones, *Owain Glyndŵr*, c.1354–1416, pp. 8/9, 42/43.

[17]   Aberystwyth, NLW Panton MS 53, pp.52–3; repeated in Thomas Ellis, *Memoirs of Owen Glendowr*, p.65.

[18]   Pennant, *Tours*, pp.307–8.

[19]   Aberystwyth, NLW Mostyn MS 158, p.286; this passage is labelled in the margin as 'Comet y seren ben grech'.

[20]   Ashton, ed., *Gweithiau Iolo Goch*, XI, 'co. i Seren Gynffonog', pp.183–92.

[21]   See discussion by Thomas Roberts in IGE², p.xvi.

[22]   Aberystwyth, NLW Peniarth MS 135, p.64.

23   Aberystwyth, NLW Panton MS 53, p.58b; repeated by Thomas Ellis, p.73.
24   Aberystwyth, NLW Panton MS 11, p.68b.
25   William Wynne, p.319.
26   Pennant, *Tours*, pp.357–8.
27   J.R.S. Phillips, 'When Did Owain Glyndwr Die?'
28   *Cambro-Briton*, I, 463.
29   Adam of Usk, p.313.
30   Thomas Thomas, *Memoirs of Owen Glendower*, p.169; *Cymru* 1 (1891), 224. Public debate about this resurfaced in the *Western Mail* as recently as January 1995 (e.g. 5, 11, 12 January).
31   BL MS Harleian 6832, taken from Thomas, *Memoirs of Owen Glendower*, p.169.
32   Thomas, *Memoirs of Owen Glendower*, pp.169–70; Tomes, ed., *Blue Guide: Wales and the Marches*, pp.258–86.
33   *Y Llenor* 9 (1897), 79; repeated in *Cymru* 21 (1901), 247; *Cymru'r Plant* 17 (1908), 313.
34   Aberystwyth, NLW MS 39B, p.68.
35   Browne Willis, *Survey of Cathedral Church of Bangor*, pp.35–6; Thomas Evans, *Cambrian Itinerary, or Welsh Tourist*, p.285; Nicholas Owen, *Caernarvonshire*, pp.49–50.
36   Field tapes, 1982, transcription, p.118. All transcriptions have been made as accurate as possible, without editing or polishing.
37   Field tapes, 1982, transcription, p.44.
38   Field tapes, 1982, transcription, p.72.
39   Owen Rhoscomyl, *Flame-Bearers of Welsh History*, pp.227–8.
40   Gwyn Thomas, *A Welsh Eye*, p.110.
41   Field tapes, 1982, transcription, p.108.
42   Field tapes, 1982, transcription, p.109.
43   Thomas, *A Welsh Eye*, p.110.
44   Field tapes, 1982, transcription, p.85 (pseudonym used).
45   Field tapes, 1982, transcription, p.93 (pseudonym used).
46   Field tapes, 1982, transcription, p.195.
47   Aberystwyth, NLW Mostyn MS 158, p.285b.
48   Field tapes, 1982, transcription, p.164.
49   Meirwen Hughes, 'Brwydr Hyddgen', *Y Cymro*, 29 Hydref (October) 1974.
50   Field tapes, 1982, transcription, p.97.
51   Field tapes, 1982, transcription, p.131.
52   T. Gwynn Jones, 'Ryw Fore Oer ar Ferwyn', *Barddoniaeth y Plant* III (1935), pp.9–10. Also published in another, earlier anthology of poetry for use in schools, *O Oes i Oes* (1917).
53   Field tapes, 1982, transcription, p.181.
54   Field tapes, 1982, transcription, p.181.
55   Adam of Usk, p.298 (under 1409).
56   'An Ode to Owen Glendower, after His Disappearance', *Y Cymmrodor*, 4 (1881), 230–2. For the Welsh text, see Henry Lewis,

'Cywyddau Brud', pp.305–7, and for discussion, see W.J. Gruffydd, 'Iolo Goch's "I Owain Glyndwr ar ddifancoll"'.

57 John Barbour, *The Bruce, an Epic Poem*, pp.79–82; Ronald McNair Scott, *Robert the Bruce, King of Scots*, pp.79–92.

58 *Y Llenor Cymreig*, 1 (1882), 111.

59 Field tapes, 1982, transcription, pp.81–2.

60 Cledwyn Fychan, notes on conversation with George Pugh, Rhiwgam, Aberhosan (February 1966).

61 *Y Brython*, 4 (1861), 212–13; *Cymru*, 10 (1896), 32; a full text for this is given in Chapter 4, where Glyndŵr as an escape artist is discussed.

62 Thomas Turner, *Narrative of a Journey*, p.104.

63 Field tapes, 1982, transcription, p.173. The element of danger is officially recognized as is seen in a guide to the area, which lists under Moel Hebog, 'Beyond this mine [an old asbestos mine] OWEN GLYNDWR'S CAVE may be visited by crawling along the lowest of three narrow ledges for about twenty yards'. (*Snowdon and Welsh Highland Holiday Book*, p.49).

64 Pennant, *Tours*, p.334; the same information is recorded in *Y Brython*, 4 (1861), 213, in which the name is given as Ednyfed ab Caron, and reprinted in William Jones, *Plwyf Beddgelert*, p.29; Robert Prys Morris, *Cantref Meirionydd*, pp.317, 360; *Y Llenor*, 9 (1897), 76; *Cymru'r Plant*, 17 (1908), 313; *Bye-Gones*, 12, New Series (1911–12), 148; *Y Geninen*, 32 (1914), 280.

65 J.Y.W. Lloyd, *The History of Powys Fadog*, V, 102.

66 *Baner ac Amserau Cymru*, 3 Ionawr (January) 1894, p.4, col.4.

67 Field tapes, 1982, transcription, p.289.

68 Field notes, II, 13.

69 AWC, MS 2593/81, pp.105–6.

70 Field tapes, 1982, transcription, p.162.

71 John Rhŷs, *Celtic Folklore*, II, 487, though Rhŷs doubts the identification of Glyndŵr made by his informant Craigfryn Hughes.

72 Field tapes, 1982, transcription, p.85.

73 Ogof y Ddinas is a name applied to more than one place. Gwyn Thomas recalls his schoolteacher suggesting that Glyndŵr might be lying at Ogof y Ddinas, 'a cave to the west of here'. (Thomas, *A Welsh Eye*, p.110.) The hero in Elwyn Thomas's novel, *The Forerunner*, remembers being told of a cave running under the hilltop Dinas from Cilrychen to the Pantyllyn Rocks: 'It had been used by the old Britons during the Roman invasion, and later by his more immediate forebearers who fought under Owen Glyndwr, and it was inhabited at that very hour . . .' (p.100).

74 Field tapes, 1982, transcription, p.291, told by the Reverend Ron Hughes, a retired parish priest, who more commonly tells the story in Welsh.

75 In the earliest and non-Welsh forms of the legend, a groom follows a runaway horse (the earliest record of the cave legend, made by Gervase of Tilbury in 1211: Arthur sleeps in a cave in Mount Etna),

or one of Arthur's servants buys a horse from a passing mortal who accompanies him back to the cave for payment, and there sees the sleeping warriors (Elis Gruffydd reported this being told 1518–24 about a cave near Glastonbury, and nineteenth-century variants have been collected in England). See Thomas Jones, 'A Sixteenth Century Version of the Arthurian Cave Legend'.

[76] Arnold Van Gennep, *La Formation des Légendes*, p.194.

[77] For an early discussion of this connection, see Edwin Sidney Hartland, *The Science of Fairy Tales*, pp.170ff.

[78] Not too much significance, however, should be attributed to the frequency of each hero's appearance in this set of materials, because the nineteenth-century antiquarians borrowed so much from each other that one person's identification of Arthur as the hero almost automatically means his identification by half a dozen other antiquarians.

[79] There is more than one Craig y Dinas told of in Welsh legendry.

[80] William Howells, *Cambrian Superstitions*, p.104; Gomer Roberts, *Chwedlau Dau Fynydd*, pp.21–4, who notes that the tale is sometimes told of Owain Glyndŵr. The separate parts appear in numerous places.

[81] *Y Brython*, 4 (1861), 371; reprinted in William Jones, *Plwyf Beddgelert*, p.59.

[82] Ibid.; *Cymru*, 3 (1892), 215; J. Jones (Myrddin Fardd), *Llên Gwerin Sir Gaernarfon*, p.233; *Bye-Gones*, 13, New Series, (1913–15), 23. Note also that again the hazel appears to have particular, though unexplained, significance.

[83] Field notes, I, 37.

[84] Field tapes, 1982, transcription, pp.85–7.

[85] Field tapes, 1982, transcription, pp.27–8.

[86] This description, which may be strongly influenced by Iolo Morganwg, appears in such places as *Y Brython*, 1 (1885), 112–13; *Cofnodion a Chyfansoddiadau Buddugol Eisteddfod Aberdar, 1885*, pp.227–9, where it is listed as 'A Popular Tale in Glamorgan' by Iolo Morganwg; Marie Trevelyan, *Folk-Lore and Folk-Stories of Wales*, pp.135–7; Isaac, *Coelion Cymru*, pp.102–4.

[87] Field tapes, 1982, transcription, p.82.

[88] In English tradition, see for example Charles Hardwick, *Traditions, Superstitions, and Folk-Lore*, pp.167–8 or James Hardy, ed., *The Denham Tracts*, pp.125–7, both quoting from Hodgson's *History of Northumberland*, part ii, vol.iii, p.287; *Folklore Journal*, 1 (1883), 193–4; *County Folklore*, 2 (1901), 406–7. In German tradition, see for example, Donald Ward, ed. and trans., *The German Legends of the Brothers Grimm*, nos.23, 28. In Jewish tradition, see for example Dov Noy, ed., *Folktales of Israel*, no.3. Even in a Lithuanian variant, where the intruder is asked, 'Is it time?', it is the intruder's failure to do the right thing which keeps the army asleep, because: 'Misunderstanding the question, the man answers: "No, not yet" – the army remains in enchantment.' (Jonas Balys, *Motif-Index of Lithuanian*

Narrative Folk-Lore, no.3595.) A Polish folktale, 'Old Fakla and the Sleeping Knights', which is closer than most European variants to the Welsh legend, raises another point about the development of this motif. A blacksmith is brought to put golden shoes on the horses of the sleepers, who are supposed to wake up 'when the time comes to go fight for the faith in a war that will begin somewhere far away and end on the steel bridge in Kuznice'. The blacksmith, who had been warned against cursing, cuts his hand and curses loudly, awakening the soldiers, one of whom asks his leader, 'Brother, is it time?' and receives the reply, 'Not yet, sleep on!' In both narratives, warriors who are awaiting some final battle waken when an intruder breaks a taboo (touching the bell, cursing) and then determine through question and answer that the time is not right for their rising. However, the details of the Polish tales show that the motif cluster can move towards fantasy and *Märchen*, something it has clearly not done in the Glyndŵr tradition. The Welsh hope for the redeemer may be too strong to let it stray from legend into fantasy. The Polish tale is recorded in Richard M. Dorson, ed., *Folktales Told around the World*, pp.101–4.

89   W. Jenkyn Thomas, *The Welsh Fairy Book*, pp.11–16.

4   *The Multifaceted Character of Owen Glyndŵr*

1   Owen Thomas, 'Glyndyfrdwy'.
2   *Y Geninen*, 22 (1904), 108. An Anglo-Saxon analogue is provided by Hereward the Wake, whose men reversed their horses' shoes in order to evade their Norman enemies. This is discussed in Keen, *The Outlaws of Medieval Legend*, p.20.
3   There is, however, some disagreement as to the exact location of Dôl Pennau, with reports placing it, for example, in Corwen, near Llansantffraid Glyn Dyfrdwy, and near Caer Drewyn.
4   Field notes II, 16.
5   Field tapes, 1982, transcription, p.114–15. This account places Dôl Pennau near Llansantffraid Glyn Dyfrdwy.
6   Cernyw, *Hynafiaethau Edeyrnion*, pp.6–7.
7   Hewett, *Walking Through Merioneth*, pp.80–1.
8   Bowen, ed., *Atlas Meirionnydd*, p.193.
9   Owen Thomas, 'Glyndyfrdwy'.
10   Field notes II, 20.
11   Aberystwyth, NLW Peniarth MS 135B, pp.62–3; also, printed in Lloyd, *Owen Glendower*, p.153 and in William Richards, 'The Works of Gruffydd Hiraethog', p.29; essentially the same text appears in Aberystwyth, NLW Panton MS 22 and Panton MS 53, both in the hand of Evan Evans, the former in 1776 and the latter at approximately the same time.

[12]   Holinshed, 1808 edition, III, 44.
[13]   Aberystwyth, NLW Panton MS 53, p.58; repeated by Thomas Ellis in his *Memoirs of Owen Glendowr*, p.72.
[14]   William Wynne, *The History of Wales*, pp.318–19.
[15]   Pennant, *Tours in Wales*, pp.342–3
[16]   Iolo Morganwg, *Iolo Manuscripts*, pp.98–9/493–4.
[17]   *Y Gwyddoniadur Cymreig*, V, 92; *Y Llenor Cymreig*, 1 (1882), 111–12; *Y Geninen*, 22 (1904), 108.
[18]   J.Y.W. Lloyd, *The History of Powys Fadog*, III, 206–7; C.J. Evans, *Story of Glamorgan*, p.304.
[19]   'Owain Glyn Dwr a Syr Lawrence', in T. Gwynn Jones, ed., *Ceiriog*, p.56. The story is told again in another ballad, 'Syr Lawrens Berclos', by John Morris Jones, *Caniadau*, pp.25–6.
[20]   Field tapes, 1982, transcription, pp.214–15.
[21]   Field tapes, 1982, transcription, p.96.
[22]   Field tapes, 1982, transcription, p.287.
[23]   Field tapes, 1982, transcription, pp.175–6.
[24]   Keen, *The Outlaws of Medieval Legend*, pp.18–19, 70, 117–18.
[25]   George Johnston, trans., *The Saga of Gisli the Outlaw*, pp.29–30, 39; Chodzko, *Specimens of the Popular Poetry of Persia*, pp.13, 35, 89.
[26]   Aberystwyth, NLW Panton MS 11, pp.41b–2. Later versions, ranging up through Pennant in 1778, have slight variations on the verse, but essentially the mockery is the same.
[27]   Aberystwyth, NLW Mostyn MS 158, pp.285–5b. Hereward the Wake provides a partial analogue. He, too, agreed to release one of his greatest enemies, Abbot Turold, for a ransom, which was, however, not properly paid. Hereward responded by burning the town and looting the monastery. Keen, *Outlaws*, p.20.
[28]   Pennant, *Tours*, pp.310–11.
[29]   Aberystwyth, NLW Peniarth MS 135, p.60; later in Aberystwyth, NLW Panton MS 53, p.52 (c.1650); Ellis, *Memoirs of Owain Glendowr*, p.65 (1775); Pennant, *Tours*, p.306 (1778); *Y Llenor Cymreig*, 1 (1882), 110, where Owain Glyndŵr is said to have had 500 men and the Flemings to have lost between 500 and 600 of their 1,500.
[30]   Aberystwyth, NLW Mostyn MS 158, p.285b (1548).
[31]   Aberystwyth, NLW Panton MS 53, p.51b (seventeenth-century text in an eighteenth-century manuscript); repeated in Ellis, *Memoirs of Owen Glendowr*, p.64; Pennant, *Tours*, p.301. A much earlier account of Glyndŵr's escape from Talbot and Grey and into the woods appears in Aberystwyth, NLW Peniarth MS 135, pp.59–60, but lacks the detail of their surprising him at home.
[32]   *Y Brython*, 4 (1861), 212–13. Further versions are found in *Cymru*, 10 (1896), 32; *Bye-Gones*, 10, New Series (1907–8), 67; *Cymru*, 50 (1916), 173; Firbank, *A Country of Memorable Honour*, p.70. Partial analogues are recorded for the tenth-century Icelandic hero and outlaw Gisli who, on at least one occasion, climbed a cliff and swam through the sea from the island to the mainland and who fought his last battle at

the cliffs where he had a hiding place. George Johnston, trans., *The Saga of Gisli the Outlaw*, pp.42, 55–8.

33 Aberystwyth, NLW Panton MS 11, pp.67–7b; see also *Y Llenor Cymreig*, 1 (1882), 108–9.
34 Borrow, *Wild Wales*, pp.444–50; Meyrick, *The History and Antiquities of the County of Cardigan*, pp.240–1; see also Dafydd H. Evans, 'Twm Siôn Cati', pp.8–19.
35 *Y Brython*, 3 (1860), 100.
36 J.Y.W. Lloyd, *History of Powys Fadog*, IV, 273–4; *Y Brython*, 3 (1860), 100.
37 Field notes, 1982, transcription, p.75.
38 T. Gwynn Jones, *Welsh Folklore and Folk-Custom*, p.54; Owen Jones, ed., *Cymru: yn Hanesyddol*, I, 443.
39 Thompson, *The Folktale*, p.319. See also Radin, *The Trickster*.
40 See Klapp's discussion of 'The Clever Hero'.
41 See Babcock-Abrahams, '"A Tolerated Margin of Mess": The Trickster and His Tales Reconsidered'.
42 Keen, *Outlaws*.
43 Hobsbawm, *Bandits*, p.35. This material is also developed in his *Primitive Rebels*, esp. pp.19–20.
44 *Baner ac Amserau Cymru*, 3 Ionawr (January) 1894, p.4, col.4.
45 Field tapes, 1982, transcription, p.288.
46 BL MS Harleian 2261 (15c.), printed in Higden, *Polychronicon Ranulphi Higden*, VIII, 515; Pennant, *Tours*, p.307.
47 J.E. Lloyd, *Owen Glendower*, pp.143–4; Glanmor Williams, *Owen Glendower*, p.56.
48 Ceinwen Thomas, 'From the Fall of Llywelyn to the Tudor Period', p.71.
49 Cledwyn Fychan, 'Llywelyn ab y Moel a'r Canolbarth'. See reference in Gwyndaf, 'The Cauldron of Regeneration', p.436, to a folksong associated with *gwerin Owain*.
50 Field tapes, 1982, transcription, p.289.
51 Hobsbawm, *Primitive Rebels*, p.19.
52 Ibid., p.24. For a discussion of the socio-economic conditions which gave rise to sixteenth-century bands of Welsh bandits, responding to the social upheaval ongoing since Glyndŵr's time and intensified with the Acts of Union, see Glyn Williams, *Y Gwylliaid*.
53 Hereward the Wake and William Wallace parallel Glyndŵr as outlaws fighting to preserve their cultures from alien invaders. Hereward led the Saxons against the Normans in the eleventh century, and Wallace similarly led the Scottish in a guerilla war against the English in the late thirteenth century. (Keen, *Outlaws*, pp.14ff., 64ff.) The three men, in addition to sharing the outlaws' stories of disguise, trickery and escape, are also the aristocratic conservators of a tradition being overwhelmed by invaders.
54 IGE², xxxvii, p.109, ll.3–4, and quoted in R. Rees Davies, 'Race Relations in Post-Conquest Wales'.

55 Pierce, 'The Social Scene in the Fourteenth Century', p.159. See also Glanmor Williams, *The Welsh Church*, pp.212–18. See R.Rees Davies, *The Age of Conquest: Wales*, 1063–1415, pp.431–59 especially, for discussion of the economic and legal tensions surrounding the revolt.

56 For example, Ffos Owen Glyndwr in *Y Brython*, 4 (1961), 253; Cadair Glyndwr in Owen Jones, ed., *Cymru: yn Hanesyddol*, I, 333, and Bowen, *Atlas Meirionnydd*, p.107; Glyndwr's Way in Hewett, *Walking through Merioneth*, pp.80–1.

57 For example, field tapes, 1982, transcription, pp.93, 131, 183, 287.

58 IGE², xiii, p.36, ll.19–20.

59 Iolo Goch, 'I Owain Glyndwr', IGE², xii, p.35, ll.1–10.

60 Gruffydd Llwyd, 'I Owain Glyndwr', IGE², xli, p.123, ll.23–36.

61 Islwyn Jones, ed., *Gwaith Hywel Cilan* (GHC), xxiii, p.39, ll.21–2.

62 GHC, xxi, p.36, ll.9–12.

63 GHC, xxii, p.38, l.9.

64 John Llywelyn Williams, coll. and Ifor Williams, ed., *Gwaith Guto'r Glyn*, xxiii, p.63, ll.49–50.

65 Rowlands, ed., *Gwaith Lewys Môn* (GLM), xxii, p.81, l.3.

66 GHC, vi, p.11, ll.47–8. See note on p.54.

67 T. Gwynn Jones, ed., *Gwaith Tudur Aled* (GTA), vol.I, xx, p.101, ll.91–2.

68 GLM, viii, pp.28–9, ll.37–8.

69 IGE², xxxvii, p.109, ll.27–8. Though included with the Iolo Goch manuscripts, this *cywydd* is of uncertain authorship. This *cywydd* and one to Rhys Gethin's brother Hywel Coetmor (IGE², xxxvi) may well be amongst the few surviving war-period compositions.

70 GTA, xlii, p.178, ll.15–16, 27–8.

71 GTA, xiii, p.75, ll.77–8.

72 GLM, ix, pp.32–3, l.18, 51, 55–6. The comparison to *y mab darogan* runs ll.51–64. See note on p.390. The term 'cyw Owain Glyn' appears elsewhere, as for example in GTA, xlvii, p.196, l.72, in a work which suggests that Glyndŵr's struggle was not in vain but rather continued by the Tudors. See note on p.592.

73 AWC, MS 2593/81, p.67.

74 *Y Brython*, 4 (1861), 212–13; J.Y.W. Lloyd, *History of Powys Fadog*, V, 102; Robert Prys Morris, *Cantref Meirionydd*, pp.317, 360; *Cymru'r Plant*, 17 (1908), 313; *Bye-Gones*, 12, New Series, (1911–12), 148; *Y Geninen*, 32 (1914), 280.

75 J.Y.W. Lloyd, *History of Powys Fadog*, IV, 155.

76 AWC, MS 2593/81, pp.57–8.

77 J.Y.W. Lloyd, *History of Powys Fadog*, I, 206.

78 Iolo Morganwg, *Iolo Manuscripts*, pp.97–8/492–3.

79 Aberystwyth, NLW Panton MS 53, p.52; later Ellis, *Memoirs of Owen Glendowr*, p.65; Pennant, *Tours*, p.305.

80 Aberystwyth, NLW Panton MS 53, pp.56–6b; later Pennant, *Tours*, pp.330–1.

[81] Aberystwyth, NLW Panton MS 53, p.56b; later Ellis, *Memoirs of Owen Glendowr*, pp.70–1; Pennant, *Tours*, p.333.

[82] Aberystwyth, NLW Panton MS 11, p.69.

[83] William Wynne, *The History of Wales*, pp.317–18; Samuel Lewis, *A Topographical Dictionary of Wales*, s.v. Bangor; Owen Jones, ed., *Cymru: yn Hanesyddol*, I, 109; John Ingman, 'Notes on Some Old Bangor Inns', p.42; also Holinshed, 1587 edition, p.521.

[84] Thomas Turner, *Narrative of a Journey*, pp.203–4.

[85] Arch Camb 5:11 (1894), 56; *Baner ac Amserau Cymru* 24 Ebrill (April) 1967, p.5, col.3 again records Glyndŵr watching the battle from Derwen Owain Glyndŵr (Owain Glyndŵr's oak tree).

[86] Aberystwyth, NLW Panton MS 53, pp.55–5b; also in William Wynne, *History of Wales*, p.318; Ellis, *Memoirs of Owen Glendowr*, pp.68–9; Pennant, *Tours*, p.326.

[87] Aberystwyth, NLW Panton 53, p.59; followed by Ellis, *Memoirs of Owen Glendowr*, p.73.

[88] William Wynne, *The History of Wales*, p.318.

[89] Pennant, *Tours*, pp.326–7.

[90] *Y Gwyddoniadur Cymreig*, V, 93–4.

[91] J.E. Lloyd, *Owen Glendower*, p.71; Gwilym Arthur Jones, *Owen Glendower c.1354–1416*, p.42/43.

[92] Pennant, *Tours*, pp.351–2.

[93] Cernyw, *Hynafiaethau Edeyrnion*, p.6.

[94] *Cymru'r Plant*, 17 (1908), 217–18.

[95] Field notes II.

[96] Borrow, *Wild Wales*, pp.124–5.

[97] See for example, *Y Llenor Cymreig*, 1 (1882), 108.

[98] Field notes II, 9.

[99] Field notes II, 16.

[100] Fenton, *Tours in Wales (1804–1813)*, p.343, Appendix – notes from printed sources.

[101] Hobley, *Hanes Methodistiaeth Arfon*, p.25.

[102] Pennant, *Tours*, p.301.

[103] Ellis, *Memoirs of Owen Glendowr*, p.66; Cernyw, *Hynafiaethau Edeyrnion*, pp.8–9, gives a more complete description of the ruins, including measurements of the walls.

[104] Field tapes, 1982, transcription, pp.92, 120.

[105] *Baner ac Amserau Cymru*, 11 Hydref (October) 1927, p.6, col.4.

[106] Foulkes, 'Dyffryn Olwyd: Ei Ramantau a'i Lafar Gwlad', p.89–90.

[107] Field tapes, 1982, transcription, p.164.

[108] Personal note (9 May 1982) from Robin Gwyndaf, who learned it as a child from his father.

[109] IGE^2 XII, p.35, ll.29–32. According to one of the Triads, Arthur was viewed as causing the same type of destruction:

Tri Ruduoavc Ynys (Brydein):
Run ap Beli,

a Llew Llaw Gyffes
a Morgan Mwynuawr,

ac vn a oed ruduogach no'r tri. Arthur oed y henw; blvydyn ny doy na gvellt na llysseu y ford y kerdei yr vn o'r tri. a seith mlyned ny doy y ford y kerdei Arthur.

Three Red Ravagers of the Island of Britain:
Rhun son of Beli,
and Lle(u) Skilful Hand,
and Morgan(t) the Wealthy.

But there was one who was a Red Ravager greater than all three: Arthur was his name. For a year neither grass nor plants used to spring up where one of the three would walk; but where Arthur went, not for seven years. (TYP 20W, p.35.)

[110] Fenton, *Tours in Wales*, p.352, Appendix – notes from printed sources.
[111] Glanmor Williams, *The Welsh Church*, p.214.
[112] Hayward, *The Life and Raigne of King Henrie the IIII*, p.143.
[113] Aberystwyth, NLW Panton MS 11, p.41.
[114] Aberystwyth, NLW MS 3064B (Mostyn 204), p.119. This proverb was generously brought to my attention by Mary Burdett-Jones along with another proverb from the same manuscript (p.123): 'Nid erys Malldraeth ar Owain' (Malltraeth does not wait on Owain). Again we cannot be certain, but the suggestion is that when the tidal marsh Malltraeth, on Anglesey, floods (as it used to, almost splitting the island), it waits for no one, not even Owain, the redeemer for whom everyone else waits.
[115] Arch Camb 5:11 (1894), 64.
[116] Arch Camb 6:10 (1910), 423.
[117] *Camden's Britannia*, p.65; the burning of Bangor is also noted by Thomas Evans, *Cambrian Itinerary*, p.285.
[118] For example, Aberystwyth, NLW Peniarth MS 135, p.61; Aberystwyth, NLW Panton MS 53, p.54; Ellis, *Memoirs of Owen Glendowr*, p.67; Pennant, *Tours*, p.302; C.J. Evans, *The Story of Glamorgan*, p.304.
[119] Thomas Evans, *Cambrian Itinerary*, p.112; C.J. Evans, *The Story of Glamorgan*, pp.303–4.
[120] Pennant, *Tours*, p.302.
[121] Hague, 'The Bishop's Palace', p.10.
[122] Llywelyn-Williams, *Crwydro Brycheiniog*, p.46.
[123] Ibid., p.59.
[124] Ibid., p.63.
[125] AWC, tape 4625 (10/6/75).
[126] Dafydd Gam: Aberystwyth, NLW Panton MS 11, p.42; Aberystwyth, NLW Panton MS 53, p.55; Edward Lhuyd, *Camden's Britannia*, taken from R. Vaughan (cf. Panton 53), p.592; William Wynne, *The History of Wales*, pp.320–2; Ellis, *Memoirs of Owen Glendowr*, pp.67–8; Pennant, *Tours*, pp.322–4.

Hywel Sele: Aberystwyth, NLW Panton MS 53, pp.53–3b; Ellis, *Memoirs of Owen Glendowr*, p.66; Pennant, *Tours*, pp.310–11; Owen Jones (ed.), *Cymru: yn Hanesyddol*, I, 564.

127   Sir John Wynne, *History of the Gwydir Family*, p.33, quoted in A.H.A. Hogg, 'A 14th Century House-Site . . .', p.1.

128   See for example, Pennant, *Tours*, p.310; P.B. Williams, *The Tourist's Guide through the County of Caernarvon*, pp.75–6; *Y Brython*, 1 (1858), 5; *Y Brython*, 3 (1860), 291–2.

129   Gresham, 'Platform Houses in North-West Wales', pp.36–7.

130   Hogg, 'A 14th Century House-Site . . .', p.6.

131   See for example, Kinsella, trans., *The Táin*, p.150, where part of one description of Cú Chulainn's war-fury reads thus:

> His face and features became a red bowl: he sucked one eye so deep into his head that a wild crane couldn't probe it onto his cheek out of the depths of his skull; the other eye fell out along his cheek. His mouth weirdly distorted: his cheek peeled back from his jaws until the gullet appeared, his lungs and liver flapped in his mouth and throat, his lower jaw struck the upper a lion-killing blow, and fiery flakes large as a ram's fleece reached his mouth from his throat . . .

132   Aberystwyth, NLW Panton MS 53, pp.53–3b.

133   Arch Camb 9 (1863), 132, from the pedigree of 'Colonel Jones the Regicide', prepared by Robert Vaughan of Hengwrt, finished 30 Jan. 1649.

134   Pennant, *Tours*, pp.310–11.

135   Fenton, *Tours in Wales*, p.127.

136   Field notes, II, 43–5. Some of the printed sources are: Turner, *Narrative of a Journey*, pp.59–60, 66; *Y Llenor Cymreig*, 1 (1882), 110; *Cymru*, 5 (1893), 249; *Y Geninen*, 26 (1908), 287.

137   *Y Geninen*, 26 (1908), 287.

138   Adam of Usk, pp.78/247.

139   Holinshed, p.520; 1808 edition, III, 20.

140   Holinshed, p.528; 1808 edition, III, 34.

141   Hayward, *The Life and Raigne of King Henrie the IIII*, p.142.

142   Pennant, *Tours*, p.315.

143   Aberystwyth, NLW Panton MS 53, p.59.

144   Field tapes, 1982, transcription, p.173.

145   Holinshed, p.520; 1808 edition, III, 20.

146   *Henry IV*, Part I, Act 3, sc.1, ll.52, 55, 63–6.

147   Aberystwyth, NLW Panton MS 53, p.54b, repeated by Ellis, *Memoirs of Owen Glendowr*, p.67.

148   Abersytwyth, NLW Panton MS 53, p.57.

149   William Wynne, *The History of Wales*, p.317.

150   Pennant, *Tours*, pp.306, 318, 335, (taking it from Walsingham, p.566).

151   *Y Llenor*, 9 (1897), 71.

152   *Y Llenor Cymreig*, 1 (1882), 110–11.

[153] J.E. Lloyd, *Owen Glendower*, pp.31, 35, 68–9; Gwilym Arthur Jones, *Owain Glyndŵr c.1354–1416*, pp.8/9, 42/43.

[154] Hahn, *Sagwissenschaftliche Studien*; Rank, *The Myth and Birth of the Hero*; Raglan, *The Hero, A Study in Tradition, Myth, and Drama*; Rees, 'The Ritual Background of Celtic Heroes and Saints'; Campbell, *The Hero with a Thousand Faces*; Propp, *Morphology of the Folktale*. For discussion of these, see Archer Taylor, 'The Biographical Pattern in Traditional Narrative'. As has happened with so many theories developed first through examination of Indo-European materials, the hero's biographical pattern, often referred to as the Indo-European heroic pattern, is now recognized as having a much more extensive international scope, especially in Semitic materials. However, examination of non Indo-European materials has been insufficient to establish any claim for a universal pattern.

[155] His father was Gruffydd Fychan ap Madog ap Gruffydd Fychan, barons of Glyndyfrdwy and Cynllaith Owain and descended from Madog ap Maredudd, king of Powys. His mother Helen was daughter of Thomas ap Llywelyn ab Owen, of the royal line of Deheubarth.

[156] Holinshed, p.521; 1808 edition, III, 21.

[157] J.E. Lloyd points out that the portent was originally connected with Mortimer, but that an unclear reference created confusion between the two men because: '*Ann. Hen. IV*, 349 (followed by Walsingham, ii.254) has an ambiguous "hujus"'. (J.E. Lloyd, *Owen Glendower*, p.52, n.3.)

[158] Pennant, *Tours*, p.290, quoting Holinshed; *Y Llenor* 9 (1897), 71.

[159] Field tapes, 1982, transcription, p.287.

[160] *Henry IV*, Part I, Act 3, sc.1, ll.12–16, 20, 23, 35–42.

[161] Trevelyan, *Folk-Lore and Folk-Stories of Wales*, p.41.

[162] Arch Camb 110 (1961), 113, quoting Samuel Lewis, *A Topographical Dictionary of Wales* (3rd ed., 1844), I, 306.

[163] *Bye-Gones*, 1 (1871–3), 172; Arch Camb 5:15 (1898), 284.

[164] Firbank, *Country of Memorable Honour*, p.46.

[165] Samuel Lewis, *A Topographical Dictionary of Wales*, s.v. Corwen. This legend, which was frequently printed and which is very much alive in the Corwen area, will be discussed further in the next chapter.

[166] *Y Geninen*, 10 (1892), 6.

[167] *Baner ac Amserau Cymru*, 11 Hydref (October) 1927, p.6, col.4.

[168] Field notes, II; field tapes, 1982, transcription, p.129.

[169] See Dundes, 'The Hero Pattern and the Life of Jesus'.

[170] *Y Brython*, 4 (1861), 331–2.

[171] AWC, tapes 4750 (23/9/75), 4760 (24/9/75); *Llen Gwerin Blaenau Rhymni*, p.15.

[172] Personal communication from Mary Burdett-Jones as well as her article 'Gweddi Anarferol', with references to Bodleian, Ashmole MS 1815, p.56 and Aberystwyth, NLW 10, p.42.

5   Local Hero and Nationalist Symbol

1   Field tapes, 1982, transcription, pp.194, 168.
2   Field notes II, 9. I could not see the stone because of an intractable bull in the field.
3   Field notes, II, 15, at Pen-y-bont.
4   Cledwyn Fychan, notes on conversation with John and Jim James, December 1965; field tapes, 1982, transcription, p.81.
5   Field tapes, 1982, transcription, p.164; personal communication from Robin Gwyndaf, 9 May 1982.
6   *Y Brython*, 4 (1961), 253; William Jones, *Plwyf Beddgelert*, p.37; Hewett, *Walking through Merioneth*, pp.80–1; Bowen, *Atlas Meirionnydd*, p.193. Aberystwyth, NLW 39B, compiled at the end of the eighteenth century, contains on p.68 the note: 'Near Corwen there is a place called pigyn Craig Owen [tip/peak of Owen's Rock], which is the highest part of the rock above the town, of Corwen, where there is a Stone Chair, call'd *Cadair Owen*, and in that, it is said Owen Glyndwr frequently used to sit.'
7   Thomas Evans, *Cambrian Itinerary*, p.170; W.J. Lewis, *Born on a Perilous Rock*, p.6. The ruins were razed in 1967.
8   AWC, MS 2593/84, pp.2–3, 7.
9   Field tapes, 1982, transcription, pp.116, 139, for example.
10   Field tapes, 1982, transcription, p.112.
11   Field tapes, 1982, transcription, p.137.
12   Field notes, II, 9.
13   Cernyw, *Hynafiaethau Edeyrnion*, p.9.
14   Field tapes, 1982, transcription, p.137.
15   Field tapes, 1982, transcription, pp.112–13.
16   Field tapes, 1982, transcription, p.128.
17   Field tapes, 1982, transcription, p.159.
18   Field tapes, 1982, transcription, p.144.
19   Field tapes, 1982, transcription, p.113.
20   Field tapes, 1982, transcription, p.138.
21   AWC, MS 2593/81, p.90.
22   Cledwyn Fychan, notes on conversation with John and Jim James, 1965. The stones are described as two white stones on the bank of the Hyddgen river between Nantyllyn and Hyddgen.
23   Cledwyn Fychan, notes on conversations with Mr Olwen, 1966, and with Meirwen Hughes, 1980.
24   Cledwyn Fychan, notes on conversation with Mrs A. Evans, Machynlleth, c.1967.
25   Aberystwyth, NLW 39B, p.68.
26   Thomas Evans, *Cambrian Itinerary*, p.266; Thomas Thomas, *Memoirs of Owen Glendower*, p.66, which adds about Glyndŵr, 'whose memory is still dear to the natives, and his exploits related with raptures'.

27 Lewis, *A Topographical Dictionary of Wales*, s.v. Corwen; Owen Jones, *Cymru: yn Hanesyddol*, I, 333; Cernyw, *Hynafiaethau Edeyrnion*, p.9.
28 Field tapes, 1982, transcription, p.289.
29 Field tapes, 1982, transcription, p.145.
30 Field tapes, 1982, transcription, p.88.
31 Field tapes, 1982, transcription, p.119.
32 Field notes, II, 16.
33 Field notes, II, 16; field tapes, 1982, transcription, pp.114–15.
34 Field tapes, 1982, transcription, p.94.
35 Field tapes, 1982, transcription, p.145.
36 Field notes, II, 41.
37 Field notes, II, 45.
38 Field tapes, 1982, transcription, pp.287–8.
39 Field tapes, 1982, transcription, pp.49–50.
40 Field tapes, 1982, transcription, p.168.
41 Field tapes, 1982, transcription, p.120. All he had to say about Caer Drewyn was 'Clŵas ddeud fod Owain Glyndŵr 'di bod yno' (I heard it said that Owain Glyndŵr had been there), p.145.
42 Field tapes, 1982, transcription, p.138.
43 Field notes, II, 29.
44 Field tapes, 1982, transcription, p.92.
45 Field tapes, 1982, transcription, pp.75–7.
46 Field tapes, 1982, transcription, p.219.
47 Rhŷs, *Celtic Folklore*, I, 125–6.
48 *Western Mail*, 12 January 1995.
49 For fuller discussion of the significance and impact of 'Brad y Llyfrau Gleision', see Prys Morgan, 'From Long Knives to Blue Books', pp.199–215, and idem, *Brad y Llyfrau Gleision*.
50 For history of the nationalist movement in Wales and discussion of its background and history, see: David Williams, *A History of Modern Wales*; Roderick, ed., *Wales Through the Ages*, vol.II; P. Berresford Ellis, *Wales – A Nation Again!*; Gwynfor Evans, *Wales Can Win*; idem, *Land of My Fathers*; R. Tudur Jones, *The Desire of Nations*; John Davies, ed., *Cymru'n Deffro*; Kenneth O. Morgan, *Rebirth of a Nation: Wales 1880–1980*. I am grateful to Ned Thomas for further explanation.
51 Field tapes, 1982, transcription, p.291.
52 David Williams, *A History of Modern Wales*, p.271.
53 Griffith John Williams, *Edward Lhuyd ac Iolo Morganwg*, p.28.
54 Ibid., p.21.
55 *Cambro-Briton*, III, 17.
56 Ibid., pp.25–6.
57 Ibid., p.26.
58 *Transactions of the Cymmrodorion or Metropolitan Cambrian Institution*, 2 (1828), 173.
59 *Lleuad yr Oes*, 3:10 (1829), cols.513, 581.
60 *Y Llenor Cymreig*, 1 (1882), 109–10.
61 *Y Llenor*, 9 (1897), 65–6.

62 *Y Llenor*, 9 (1897), 78. The use of the word *(g)werin* in this and the following quotation and which is here translated as 'people', has the connotation of 'folk' and is indicative of the egalitarian attitudes which were becoming more prevalent in the nineteenth century, when the folk or common people were idealized as the conservators of Welsh culture. When Owain Glyndŵr becomes the saviour of the *gwerin*, he is being placed in acceptable nineteenth-century social terms for O.M. Edwards and his kind.

63 *Y Llenor*, 9 (1897), 79.

64 *Bye-Gones*, 5, Second Series (1897), 118. Owen Rhoscomyl is the pen-name of the adventurer Arthur Owen Vaughan.

65 Ibid., 117.

66 John Edward Lloyd, *A History of Wales*.

67 Rhŷs, *Celtic Folklore*.

68 *Cymru'r Plant*, 17 (1908), 217–18, 313.

69 *Cymru*, 5 (1893), 249–51.

70 Meirwen Hughes, 'Brwydr Hyddgen', *Y Cymro*, 29 Hydref (October) 1974.

71 *Cymru*, 4 (1893), 173; reprinted in *Y Geninen*, 33 (1915), 152.

72 Ibid.

73 Eifion Wyn, 'Owain Glyndwr', *Cymru*, 13 (1897), 188; also printed in Eifion Wyn, *O Drum i Draeth*, pp.156–66.

74 Ap Ceredigion, 'Owen Glyndwr', *Cymru*, 38 (1910), 60.

75 J.E. Lloyd, 'Owen Glyn Dŵr: His Family and Early History', p.128. Mynyddog is the bardic name of Richard Davies (1833–77).

76 Owen Rhoscomyl, *Flame-Bearers of Welsh History*, p.219.

77 Ibid., p.228.

78 Millward, '"Cenedl o Bobl Ddewrion": Y Rhamant Hanesyddol yn Oes Victoria'.

79 'Owain Glyndwr', *Tarian y Gweithiwr*, 6 Mehefin (June) 1878, p.2; Wiliam Pritchard, *Owain Tudur*, p.115.

80 *Cymru*, 44 (1913).

81 *Tarian y Gweithiwr*, 8 Chwefror (February) 1878, p.2.

82 J.E. Lloyd, *Owen Glendower*, p.146.

83 The quotation is from a lecture by Gwyn A. Williams. It and the photograph appear in Gwynfor Evans, *Rhagom i Ryddid*, facing p.33.

84 Geary, 'Meibion Glyndŵr: Folk-Devils or Folk-Heroes?'

85 Iorwerth Feddyg, *Yspryd Glyndŵr*.

86 The quotation is taken from a letter (originally in Latin) to Glyndŵr's friend and supporter Henry Don. The full text appears in Matthews, *Welsh Records in Paris*, pp.105–6/113–14, and is discussed in Lloyd, *Owen Glendower*, p.40. The symbolic nature of invoking Glyndŵr is stressed by the quotation's placement next to a red dragon raising pennants inscribed, 'Annibyniaeth 2000', 'Rhyddid', 'Cyfiawnder', and 'Brawdoliaeth' (Independence 2000, Freedom, Justice, Brotherhood).

87 'Dydd y Cenhedloedd Bychain', *Cymru*, 47 (November 1914), 205.

88 Gwynfor Evans, *Wales Can Win*, p.79.

[89] Ibid., p.140.
[90] P. Berresford Ellis, *Wales – A Nation Again!*, p.138. The Free Wales Army further identified with Glyndŵr in the suggestion that the capital of Wales should be moved from Cardiff to Machynlleth, the site of Glyndŵr's parliament (ibid, p.140).
[91] Emyr Llewelyn, 'Sut Chwyldro', *Areithiau*, p.10. This speech was given at Glyndŵr's Parliament House in March 1969 and was thus also reacting to the impending investiture of Prince Charles.
[92] Emyr Llewelyn, 'Mi a Wn y Daw', *Areithiau*, pp.13–16. The *cywydd brud* appears in Aberystwyth, NLW MS 6209, pp.336–7.
[93] Dafydd Iwan, 'Myn Duw Mi a Wn y Daw', *Cant o Ganeuon*, pp.91–3.
[94] Geraint H. Jenkins, ed., *Cof Cenedl: Ysgrifau ar Hanes Cymru*.
[95] Field tapes, 1982, transcription, p.171.
[96] Field tapes, 1982, transcription, p.171.
[97] Field tapes, 1982, transcription, p.169.
[98] Field tapes, 1982, transcription, pp.202–3. This and the following transcriptions were reviewed by Mr Evans and lightly edited for transcription errors and clarity.
[99] Field tapes, 1982, transcription, pp.203–4.
[100] Field tapes, 1982, transcription, p.170.
[101] *Welsh Historical Sculpture*, p.60.
[102] Gwyn A. Williams, 'Owain Glyn Dŵr', p.183.
[103] Field tapes, 1982, transcription, p.172.
[104] Field tapes, 1982, transcription, pp.23, 26.
[105] Field tapes, 1982, transcription, p.134.
[106] Field tapes, 1982, transcription, p.191.
[107] Field tapes, 1982, transcription, p.287.
[108] Emyr Llewelyn, 'Mi a Wn y Daw', pp.13–16.
[109] *Y Llenor*, 9 (1897), 80.
[110] Field tapes, 1982, transcription, p.92–3.
[111] Field tapes, 1982, transcription, p.183.
[112] Field tapes, 1982, transcription, p.287.
[113] Frank Price Jones, 'Pam Llywelyn?', *Y Genhinen*, 19 (1969), 247.
[114] Field tapes, 1982, transcription, p.287.
[115] Field tapes, 1982, transcription, p.291.
[116] Field notes, II, 49.
[117] Field notes, I, 35.
[118] Field notes, I, 11.
[119] Field tapes, 1982, transcription, p.14.
[120] Field tapes, 1982, transcription, p.291.
[121] Field tapes, 1982, transcription, p.9.
[122] Field tapes, 1982, transcription, pp.62–3.
[123] Field tapes, 1982, transcription, p.5.
[124] Goronva Camlan, *Owen Glendower, a Dramatic Biography*, pp.xi, xix, xxii.
[125] Script of pageant, written and performed in Corwen, *c*.1967.
[126] Dafydd Penri Roberts and Derec Williams, *Y Mab Darogan* (unpublished script, 1981).

127   Ibid.
128   *Y Mab Darogan*, programme, p.6.
129   Field tapes, 1982, transcription, p.243.
130   Berthoff, *British Immigrants in Industrial America*, p.145. The author also notes 'Owain Glyndŵr' as the name of a fraternal order's lodge in a Pennsylvania coalmining town (p.180).
131   Green, *The Vale of Rheidol Light Railway*, pp.192–9.
132   *Welsh Historical Sculpture*, p.59.
133   Personal communication by Brynley F. Roberts of information learned from E.G. Millward, 1994. The verse is apparently related to a nineteenth-century English rhyme, which begins with the lines, 'Where are you going to, my pretty maid?/ I'm going a-milking, sir, she said', and concludes, after the maid states that her father is a farmer and her face is her fortune, with the lines, 'Then I can't marry you, my pretty maid./ Nobody asked you, sir, she said.' The rhyme has a history of at least several centuries, traced in Opie and Opie, *The Oxford Dictionary of Nursery Rhymes*, pp.281–3. The relationship between the postcard verse and the English rhyme is further accentuated by the fact that some of the postcards depict the maid carrying a milk-pail.
134   I interviewed mainly at two Welsh schools in Aberystwyth – Penweddig and Yr Ysgol Gymraeg. Field tapes, 1982.
135   Field notes, I, 37.
136   Field notes, I, 51.
137   Field notes, I, 55.

Bibliography

Aarne, Antti, and Stith Thompson, *The Types of the Folktale*, Folklore Fellows Communication 184 (Helsinki, 1961).

Adam of Usk, *Chronicon Adae de Usk*, ed. and trans. Edward Maunde Thompson, 2nd ed. (London: Henry Frowde, 1904).

Ashe, Geoffrey, *The Discovery of King Arthur* (Garden City, New York: Anchor Press/Doubleday, 1985).

Ashton, Charles, ed., *Gweithiau Iolo Goch* (Croesoswallt: Anrhydeddus Gymdeithas y Cymmrodorion, 1896).

Babcock-Abrahams, Barbara, ' "A Tolerated Margin of Mess": The Trickster and His Tales Reconsidered', JFI 11 (1975), 147–86.

Balys, Jonas, *Motif-Index of Lithuanian Narrative Folk-Lore*, Folklore Studies, (Kaunus: Lithuanian Folklore Archives, 1936), vol.2.

Barbour, John, *The Bruce, an Epic Poem*, trans. and ed. Archibald A.H. Douglas (Glasgow: William Maclellan, 1964).

Barddoniaeth y Plant III (Wrexham, 1935).

Baughman, Ernest Warren, *Type and Motif-Index of the Folktales of England and North America* (The Hague: Mouton & Co., 1966).

Berthoff, Rowland Tappan, *British Immigrants in Industrial America, 1790–1950* (Cambridge: Harvard University Press, 1953).

Borrow, George, *Wild Wales* (Glasgow: Fontana/Collins, [1862], 1977).

Bowen, Geraint, ed., *Atlas Meirionnydd* (Y Bala: Gwasg y Sir, [?1974]).

Bradley, Arthur Granville, *Owen Glyndwr and the Last Struggle for Welsh Independence* (New York: G.P. Putnam's Sons, 1902).

Bromwich, Rachel, ed., *Trioedd Ynys Prydein* (Cardiff: University of Wales Press, 1978).

Bullock-Davies, Constance, ' "*Exspectare Arturum*": Arthur and the Messianic Hope', BBCS 29 (1981), 432–40.

Burdett-Jones, Mary, 'A Note on a Welsh Legal Manuscript, British Library, Cotton Caligula A iii', *Journal of the National Library of Wales* 28 (1987–8), 349–51.

——,'Gweddi Anarferol', *Y Cylchgrawn Catholig* 3 (1994), 35–6.

The Cambro-Briton, 3 vol. (London: W. Simpkin and Marshall, 1820–2).

Camden's Britannia (London: F. Collins, 1695).

Campbell, Joseph, *The Hero with a Thousand Faces* (New York: Meridian Books, 1956).

Carr, A.D., *Medieval Anglesey* (Llangefni: Anglesey Antiquarian Society, 1982).

——, 'Who was Owen of Wales?', *La Société Guernesiaise Report and Transactions* 22, 1 (1986), 77–90.

——, 'Owain Lawgoch: Yr Etifedd Olaf', *Cof Cenedl V* (Llandysul: Gwasg Gomer, 1990), pp.1–27.

Cernyw, Hywel, *Hynafiaethau Edeyrnion* (Corwen: R. Hughes, 1878).

Chambers, E.K., *Arthur of Britain* (London: Sidgwick and Jackson, 1927).

Chodzko, Alexander, coll. and trans., *Specimens of the Popular Poetry of Persia as Found in the Adventures and Improvisations of Kurroglou, the Bandit-Minstrel of Northern Persia* (London: Oriental Translation Fund, 1842).

Cofnodion a Chyfansoddiadau Buddugol Eisteddfod Aberdar, 1885 (Caerdydd: Meistri D. Duncan a'i Feibion, 1887).

Cofnodion a Chyfansoddiadau Buddugol Eisteddfod Bangor, 1902 (Liverpool: I. Foulkes, 1903).

Cofnodion a Chyfansoddiadau Buddugol Eisteddfod Llanelli, 1895 (Cymdeithas yr Eisteddfod Genedlaethol, 1898).

Cohn, Norman, *The Pursuit of the Millenium* (London: Secker & Warburg, 1957).

Davidson, Hilda, 'Folklore and History', *Patterns of Folklore* (Ipswich: D.S. Brewer, 1978).

Davies, A. Stanley, ed., *Ballads of Montgomeryshire* (Welshpool, 1938).

Davies, J.H., 'A Welsh Version of the Birth of Arthur', *Y Cymmrodor* 24 (1913), 247–64.

Davies, John, ed., *Cymru'n Deffro* (Talybont: Y Lolfa, 1981).

——, *Hanes Cymru* (London: Penguin Books, 1992).

Davies, Jonathan Ceredig, *Folk-Lore of West and Mid-Wales* (Aberystwyth: Welsh Gazette, 1911).

Davies, R. Rees, 'Race Relations in Post-Conquest Wales: Confrontation and Compromise', THSC (1975), 32–56.

——, 'Law and National Identity in Thirteenth-Century Wales', *Welsh Society and Nationhood: Historical Essays Presented to Glanmor Williams*, ed. R.R. Davies, Ralph A. Griffiths, Ieuan Gwynedd Jones, and Kenneth O. Morgan (Cardiff: University of Wales Press, 1984), pp.51–69.

——, 'Ar Drywydd Owain Glyndŵr', *Cof Cenedl II* (Llandysul: Gwasg Gomer, 1987), pp.1–26.

——, *The Age of Conquest: Wales, 1063–1415* (Oxford: Oxford University Press, 1991).

Dictionary of Welsh Biography Down to 1940 (London: Honourable Society of Cymmrodorion, 1959).

Dodd, A.H., 'Nationalism in Wales: A Historical Assessment', THSC (1971); 33–49.

Dorson, Richard M., ed., *Folktales Told around the World* (Chicago: University of Chicago Press, 1975).

Dundes, Alan, 'The Hero Pattern and the Life of Jesus', *Interpreting Folklore* (Bloomington: Indiana University Press, 1980), pp.223–61.

[Edwards, O.M.], 'Dydd y Cenhedloedd Bychain', *Cymru* 47 (November, 1914), 201–5.

Eifion Wyn, *O Drum i Draeth* (Llundain: Gwasg Gymraeg Foyle, 1929).

Eliade, Mircea, *Myth and Reality* (New York: Harper & Row, 1963).

Ellis, P. Berresford, *Wales – A Nation Again!* (London: Tandem Books, 1968).

Ellis, Thomas, *Memoirs of Owen Glendowr*, printed in *A History of the Island of Anglesey* (London: J. Dodsley, 1775).

Evans, C.J., *The Story of Glamorgan* (Cardiff: Educational Publishing Company, 1908).

Evans, Dafydd H., 'Twm Siôn Cati', *Coleg Dewi a'r Fro*, ed. D.P. Davies (Llanbedr Pont Steffan: Coleg Prifysgol Dewi Sant, 1984), pp.8–19.

Evans, Griffith, *The Arthurian Legend: Its Message for Today*, United Wales Pamphlets, No. 1 (Caernarvon: The Gwenlyn Press, n.d.).

Evans, Gwynfor, *Rhagom i Ryddid* (Bangor: Plaid Cymru, 1964).

——, *Wales Can Win* (Llandybie: Christopher Davies, 1973).

——, *Land of My Fathers* (Swansea: John Penry Press, 1974).

Evans, J. Gwenogvryn, ed., *Black Book of Carmarthen* (Pwllheli, 1906).

——, ed., *Book of Taliesin* (Llanbedrog, 1910).

——, ed., *The Poetry in the Red Book of Hergest* (Llanbedrog, 1911).

——, ed., *Llyfr Gwyn Rhydderch* (Caerdydd: Gwasg Prifysgol Cymru, 1973).

Evans, Myra, *Casgliad o Chwedlau Newydd* (Aberystwyth: Cambrian News [1926]).

Evans, R. Wallis, 'Trem ar y Cywydd Brud', *Harlech Studies: Essays Presented to Dr. Thomas Jones*, ed. B.B. Thomas (Cardiff: University of Wales Press Board, 1938), pp.149–63.

——, 'Prophetic Poetry', *A Guide to Welsh Literature*, vol.2, ed. A.O.H. Jarman and Gwilym Rees Hughes (Swansea: Christopher Davies, 1979), pp.278–97.

Evans, Thomas, *Cambrian Itinerary, or Welsh Tourist* (London: C. Whittingham, 1801).

Fenton, Richard, *Tours in Wales (1804–1813)* (London: The Bedford Press, 1917).

Fentress, James, and Chris Wickham, *Social Memory* (Oxford: Blackwell, 1992).

Firbank, Thomas, *A Country of Memorable Honour* (Bath: Cedric Chivers Ltd, [1953], 1971).

Fisher, J., ed., *Cefn Coch MSS* (Liverpool: I. Foulkes, 1899).

Foulkes, Isaac, 'Dyffryn Olwyd: Ei Ramantau a'i Lafar Gwlad', THSC (1893), 88–103.

Friedman, Albert B., 'The Usable Myth: The Legends of Modern Mythmakers', *American Folk Legend: A Symposium*, ed. Wayland D. Hand (Berkeley: University of California Press, 1971).

Fychan, Cledwyn, 'Llywelyn ab y Moel a'r Canolbarth', *Llên Cymru* 15 (1987–8), 289–307.

Geary, Roger, 'Meibion Glyndŵr: Folk-Devils or Folk-Heroes?', *Planet* 92 (April/May 1992), 39–44.

Geoffrey of Monmouth, *The Historia Regum Britanniae of Geoffrey of Monmouth*, ed. Acton Griscom (London: Longmans, Green and Co., 1929).

——, *History of the Kings of Britain*, trans. Lewis Thorpe (Harmondsworth: Penguin Books Ltd., [1966], 1976).

——, *Life of Merlin, Vita Merlini*, ed. and trans. Basil Clarke (Cardiff: University of Wales Press, 1973).

Gerald of Wales, *The Journey through Wales and The Description of Wales*, trans. Lewis Thorpe (Harmondsworth: Penguin Books Ltd, 1978).

——, *De Principis Instructione*, vol.8 (1891), ed. George F. Warner, in *Giraldi Cambrensis Opera*, ed. J.S. Brewer, 8 vol., Rolls Series 21 (London, 1861–91).

——, *Speculum Ecclesiae*, vol.4 (1873) in *Giraldi Cambrensis Opera*, ed. J.S. Brewer, 8 vols., Rolls Series 21 (London, 1861–91).

Gildas, *The Ruin of Britain*, ed. and trans. Michael Winterbottom (Totowa, New Jersey: Rowman and Littlefield, 1978).

Goronva Camlan [Rowland Williams], *Owen Glendower, a Dramatic Biography* (London: Williams and Norgate, 1870).

Green, C.C., *The Vale of Rheidol Light Railway* (Didcot, Oxon: Wild Swan Publications, 1986).

Gresham, Colin A., 'Platform Houses in North-West Wales', Arch Camb 103 (1954), 18–53.

Griffiths, Margaret Enid, *Early Vaticination in Welsh* (Cardiff: Gwasg Prifysgol Cymru, 1937).

Grinsell, Leslie V., *Folklore of Prehistoric Sites in Britain* (Newton Abbot: David & Charles, 1976).

Gruffydd, W.J., ed., 'Iolo Goch's "I Owain Glyndwr ar ddifancoll"', *Y Cymmrodor* 21 (1908), 105–12.

——, *Y Flodeugerdd Newydd* (Caerdydd: Cwmni Cyhoeddiadol Addysgol, 1909).

Gwaith Lewis Glyn Cothi (Oxford: The Cymmrodorion, 1837).

Y Gwyddoniadur Cymreig, (1866).

Gwyndaf, Robin, 'The Cauldron of Regeneration: Continuity and Function in the Welsh Folk Epic Tradition', *The Heroic Process*, ed. Bo Almqvist, Séamus Ó Catháin, Pádraig Ó Héalaí (Dublin: The Glendale Press, 1987), pp.413–51.

Hague, Douglas B., 'The Bishop's Palace, Gogarth, Llandudno, Caernarvonshire', *Transactions of the Caernarvonshire Historical Society* 17 (1956), 9–22.

Hahn, J.G. von, *Sagwissenschaftliche Studien* (Jena, 1871–6).

Hardwick, Charles, *Traditions, Superstitions, and Folk-Lore* (Simpkin, Marshall & Co., 1872).

Hardy, James, ed., *The Denham Tracts* (London: David Nutt, 1895).

Harries, Leslie, ed., *Gwaith Huw Cae Llwyd ac Eraill* (Caerdydd: Gwasg Prifysgol Cymru, 1953).

Hartland, Edwin Sidney, *The Science of Fairy Tales* (London: Walter Scott Publishing Co., 1914).

Haycock, Marged, 'Llyfr Taliesin: astudiaethau ar rai agweddau' (Ph.D. dissertation, University of Wales, 1982).

Hayward, John, *The First Part of the Life and Raigne of King Henrie the IIII* (London: Iohn Wolfe, 1599) in *The First Volume of the Works of Sir Iohn Hayward Knight, hitherto published*, coll. Iohn Bill (1623).

Headley, Mary Gwendoline, 'Barddoniaeth Llawdden a Rhys Nanmor' (MA thesis, University of Wales, 1938).

Henry of Huntingdon, *Epistola ad Warinum*, vol.4 (1889) in *Chronicles of the Reigns of Stephen, Henry II, and Richard I*, ed. Richard Howlett, 4 vols., Rolls Series 82 (London, 1884–9), pp.65–75.

Hewett, Hope, *Walking through Merioneth* (Newton: The Welsh Outlook Press, n.d.).

Higden, Ranulf, *Polychronicon Ranulphi Higden*, ed. Joseph Rawson Lumby, Rolls Series 41 (London: Longman & Co, 1882), vol.8.

Hobley, W., *Hanes Methodistiaeth Arfon* (Caernarfon: Cyfarfod Misol Arfon, 1924).

Hobsbawm, Eric, *Primitive Rebels, Studies in Archaic Forms of Social Movement in the 19th and 20th Centuries* (New York: Frederick A. Praeger, 1959, [1963]).

——, *Bandits* (Delacorte Press, 1969).

——, *Nations and Nationalism since 1780* (Cambridge: Cambridge University Press, 1990).

Hogg, A.H.A., 'A 14th Century House-Site at Cefn-y-Fan Near Dolbenmaen, Caernarvonshire', THSC 15 (1954), 1–7.

Holinshed, Raphael, *The Chronicles of England, Scotland, and Ireland* (London: 1587).

——, *Holinshed's Chronicles of England, Scotland, and Ireland*, 6 vol. (London: J. Johnson, 1808).

Howells, William, *Cambrian Superstitions* (London: Longman & Co., 1831).

Hughes, Hugh Derfel, *Hynafiaethau Llandegai a Llanllechid* (Bethesda: R. Jones, Y Swyddfa 'Yr Ardd.', [1866], 1979).

Ingman, John, 'Notes on Some Old Bangor Inns', *Transactions of the Caernarvonshire Historical Society* 10 (1949), 38–52.

Iolo Morganwg, *Iolo Manuscripts*, ed. and trans. Taliesin Williams (Llandovery: Welsh MSS. Society, 1848).

Iorwerth Feddyg, *Ysbryd Glyndŵr: neu y clêdd lle metho hêdd* (Gwrecsam: Hughes a'i Fab, 1911).

Isaac, Evan, *Coelion Cymru* (Aberystwyth: Gwasg Aberystwyth, 1938).

Iwan, Dafydd, 'Myn Duw Mi a Wn y Daw', *Cant o Ganeuon* (Talybont: Y Lolfa, 1982), pp.91–3.

Jarman, A.O.H., 'Wales a Part of England 1485–1800', in *The Historical Basis of Welsh Nationalism* (Cardiff: Plaid Cymru, 1950), pp.79–98.

—— and Gwilym Rees Hughes, *A Guide to Welsh Literature*, vol.1 (Swansea: Christopher Davies, 1976).

——, ed., *Llyfr Du Caerfyrddin* (Caerdydd: Gwasg Prifysgol Cymru, 1982).

Jenkins, Abraham, 'The Works of Tudur Penllyn and Ieuan Brydydd Hir Hynaf' (MA thesis, University of Wales, 1921).

Jenkins, Geraint H., ed., *Cof Cenedl: Ysgrifau ar Hanes Cymru* (Llandysul: Gwasg Gomer, 1986–).

Johnston, David, 'Iolo Goch and the English: Welsh Poetry and Politics in the Fourteenth Century', CMCS 12 (1986), 73–98.

Johnston, George, trans., *Saga of Gisli the Outlaw* (Toronto: University of Toronto Press, [1963], reprint 1984).

Jones, Bedwyr Lewis, 'Sion ap Howel ap Owen, Cefn Treflaeth', *Trafodion Cymdeithas Hanes Sir Gaernarfon* 21 (1960), 63–9.

Jones, E.D., ed., *Gwaith Lewis Glyn Cothi* (Caerdydd: Gwasg Prifysgol Cymru, 1953).

Jones, Frank Price, 'Pam Llywelyn?', *Y Genhinen* 19 (1969), 244–7.

Jones, Geraint Percy, 'Astudiaeth destunol o ganu Wiliam Cynwal yn Llawysgrif (Bangor) Mostyn 4' (MA thesis, University of Wales, 1969).

Jones, Gwilym Arthur, *Owain Glyndŵr, c.1354–1416* (Cardiff: University of Wales Press, 1962).

Jones, Gwyn and Thomas Jones, trans., *Mabinogion*, Everyman's Library (London: Dent, 1949).

Jones, Howell Llewellyn, 'Bywyd a barddoniaeth Iorwerth Fynglwyd' (MA thesis, University of Wales, 1970).

Jones, Islwyn, ed., *Gwaith Hywel Cilan* (Caerdydd: Gwasg Prifysgol Cymru, 1963).

Jones, J. (Myrddin Fardd), *Llên Gwerin Sir Gaernarfon* (Caernarfon: Cwmni y Cyhoeddwyr Cymreig, [1908]).

Jones, John Morris, *Caniadau* (Rhydychen: Fox, Jones, & Co, 1907).

Jones, Owen, 'Owain Glyndwr a'i Amserau' in his *Pymtheg o Ddarlithiau ar Hanes y Cymry* (Pwllheli: W. Edwards & Co., 1853).

——, ed., *Cymru: yn Hanesyddol, Parthedegol, a Bywgraphyddol*, 2 vol. (Llundain: Blackie a'i Fab, 1875).

——, ed., *Ceinion Llenyddiaeth Gymreig*, 2 vol. (Llundain: Blackie a'i Fab, 1876).

Jones, R. Tudur, *The Desire of Nations* (Llandybie: Christopher Davies, 1974).

Jones, Richard Lewis, 'Astudiaeth destunol o awdlau, cywyddau ac englynion gan Wiliam Cynwal' (MA thesis, University of Wales, 1969).

Jones, T. Gwynn, ed., *Ceiriog* (Wrecsam: Hughes a'i Fab, n.d.).

——, 'Cultural Bases: A Study of the Tudor Period in Wales', *Y Cymmrodor* 31 (1921), 161–73.

——, ed., *Gwaith Tudur Aled*, 2 vol. (Caerdydd: Gwasg Prifysgol Cymru, 1926).

Jones, Thomas, 'A Sixteenth Century Version of the Arthurian Cave Legend', *Studies in Language and Literature in Honor of Margaret Schlauch*, ed. Mieczyslaw Brahmer, Stanislaw Helsztynski, Julian Krzyzanowski (Warszawa: Polish Scientific Publishers, 1966).

——, ed. and trans., *Brehinedd y Saesson*, Board of Celtic Studies, University of Wales, History and Law Series, No. 25 (Cardiff: University of Wales Press, 1971).

Jones, W. Garmon, 'Welsh Nationalism and Henry Tudor', THSC (1919), 1–59.

Jones, W. Lewis, *King Arthur in History and Legend* (Cambridge: University Press, 1911).

Jones, William (Bleddyn), *Plwyf Beddgelert: ei hynafiaethau a'i gofiannau* (Tremadog: Swyddfa'r Brython, 1862).

Keen, Maurice, *The Outlaws of Medieval Legend* (London: Routledge & Kegan Paul, 1961, rev. 1987).

Kinsella, Thomas, trans., *The Táin* (London: Oxford University Press, 1970).

Klapp, Orrin E., 'The Clever Hero', JAF 67 (1954), 21–34.

Lanczkowski, Günter, *Verborgene Heilbringer* (Darmstadt: Wissenschaftliche Buchgesellschaft, 1977).

Lewis, Ceri W., 'The Court Poets: Their Function, Status and Craft', *A Guide to Welsh Literature*, vol.1, ed. A.O.H. Jarman and Gwilym Rees Hughes (Swansea: Christopher Davies, 1976), pp.123–56.

Lewis, Henry, 'An Ode to Owen Glendower, after His Disappearance', in 'A Historical Poem by Iolo Goch', *Y Cymmrodor* 4 (1881), 230–2.

——, 'Rhai Cywyddau Brud', BBCS 1, No.3 (1922), 240–55.

——, 'Cywyddau Brud', BBCS 1, No.4 (1923), 296–309.

—— and Thomas Roberts, Ifor Williams, eds., *Cywyddau Iolo Goch ac Eraill* (Caerdydd: Gwasg Prifysgol Cymru, [1925], 1972).

Lewis, Samuel, *A Topographical Dictionary of Wales*, 2 vol. (London: S. Lewis and Co., 1833).

Lewis, W.J., *Born on a Perilous Rock: Aberystwyth Past and Present* (Aberystwyth: Cambrian News, 1980).

Lhuyd, Edward, 'Additions to Brecknockshire', in *Camden's Britannia* (London: F. Collins, 1695).

——, *Parochialia*, ed. Rupert H. Morris (London: Cambrian Archaeological Association, 1909–11).

Llen Gwerin Blaenau Rhymni (Pengam: Ysgol Lewis, 1912).

Llewelyn, Emyr, *Areithiau* (Talybont: Y Lolfa, 1970).

Lloyd, J.Y.W., *The History of Powys Fadog*, 6 vol. (London: T. Richards, 1881–7).

Lloyd, John Edward, *A History of Wales* (London: Longmans, Green, and Co., 1912).

——, 'Owen Glyn Dŵr: His Family and Early History', THSC (1920), 128–45.

——, *Owen Glendower / Owen Glyn Dŵr* (Oxford: Clarendon Press, 1931).

Llywelyn-Williams, Alun, *Crwydro Brycheiniog* (Llandybie: Llyfrau'r Dryw, 1964).

Loomis, Roger Sherman, ed., *Arthurian Literature in the Middle Ages* (Oxford: Clarendon Press, 1959).

Madgwick, P.J., Non Griffiths, and Valerie Walker, *The Politics of Rural Wales: A Study of Cardiganshire* (London: Hutchinson & Co, 1973).

Matthews, T., ed., *Welsh Records in Paris* (Carmarthen: W. Spurrell and Son, 1910).

Meyrick, Samuel Rush, *The History and Antiquities of the County of Cardigan* (Brecon: Davies and Co., 1907).

Millward, E.G., '"Cenedl o Bobl Ddewrion": Y Rhamant Hanesyddol yn Oes Victoria', *Ysgrifau Beirniadol XVII*, ed. J.E. Caerwyn Williams (Dinbych: Gwasg Gee, 1990), pp.131–47.

Morgan, Kenneth O., *Rebirth of a Nation: Wales 1880–1980* (Oxford: Oxford University Press, 1982).

Morgan, Prys, 'Rhag Pob Brad', *Y Traethodydd* (April 1982), 80–91.

——, 'From Long Knives to Blue Books', *Welsh Society and Nationhood: Historical Essays Presented to Glanmor Williams*, ed. R.R. Davies, Ralph A. Griffiths, Ieuan Gwynedd Jones, and Kenneth O. Morgan (Cardiff: University of Wales Press, 1984), pp.199–215.

——, ed., *Brad y Llyfrau Gleision* (Llandysul: Gwasg Gomer, 1991).

Morrice, J.C., ed., *Barddoniaeth Wiliam Llŷn a'i Eirlyfr Gyda Nodiadau* (Bangor: Jarvis a Foster, 1908).

Morris, Jan, *The Matter of Wales* (Oxford: Oxford University Press, 1984).

Morris, Lewis, *Celtic Remains* (London: J. Parker, 1878).

Morris, Robert Prys, *Cantref Meirionydd: ei chwedlau, ei hynafiaethau, a'i hanes* (Dolgellau: E.W. Evans, 1890).

Nagy, Joseph Falaky, *The Wisdom of the Outlaw: The Boyhood Deeds of Finn in Gaelic Narrative Tradition* (Berkeley: University of California Press, 1985).

Nennius, *British History and the Welsh Annals*, ed. and trans. John Morris (London and Chichester: Phillimore, 1980).

Noy, Dov, ed., *Folktales of Israel* (Chicago: University of Chicago Press, 1963).

Ó Cathasaigh, Tomás, *The Heroic Biography of Cormac mac Airt* (Dublin: Institute for Advanced Studies, 1977).

L'Oeuvre Poétique de Gutun Owain, ed. E. Bachellery, 2 vol. (Paris: Librairie Ancienne Honoré Champion, 1950, 1951).

Oinas, Felix J., 'Kalevipoeg and His South Slavic Relations', *Journal of Baltic Studies* 10 (1979), 369–80.

Opie, Iona, and Peter Opie, eds., *The Oxford Dictionary of Nursery Rhymes* (Oxford: Clarendon Press, 1951).

'Owain Glyndwr', *The Cambro-Briton* 3 (1822), 17–26.

'Owain Glyndwr', *Tarian y Gweithiwr* (1877–8).

Owen, Edward, 'Owain Lawgoch – Yeuain de Galles: Some Facts and Suggestions', THSC (1901), 6–105.

——, 'Owain Lawgoch – A Rejoinder', THSC (1902), 98–113.

Owen, Elias, *Welsh Folklore* (Oswestry and Wrexham: Woodall, Minshall, and Co., [1896]).

Owen, Nicholas, *Caernarvonshire: A Sketch of its History, Antiquities, Mountains, and Productions* (London: J. Debrett, 1792).

Owen, William, *Hanes Owain Glandwr* (Caernarfon: Peter Evans, 1833).

Owen, William, *History of Dolbadarn Castle, Llanberis* (Llanberis: W.H. Jones, n.d.).

Parry, G. Tecwyn, *Llanberis: ei hanes, ei phobl, a'i phethau* (Caernarfon: Cwmni y Cyhoeddwyr Cymreig, 1908).

Parry, Thomas, *A History of Welsh Literature* (Oxford: Clarendon Press, 1970).

Pennant, Thomas, *Hanes Owen Glyndwr, Tywysog Cymru* (Caernarfon: Cwmni y Cyhoeddwyr Cymru, n.d.).

——, *Tours in Wales*, ed. John Rhŷs (Caernarvon: H. Humphreys, 1883), vol.III, App. VII, 'of Owen Glyndwr'.

Phillips, D. Rhys, *A Select Bibliography of Owen Glyndŵr* (Swansea: Beili Glas, 1915).

Phillips, J.R.S., 'When Did Owain Glyndwr Die?', BBCS 24 (1972), 59–77.

Pierce, T. Jones, 'The Social Scene in the Fourteenth Century', *Wales Through the Ages*, ed. A.J. Roderick, 2 vol. (Llandybie: Christopher Davies, Ltd., [1959], 1973), vol.1, pp.153–9.

Powel, David, *The Historie of Cambria, now called Wales* (London, 1584).

Powys, John Cowper, *Owen Glendower* (New York: Simon and Schuster, 1940).

Pritchard, Wiliam, *Owain Tudur: Rhamant Hanesyddol* (Llanerchymedd: L. Jones, 1874).

Propp, Vladimir, *Morphology of the Folktale* (Austin: University of Texas Press, 1970).

Radin, Paul, *The Trickster* (London: Routledge and Kegan Paul, 1956).

Raglan, Lord, *The Hero, A Study in Tradition, Myth, and Drama* (New York: Vintage Books, 1956).

Rank, Otto, *The Myth and Birth of the Hero*, ed. Philip Freund (New York: Random House, Vintage Books, 1964).

Rees, Alwyn, 'The Ritual Background of Celtic Heroes and Saints' (MA thesis, University of Wales, 1937).

Rhoscomyl, Owen (Arthur Owen Vaughan), *Flame-Bearers of Welsh History* (Merthyr Tydfil: Welsh Educational Publishing Co., 1905).

Rhŷs, John, *Celtic Folklore: Welsh and Manx*, 2 vol. (London: Wildwood House, [1901], 1980).

Richards, W. Leslie, 'Cywyddau Brud Dafydd Llwyd ap Llywelyn ap Gruffudd o Fathafarn', *Llên Cymru* 2 (1953), 244–54.

——, ed., *Gwaith Dafydd Llwyd o Fathafarn* (Caerdydd: Gwasg Prifysgol Cymru, 1964).

Richards, William, 'The Works of Gruffydd Hiraethog', (MA thesis, University of Wales, 1925).

Robbins, Keith, *Nineteenth-Century Britain* (Oxford: Oxford University Press, 1989).

Roberts, Brynley F., 'Un o Lawysgrifau Hopcyn ap Tomas o Ynys Dawy', BBCS 22 (1967), 223–8.

——, 'Astudiaeth Destunol o'r Tri Chyfieithiad Cymraeg Cynharaf o *Historia Regum Britanniae* Sieffre o Fynwy' (Ph.D. dissertation, University of Wales, 1969).

——, ed., *Brut y Brenhinedd* (Dublin: Institute for Advanced Studies, 1971).

——, 'Testunau Hanes Cymraeg Canol', *Y Traddodiad Rhyddiaeth yn yr Oesau Canol*, ed. Geraint Bowen (Llandysul: Gwasg Gomer, 1974), pp.274–302.

——, 'Geoffrey of Monmouth and Welsh Historical Tradition', *Nottingham Mediaeval Studies* 20 (1976), 29–40.

——, 'Sieffre o Fynwy a Myth Hanes Cenedl y Cymry', *Cof Cenedl VI* (Llandysul: Gwasg Gomer, 1991), pp.1–32.

Roberts, Glyn, 'Wales and England: Antipathy and Sympathy

1282–1485', in his *Aspects of Welsh History* (Cardiff: University of Wales Press, 295–318.

Roberts, Gomer Morgan, *Hanes Plwyf Llandybïe* (Caerdydd: Gwasg Prifysgol Cymru, 1939).

——, *Chwedlau Dau Fynydd* (Llandebie: Llyfrau'r Dryw, 1948).

Roberts, John W., *From Trickster to Badman: The Black Folk Hero in Slavery and Freedom* (Philadelphia: University of Pennsylvania Press, 1989).

Roberts, Thomas, ed., *Gwaith Tudur Penllyn ac Ieuan ap Tudur Penllyn* (Caerdydd: Gwasg Prifysgol Cymru, 1958).

Roberts, Thomas, ed. and Ifor Williams, rev., *Poetical Works of Dafydd Nanmor* (Cardiff: University of Wales Press Board, 1923).

Roderick, A.J., *Wales through the Ages*, 2 vol. (Llandybie: Christopher Davies, 1973).

Rosenberg, Bruce A., *Custer and the Epic of Defeat* (University Park: Pennsylvania State University Press, 1974).

——, 'Custer and the Epic of Defeat', JAF 88 (1975), 165–77.

Rowlands, Eurys, 'Dilid y Broffwydoliaeth', *Trivium* 2 (1967), 37–46.

——, 'Iolo Goch', *Celtic Studies, Essays in Memory of Angus Matheson 1912–1962*, ed. James Carney and David Greene (London: Routledge and Kegan Paul, [1968], 1969), pp.124–46.

——, ed., *Gwaith Lewys Môn* (Caerdydd: Gwasg Prifysgol Cymru, 1975).

——, 'The Continuing Tradition', *A Guide to Welsh Literature*, vol.2, ed. A.O.H. Jarman and Gwilym Rees Hughes (Swansea: Christopher Davies, 1979), pp.298–321.

Schneider, Laurence A., *A Madman of Ch'u: The Chinese Myth of Loyalty and Dissent* (Berkeley: University of California Press, 1980).

Scott, Ronald McNair, *Robert the Bruce, King of Scots* (London: Hutchinson, 1982).

Shakespeare, William, *Henry IV*, Part I.

Siddons, Michael Powell, *The Development of Welsh Heraldry*, vol.1 (Aberystwyth: The National Library of Wales, 1991).

Sikes, Wirt, *British Goblins* (London: Sampson Low, Marston, Searle & Rivington, 1880).

Skidmore, Ian, *Owain Glyndŵr, Prince of Wales* (Swansea: Christopher Davies, 1978).

Smith, J. Beverley, 'Llywelyn ap Gruffudd a Chenedligrwydd Cymru', *Cof Cenedl IV* (Llandysul: Gwasg Gomer, 1989), pp.1–28.

——, *Yr Ymwybod â Hanes yng Nghymru yn yr Oesoedd Canol / The Sense of History in Medieval Wales* (Aberystwyth: Coleg Prifysgol Cymru, [1991]).

Snowdon and Welsh Highland Holiday Book (Llanberis: Snowdon Mountain Tramroad & Hotels Company Ltd, 1923).

Steckmesser, Kent L., 'Robin Hood and the American Outlaw', JAF 79 (1966), 348–55.

Styles, Showell, *Welsh Walks and Legends* (Cardiff: John Jones Cardiff Ltd, 1972).

Taliesin ab Iolo Morganwg, *Traethawd ar Gywreinedd, Hynafiaeth, a Hen Bendefigion Glyn Nedd* (Aberdar: Jenkin Howell, 1886).

Taylor, Archer, 'The Biographical Pattern in Traditional Narrative', JFI 1 (1964), 114–29.

Taylor, John, *The Universal Chronicle of Ranulf Higden* (Oxford: Clarendon Press, 1966).

Taylor, Rupert, *The Political Prophecy in England* (New York: Columbia University Press, 1911).

Thomas, Ceinwen, 'From the Fall of Llywelyn to the Tudor Period', in *The Historical Basis of Welsh Nationalism* (Cardiff: Plaid Cymru, 1950).

Thomas, Elwyn, *The Forerunner* (London: Lynwood & Co, 1910).

Thomas, Gwyn, *A Welsh Eye* (London: Hutchinson & Co, 1964).

——, 'Sylwadau ar "Armes Prydein" ', BBCS 24 (1971), 263–7.

Thomas, Keith, *Religion and the Decline of Magic* (London: Weidenfeld and Nicolson, 1971).

Thomas, Owen, 'Glyndyfrdwy', *Y Geninen* 10 (1892), 7.

Thomas, Thomas, *Memoirs of Owen Glendower* (Haverfordwest, 1822).

Thomas, W. Jenkyn, *The Welsh Fairy Book* (London: T. Fisher Unwin, 1907).

Thompson, Stith, *Motif-Index of Folk-Literature*, 6 vol. (Bloomington: Indiana University Press, 1955).

——, *The Folktale* (Berkeley: University of California Press, [1946], 1977).

Tomes, John, ed., *Blue Guide: Wales and the Marches* (London: Ernest Benn Limited, 1979).

Trevelyan, Marie, *From Snowdon to the Sea* (London: John Hogg, [1894]).

——, *Folk-Lore and Folk-Stories of Wales* (London: Elliot Stock, 1909).

Turner, Thomas, *Narrative of a Journey* (London: C. Whittingham, 1840).

Van Gennep, Arnold, *La Formation des Légendes* (Paris: Ernest Flammarion, 1910).

Ward, Donald, ed. and trans., *German Legends of the Brothers Grimm*, 2 vol. (Philadelphia: Institute for the Study of Human Issues, 1981).

Welsh Historical Sculpture presented to . . . the City of Cardiff by Rt. Hon. Lord Rhondda of Llanwerin, M.A. October, 1916 [Illustrated Catalogue] (Cardiff, 1916).

William of Malmesbury, *De Gestis Regum Anglorum*, ed. William Stubbs, 2 vol., Rolls Series 90 (London: 1887/9).

Williams, David, *A History of Modern Wales* (London: John Murray, Ltd., [1950], 1977).

Williams, G.J., and E.J. Jones, *Gramadegau'r Penceirddiaid* (Caerdydd: Gwasg Prifysgol Cymru, 1934).

Williams, Glanmor, *Owen Glendower* (Oxford: Oxford University Press, 1966).

——, *The Welsh Church from Conquest to Reformation* (Cardiff: University of Wales Press, 1976).

——, 'Prophecy, Poetry, and Politics in Medieval and Tudor Wales', *Religion, Language and Nationality in Wales* (Cardiff: University of Wales Press, 1979), pp.71–86.

Williams, Glyn, *Y Gwylliaid* (Maentwrog: Plas Tan-y-Bwlch, 1989).

Williams, Griffith John, *Edward Lhuyd ac Iolo Morganwg* (Caerdydd: Amgueddfa Werin Cymru, 1964).

Williams, Gwyn A., 'Owain Glyn Dŵr', *Wales through the Ages*, ed. A.J. Roderick, (Llandybie: Christopher Davies Ltd., 1959), vol.1, pp.176–83.

——, *A Distant Mirror: Five Faces of Owain Glyn Dŵr* (Aberystwyth: Plaid Cymru, [?1985]).

Williams, Ifor, 'Llyma Fyd Rhag Sythfryd Sais', *Y Llenor* 1 (1922), 62–70.

——, 'Hiriell', BBCS 3 (1927), 50–2.

——, ed., *Canu Aneirin* (Caerdydd: Gwasg Prifysgol Cymru, 1961).

——, ed. and Rachel Bromwich, trans., *Armes Prydein* (Dublin: Institute for Advanced Studies, 1972).

—— and Thomas Roberts, eds., *Cywyddau Dafydd ap Gwilym a'i Gyfoeswyr*, (Caerdydd: Gwasg Prifysgol Cymru, 1935).

Williams, J.E. Caerwyn, *The Poets of the Welsh Princes*, Writers of Wales Series (Cardiff: University of Wales Press, 1978).

Williams, John Llywelyn, coll., and Ifor Williams, ed., *Gwaith Guto'r Glyn* (Caerdydd: Gwasg Prifysgol Cymru, 1961).

Williams, P.B., *The Tourist's Guide through the County of Caernarvon* (Caernarvon: J. Hulme, 1821).

Williams, W. Llewelyn, 'Owain Lawgoch', THSC (1902), 87–97.

Willis, Browne, *A Survey of the Cathedral Church of Bangor and the Edifices Belonging to It* (London: Robert Gosling, 1721).

Wynne, Sir John, *History of the Gwydir Family* (Oswestry: Woodall, 1878).

Wynne, William, *The History of Wales* (London: M. Clark, 1697).

Index